MW00606052

Focus on Grammar 3A

Marjorie Fuchs
Margaret Bonner
Miriam Westheimer

Focus on Grammar 3: An Integrated Skills Approach, Fifth Edition, Volume A

Pearson Education, 221 River Street, Hoboken, NJ 07030

Staff credits: The people who made up the ***Focus on Grammar 3, Fifth Edition, Volume A*** team, representing content creation, design, manufacturing, marketing, multimedia, project management, publishing, rights management, and testing, are Pietro Alongi, Rhea Banker, Elizabeth Barker, Stephanie Bullard, Jennifer Castro, Tracey Cataldo, Aerin Csigay, Mindy DePalma, Dave Dickey, Warren Fischbach, Pam Fishman, Nancy Flaggman, Lester Holmes, Gosia Jaros-White, Leslie Johnson, Barry Katzen, Amy McCormick, Julie Molnar, Brian Panker, Stuart Radcliffe, Jennifer Raspiller, Lindsay Richman, Robert Ruvo, Alexandra Suarez, Paula Van Ells, and Joseph Vella.

Text design and layout: Don Williams
Composition: Page Designs International
Project supervision: Bernard Seal
Contributing editors: Françoise Leffler and Bernard Seal

Cover image: Andy Roberts / Getty Images

Printed in the United States of America

ISBN 10: 0-13-413271-8
ISBN 13: 978-0-13-413271-6

2 2019

Contents

WELCOME TO FOCUS ON GRAMMAR
FIFTH EDITION

BUILDING ON THE SUCCESS of previous editions, *Focus on Grammar* continues to provide an integrated-skills approach to engage students and help them understand, practice, and use English grammar. Centered on thematic instruction, *Focus on Grammar* combines comprehensive grammar coverage with abundant practice, critical thinking skills, and ongoing assessment, helping students accomplish their goals of communicating confidently, accurately, and fluently in everyday situations.

New in the Fifth Edition

New and Updated Content

Focus on Grammar continues to offer engaging and motivating content that appeals to learners from various cultural backgrounds. Many readings and activities have been replaced or updated to include topics that are of high interest to today's learners.

Updated Charts and Redesigned Notes

Clear, corpus-informed grammar presentations reflect real and natural language usage and allow students to grasp the most important aspects of the grammar. Clear signposting draws attention to common usage, the difference between written and spoken registers, and common errors.

Additional Communicative Activities

The new edition of *Focus on Grammar* has been expanded with additional communicative activities that encourage collaboration and the application of the target grammar in a variety of settings.

Expanded Writing Practice

Each unit in *Focus on Grammar* now ends with a structured "From Grammar to Writing" section. Supported by pre-writing and editing tasks, students engage in activities that allow them to apply the target grammar in writing.

New Assessment Program

The new edition of *Focus on Grammar* features a variety of new assessment tools, including course diagnostic tests, formative and summative assessments, and a flexible gradebook. The assessments are closely aligned with unit learning outcomes to inform instruction and measure student progress.

Revised MyEnglishLab

The updated MyEnglishLab offers students engaging practice and video grammar presentations anywhere, anytime. Immediate feedback and remediation tasks offer additional opportunities for successful mastery of content and help promote accuracy. Instructors receive instant access to digital content and diagnostic tools that allow them to customize the learning environment to meet the needs of their students.

The *Focus on Grammar* Approach

At the heart of the *Focus on Grammar* series is its unique and successful four-step approach that lets learners move from comprehension to communication within a clear and consistent structure. The books provide an abundance of scaffolded exercises to bridge the gap between identifying grammatical structures and using them with confidence and accuracy. The integration of the four skills allows students to learn grammar holistically, which in turn prepares them to understand and use English more effectively.

STEP 1: Grammar in Context integrates grammar and vocabulary in natural contexts such as articles, stories, dialogues, and blog posts. Students engage with the unit reading and theme and get exposure to grammar as it is used in real life.

STEP 2: Grammar Presentation presents the structures in clear and accessible grammar charts and notes with multiple examples of form and meaning. Corpus-informed explanations and examples reflect natural usage of the target forms, differentiate between written and conversational registers whenever appropriate, and highlight common errors to help students avoid typical pitfalls in both speaking and writing.

STEP 3: Focused Practice provides numerous and varied contextualized exercises for both the form and meaning of the new structures. Controlled practice ensures students' understanding of the target grammar and leads to mastery of form, meaning, and use.

STEP 4: Communication Practice provides practice with the structures in listening exercises as well as in communicative, open-ended speaking activities. These engaging activities provide ample opportunities for personalization and build students' confidence in using English. Students also develop their critical thinking skills through problem-solving activities and discussions.

Each unit now culminates with the **From Grammar to Writing** section. Students learn about common errors in writing and how to recognize them in their own work. Engaging and motivating writing activities encourage students to apply grammar in writing through structured tasks from pre-writing to editing.

Recycling

Underpinning the scope and sequence of the *Focus on Grammar* series is practice that allows students to use target structures and vocabulary many times, in different contexts. New grammar and vocabulary are recycled throughout the book. Students have maximum exposure, leading them to become confident in using the language in speech and in writing.

Assessment

Extensive testing informs instruction and allows teachers and students to measure progress.

- **Unit Reviews** at the end of every unit assess students' understanding of the grammar and allow students to monitor their own progress.
- **Diagnostic Tests** provide teachers with a valid and reliable means to determine how well students know the material they are going to study and to target instruction based on students' needs.
- **Unit Review Tests, Mid- and End-of-Term Review Tests, and Final Exams** measure students' ability to demonstrate mastery of skills taught in the course.
- The **Placement Test** is designed to help teachers place students into one of the five levels of the *Focus on Grammar* course.

The Importance of Context

A key element of *Focus on Grammar* is presenting important grammatical structures in context. The contexts selected are most relevant to the grammatical forms being introduced. Contextualized grammar practice also plays a key role in improving fluent use of grammar in communicative contexts. It helps learners to develop consistent and correct usage of target structures during all productive practice.

The Role of Corpus

The most important goal of *Focus on Grammar* has always been to present grammar structures using natural language. To that end, *Focus on Grammar* has incorporated the findings of corpus linguistics,* while never losing sight of what is pedagogically sound and useful. By taking this approach, *Focus on Grammar* ensures that:

- the language presented reflects real, natural usage
- themes and topics provide a good fit with the grammar point and elicit the target grammar naturally
- findings of the corpus research are reflected in the syllabus, readings, charts, grammar notes, and practice activities
- examples illustrate differences between spoken and written registers, and formal and informal language
- students are exposed to common errors in usage and learn how to recognize and avoid errors in their own speech and writing

Focus on Grammar Efficacy

The fifth edition of *Focus on Grammar* reflects an important efficacy initiative for Pearson courses—to be able to demonstrate that all teaching materials have a positive impact on student learning. To support this, *Focus on Grammar* has been updated and aligned to the **Global Scale of English** and the **Common European Framework** (CEFR) to provide granular insight into the objectives of the course, the progression of learning, and the expected outcomes a learner will be able to demonstrate upon successful completion.

To learn more about the Global Scale of English, visit www.English.com.

Components

Student Books with Essential Online Resources include access codes to the course audio, video, and self-assessment.

Student Books with MyEnglishLab offer a blended approach with integration of print and online content.

Workbooks contain additional contextualized practice in print format.

Digital Teacher's Resources include printable teaching notes, GSE mapping documents, answer keys, audio scripts, and downloadable tests. Access to the digital copy of the student books allows teachers to project the pages for whole-class instruction.

***FOG Go* app** allows users to access the student book audio on their mobile devices.

* A principal resource has been Douglas Biber et al, *Longman Grammar of Spoken and Written English*, Harlow: Pearson Education Ltd., 1999.

The *Focus on Grammar* Unit

Focus on Grammar introduces grammar structures in the context of unified themes. All units follow a four-step approach, taking learners from grammar in context to communicative practice. Thematic units add a layer to learning so that by the end of the unit students will be able to discuss the content using the grammar points they have just studied.

STEP 1 GRAMMAR IN CONTEXT

Before You Read activities create interest and elicit students' knowledge about the topic.

Vocabulary exercises help students improve their command of English.

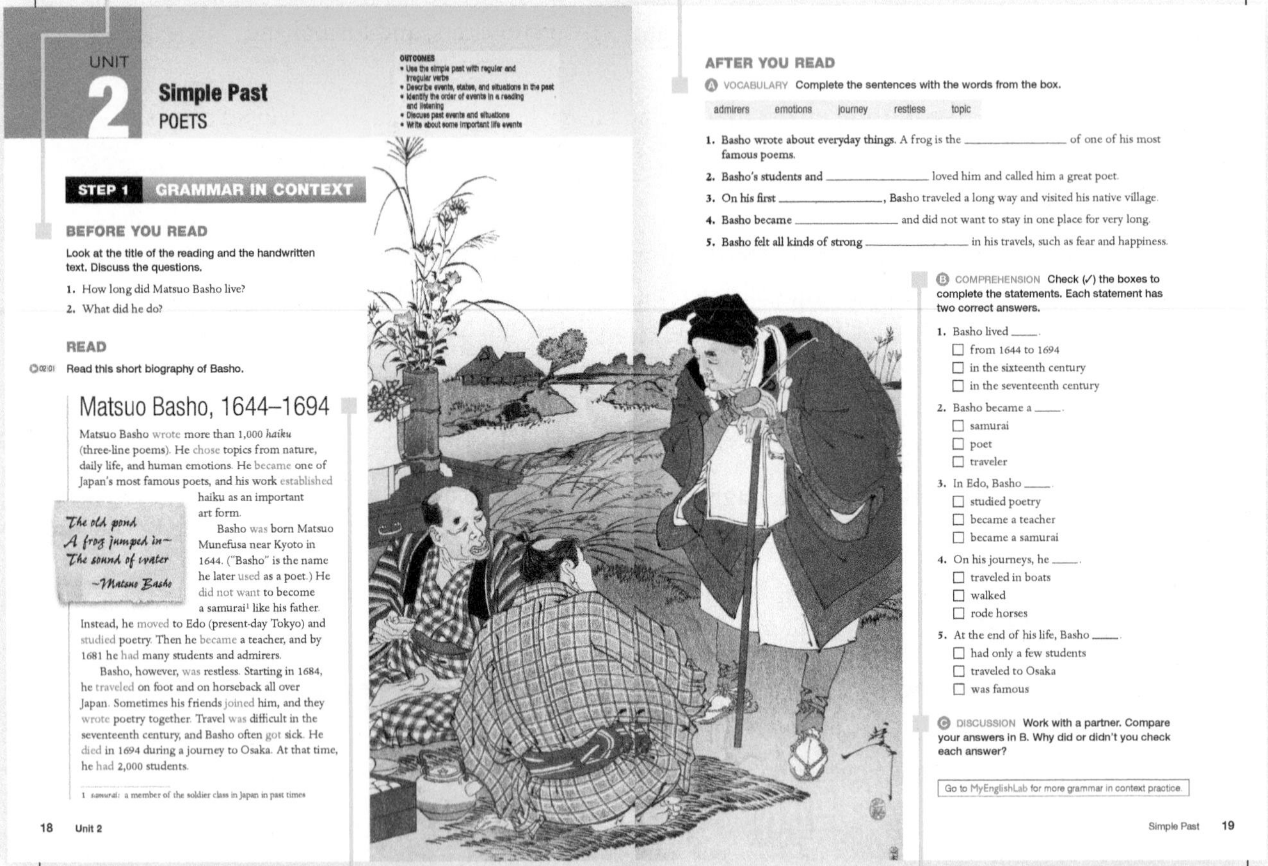
UNIT 2 Simple Past
POETS

OUTCOMES
- Use the simple past with regular and irregular verbs
- Describe events, states, and situations in the past
- Identify the order of events in a reading and listening
- Discuss past events and situations
- Write about some important life events

STEP 1 GRAMMAR IN CONTEXT

BEFORE YOU READ

Look at the title of the reading and the handwritten text. Discuss the questions.

1. How long did Matsuo Basho live?
2. What did he do?

READ

Read this short biography of Basho.

Matsuo Basho, 1644–1694

Matsuo Basho wrote more than 1,000 *haiku* (three-line poems). He chose topics from nature, daily life, and human emotions. He became one of Japan's most famous poets, and his work established haiku as an important art form.

The old pond
A frog jumped in—
The sound of water
—Matsuo Basho

Basho was born Matsuo Munefusa near Kyoto in 1644. ("Basho" is the name he later used as a poet.) He did not want to become a samurai[1] like his father. Instead, he moved to Edo (present-day Tokyo) and studied poetry. Then he became a teacher, and by 1681 he had many students and admirers.

Basho, however, was restless. Starting in 1684, he traveled on foot and on horseback all over Japan. Sometimes his friends joined him, and they wrote poetry together. Travel was difficult in the seventeenth century, and Basho often got sick. He died in 1694 during a journey to Osaka. At that time, he had 2,000 students.

1 *samurai:* a member of the soldier class in Japan in past times

18 Unit 2

AFTER YOU READ

A VOCABULARY Complete the sentences with the words from the box.

admirers emotions journey restless topic

1. Basho wrote about everyday things. A frog is the ______ of one of his most famous poems.
2. Basho's students and ______ loved him and called him a great poet.
3. On his first ______, Basho traveled a long way and visited his native village.
4. Basho became ______ and did not want to stay in one place for very long.
5. Basho felt all kinds of strong ______ in his travels, such as fear and happiness.

B COMPREHENSION Check (✓) the boxes to complete the statements. Each statement has two correct answers.

1. Basho lived ____.
   - ☐ from 1644 to 1694
   - ☐ in the sixteenth century
   - ☐ in the seventeenth century
2. Basho became a ____.
   - ☐ samurai
   - ☐ poet
   - ☐ traveler
3. In Edo, Basho ____.
   - ☐ studied poetry
   - ☐ became a teacher
   - ☐ became a samurai
4. On his journeys, he ____.
   - ☐ traveled in boats
   - ☐ walked
   - ☐ rode horses
5. At the end of his life, Basho ____.
   - ☐ had only a few students
   - ☐ traveled to Osaka
   - ☐ was famous

C DISCUSSION Work with a partner. Compare your answers in B. Why did or didn't you check each answer?

Go to MyEnglishLab for more grammar in context practice.

Simple Past 19

Engaging, high-interest **readings** in a variety of genres present the target structures in natural and realistic contexts. As students read, they encounter the form, meaning, and use of the grammar.

Comprehension and **Discussion** activities focus on the meaning of the text and draw students' attention to the target structures. NEW!

STEP 2 GRAMMAR PRESENTATION

Grammar Charts present the structures in a clear, easy-to-read format.

STEP 2 GRAMMAR PRESENTATION

PRESENT PROGRESSIVE

Affirmative Statements

Subject	Be	Base Form of Verb + -ing	
I	am	traveling	now.
You	are		
He / She / It	is		
We / You / They	are		

Negative Statements

Subject	Be	Not	Base Form of Verb + -ing	
I	am	not	traveling	now.
He	is			
We	are			

Yes/No Questions

Be	Subject	Base Form of Verb + -ing	
Is	he	traveling	now?

Short Answers

Yes,	he	is.
No,		isn't.

Wh- Questions

Wh- Word	Be	Subject	Base Form of Verb + -ing	
Where	are	you	traveling	now?

SIMPLE PRESENT

Affirmative Statements

Subject		Verb
I	often	travel.
You		
He / She / It		travels.
We / You / They		travel.

Negative Statements

Subject	Do	Not	Base Form of Verb	
I	do	not	travel	often.
He	does			
We	do			

Yes/No Questions

Do	Subject	Base Form of Verb	
Does	he	travel	often?

Short Answers

Yes,	he	does.
No,		doesn't.

Wh- Questions

Wh- Word	Do	Subject		Base Form of Verb
Where	do	you	usually	travel?

6 Unit 1

NEW!

The newly designed **Grammar Notes** highlight the main point of each note, making navigation and review easier. Simple corpus-informed **explanations** and **examples** ensure students' understanding.

GRAMMAR NOTES

1 Referring to Future Events

There are **several ways to refer to future events**. Sometimes only one form is appropriate, but in many cases more than one form is possible.

- *be going to*
- *will*
- present progressive
- simple present

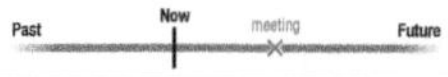

They'**re going to have** a meeting.
I think I'll **go**. **Will** you **be** there?
It'**s taking** place next week.
It **starts** at 9:00 a.m. on Monday.

2 Future Facts

For facts or events that you are **certain will happen in the future**, you can use *be going to* or *will*.

- *be going to*
- *will*

The sun **is going to rise** at 6:43 tomorrow.
The sun **will rise** at 6:43 tomorrow.

3 Predictions

For predictions about things you are **quite sure will happen in the future**, you can also use *be going to* or *will*.

- *be going to*
- *will*

I think a lot of people **are going to travel** to space.
I think a lot of people **will travel** to space.

USAGE NOTE We often use *I think* before a prediction. | ***I think*** tickets **are going to get** cheaper.

IN WRITING We use *will* more in **formal writing** and *be going to* more in **conversation**. | Prices **will drop** in time. *(formal writing)* Prices **are going to drop** in time. *(conversation)*

BE CAREFUL! Do not use *will* when something you notice right now makes you almost certain that an event is going to happen. Use *be going to*. | A: Look at that car! B: Oh, no. It'**s going to crash**! NOT ~~It'll crash~~.

4 Future Plans

For plans or things that are **already decided**, use *be going to* or the **present progressive**.

- *be going to*
- present progressive

I'm **going to fly** to Chicago next week.
I'm **flying** to Chicago next week.
NOT ~~I'll fly~~ to Chicago next week.

USAGE NOTE We often use the **present progressive** for plans that are already arranged. | I'm **flying** to Chicago next week. I already have a ticket.

USAGE NOTE When the main verb is *go*, it is more common to use the **present progressive** (*be going*) than *be going to go*. | I'm **going** to Paris tomorrow. *(more common)* I'm **going to go** to Paris tomorrow. *(less common)*

78 Unit 6

NEW!

Clear signposting provides corpus-informed notes about common usage, differences between spoken and written registers, and common errors.

PRONUNCIATION NOTE

06|02 **Pronunciation of *Going to***

In **informal conversation**, we often pronounce *going to* as "gonna." | A: What time are you **going to** be home? *(gonna)* B: I'm **going to** get home late. *(gonna)*

IN WRITING Sometimes people use *gonna* in **informal notes, text messages**, and **email** to friends. | Hi Lyn, I'm **gonna** be late. *(email)*

BE CAREFUL! Do not use *gonna* when you write to people you have a formal relationship with. | Professor, I'm **going to** be late. *(email)* NOT Professor, I'm ~~gonna~~ be late.

Also do not use *gonna* in formal writing. | According to scientists, Mars is **going to** become a tourist destination. *(paper)* NOT According to scientists, Mars is ~~gonna~~ become a tourist destination.

Pronunciation Notes are now included with the grammar presentation to highlight relevant pronunciation aspects of the target structures and to help students understand authentic spoken English.

NEW!

STEP 3 FOCUSED PRACTICE

Controlled practice activities lead students to master form, meaning, and use of the target grammar.

Discover the Grammar activities develop students' recognition and understanding of the target structures before they are asked to produce them.

STEP 3 FOCUSED PRACTICE

EXERCISE 1 DISCOVER THE GRAMMAR

GRAMMAR NOTES 1–7 Read this notice from a university bulletin board. Underline the adjectives and circle the adverbs. Then draw an arrow from the adjective or adverb to the word it is describing.

APARTMENT FOR RENT
140 Grant Street, Apt. 4B

Are you looking for a place to live? This amazing apartment is in a new building and has two large comfortable bedrooms and a small sunny kitchen. The building is very quiet—absolutely perfect for two serious students. It's near the campus on a peaceful street. There's convenient transportation. The bus stop is an easy, pleasant walk, and the express bus goes directly into town. You can run or ride your bike safely in nearby parks. The rent is very affordable. Small pets are welcome. The apartment is available on June 1. Interested students should call Megan at 555-5050. We're sure you'll be satisfied. Don't wait! This beautiful new apartment will rent fast. Nonsmokers, please.

EXERCISE 2 ADJECTIVE OR ADVERB

GRAMMAR NOTES 1–4 Circle the correct words to complete Maggie's email to her brother.

Hi Roger!

I wasn't sure I'd like living in a (1) large / largely city, but I (2) real / really love it! Maybe that's because my (3) new / newly neighborhood is located in such a (4) beautiful / beautifully residential area with lots of nice old trees.

Last Saturday, I worked (5) hard / hardly and unpacked all my stuff. Then I spent Sunday (6) happy / happily exploring my new neighborhood. I couldn't believe the (7) gorgeous / gorgeously houses on these streets. I feel very (8) lucky / luckily to live in one of them.

266 Unit 19

EXERCISE 2 COMPARISONS WITH *AS . . . AS*

GRAMMAR NOTE 1 Look at the consumer magazine chart comparing three brands of pizza cheese. Complete the sentences. Use *(just) as . . . as* or *not as . . . as* and the correct form of the words in parentheses.

PIZZA CHEESE ● Better ◐ ⟷ ○ Worse

Brand	Price (per serving)	Taste	Smell
X	45¢	◐	●
Y	30¢	◐	◐
Z	30¢	○	◐

1. Brand Z *is as expensive as* or *is just as expensive as* Brand Y. (be / expensive)
2. Brand Y ______ Brand X. (be / expensive)
3. Brand X ______ Brand Y. (taste / good)
4. Brand Z ______ Brand Y. (taste / good)
5. Brand Y ______ Brand X. (smell / delicious)
6. Brand Y ______ Brand Z. (smell / delicious)

EXERCISE 3 COMPARISONS WITH *THAN*

GRAMMAR NOTES 2–3 Look at the menu on the next page. Then complete these sentences comparing items on the menu. Use the appropriate comparative form of the adjectives in parentheses and *than* where necessary.

1. The sweet-and-sour shrimp is *more expensive than* the steamed scallops. (expensive)
2. The beef with red pepper is ______ the beef with broccoli. (hot)
3. The pork with scallions is ______ the sweet-and-sour shrimp. (expensive)
4. The chicken with orange sauce is ______ the steamed scallops. (spicy)
5. The steamed vegetables are ______ the pork with scallions. (salty)
6. The steamed vegetables are ______ the beef with red pepper. (healthy)
7. The broccoli with garlic is ______ the chicken with broccoli. (cheap)
8. The shrimp dish is ______ the scallop dish. (sweet)

282 Unit 20

A **variety of exercise types** engage students and guide them from recognition and understanding to accurate production of the grammar structures.

Editing exercises allow students to identify and correct typical mistakes.

EXERCISE 8 EDITING

GRAMMAR NOTES 1–6 Read this student's report on space travel. There are eleven mistakes in the use of the future. The first mistake is already corrected. Find and correct ten more.

Both astronauts and space tourists will ~~traveling~~ *travel* in space, but tourists are gonna have a much different experience. Space tourists is going to travel for fun, not for work. So, they will no have to worry about many of the technical problems that astronauts worry about. For example, space tourists will need not to figure out how to use tools without gravity. And they isn't going to go outside the spaceship to make repairs. For the most part, space tourists will just going to see the sights and have a good time.

Still, there will be similarities. Regular activities be the same for astronauts and space tourists. For example, eating, washing, and sleeping will turned into exciting challenges for everyone in space. And on long trips, everyone is going to doing exercises to stay fit in zero gravity. And both astronauts and space tourists will going to have many new adventures!

STEP 4 COMMUNICATION PRACTICE

Listenings in a variety of genres allow students to hear the grammar in natural contexts.

STEP 4 COMMUNICATION PRACTICE

EXERCISE 6 LISTENING

21|02 (A) A couple is trying to choose a hotel for their trip to Toronto. Listen to their conversation. Look at the list below. Then listen again and check (✓) the correct hotel for each item.

	Westin Harbour Castle	Hôtel Le Germain	Eaton Chelsea

the best view	✓		
the most convenient			
the least convenient			
the most comfortable			
the most expensive			
the least expensive			
the biggest			
the smallest			

21|02 (B) Listen to the conversation again. Then work with a partner. Compare your answers. Give reasons.

EXAMPLE: A: The Westin has the best views.
B: Yes. You can see the lake from a lot of the rooms.
A: And their restaurant has a good view, too.

(C) Work in a group. Which hotel would *you* like to stay at? Why?

EXAMPLE: A: I'd like to stay at the Hôtel Le Germain.
B: Oh. Why is that?
A: Because it's the smallest of the three. I don't like big hotels. What about you?
B: I'd prefer . . .

298 Unit 21

In the **listening activities**, students practice a range of listening skills. A **new step** has been added in which partners complete an activity that relates to the listening and uses the target grammar. **NEW!**

Engaging **communicative activities** (conversations, discussions, presentations, surveys, and games) help students synthesize the grammar, develop fluency, and build their problem-solving skills.

EXERCISE 6 ON THE WITNESS STAND

ROLE PLAY Work with a partner. Look at the excerpt from a court transcript on page 61 again. Read it aloud. Then continue the lawyer's questioning of the witness. Ask at least six more questions.

EXAMPLE: LAWYER: When did the woman leave?
WITNESS: She was still there when we heard his car speed away.
LAWYER: What happened next?
WITNESS: I saw . . .

EXERCISE 7 TO TELL THE TRUTH

(A) GAME Work in a group of three. Each student tells the group an interesting fact about his or her life. The fact can *only* be true for this student.

EXAMPLE: A: I play three musical instruments.
B: I speak four languages.
C: I have five pets.

(B) The group chooses a fact and goes to the front of the class. Each student states the same fact, but remember: Only one student is telling the truth.

EXAMPLE:

(C) The class asks the three students *wh-* questions to find out who is telling the truth.

EXAMPLE: THEA: Cezar, which four languages do you speak?
CEZAR: I speak Russian, French, Spanish, and English.
LEV: Cezar, where did you learn Russian?
CEZAR: I was born in Russia.
MEI: Cezar, who taught you French?
CEZAR: My grandmother is French. I learned it from her.
JOSÉ: Cezar, how do you say "witness" in Spanish?
CEZAR: . . .

Go to MyEnglishLab for more communication practice.

Wh- Questions 69

FROM GRAMMAR TO WRITING

A **From Grammar to Writing** section, now in every unit, helps students confidently apply the unit's grammar to their own writing. **NEW!**

FROM GRAMMAR TO WRITING

A BEFORE YOU WRITE **Think about a new experience you are having (for example, living in a new country, taking a new class, working at a new job). Complete the outline.**

____
(New Experience)

Usually	Now
______________	______________
______________	______________
______________	______________

B WRITE **Use your outline to write a paragraph about your new experience. How is it different from what you usually do? How do you feel in the new situation? Use *but* or *however* to contrast your usual experience with your new experience. Try to avoid the common mistakes in the chart.**

EXAMPLE: I usually live at home with my parents, but this month I'm living with my aunt and uncle. Everything seems different. My aunt always makes dinner at 6:00. However, at home we never eat before 8:00 p.m. . . .

Common Mistakes in Using the Present Progressive and Simple Present	
Use the **simple present** with most **non-action verbs**. Do not use the present progressive.	I **think** my aunt's dinners are great. NOT I ~~am thinking~~ my aunt's dinners are great.
Put an **adverb of frequency before** the simple present verb. Do not put it after the verb.	We ***always*** **eat** at 6:00. NOT We ~~eat always~~ at 6:00.
Put an **adverb of frequency after** the verb ***be***. Do not put it before *be*.	She **is *always*** on time. NOT She ~~always is~~ on time.

The **Before You Write** task helps students generate ideas for their writing assignment.

In the **Write** task, students are given a writing assignment and guided to use the target grammar and avoid common mistakes.

C CHECK YOUR WORK **Read your paragraph. Underline once the present progressive and underline twice the simple present forms. Circle the adverbs of frequency. Use the Editing Checklist to check your work.**

Editing Checklist

Did you use . . . ?

- ☐ the present progressive to describe something that is happening right now
- ☐ the simple present to describe what regularly happens
- ☐ the simple present with non-action verbs such as *be*, *like*, *seem*, and *want*
- ☐ adverbs of frequency in the correct position

Check Your Work includes an Editing Checklist that allows students to proofread and edit their compositions.

D REVISE YOUR WORK **Read your paragraph again. Can you improve your writing? Make changes if necessary. Give your paragraph a title.**

In **Revise Your Work**, students are given a final opportunity to improve their writing.

16 Unit 1

Go to MyEnglishLab for more writing practice.

UNIT REVIEW

Unit Reviews give students the opportunity to check their understanding of the target structures. Students can check their answers against the Answer Key at the end of the book. They can also complete the Review on MyEnglishLab.

UNIT 22 REVIEW

Test yourself on the grammar of the unit.

A **Circle the correct words to complete the sentences.**

1. Chen plays just as good / well as Sanchez.
2. Maya is a slow runner. She runs / doesn't run as fast as her teammates.
3. Dan always shoots the ball more accurately / the most accurately than Will.
4. Inez plays the most aggressively of / than all the other players.
5. Our team didn't play the worst / as well as I expected. I was disappointed.
6. The faster Tranh runs, the more tired he gets / he gets more tired.
7. We need to practice harder / hardly if we want to win.
8. You're playing well / better and better!

B **Complete the sentences with the correct form of the words in parentheses.**

1. You play just as ______________ (good) as Tomás.
2. Olga runs ______________ (fast) than any of her teammates.
3. Diego shoots the ball ______________ (accurate) of all the players.
4. He practices ______________ (hard) of all.
5. Their team played ______________ (bad) of all the teams.

C **Find and correct seven mistakes.**

Last night's game was a very exciting one. The Globes played the best they've played all season. But they still didn't play as good as the Stars. The Stars hit the ball more frequent and ran more fast than the Globes, and their pitcher, Kevin Rodriguez, threw the ball more

MyEnglishLab

MyEnglishLab delivers rich online content to engage and motivate **students**.

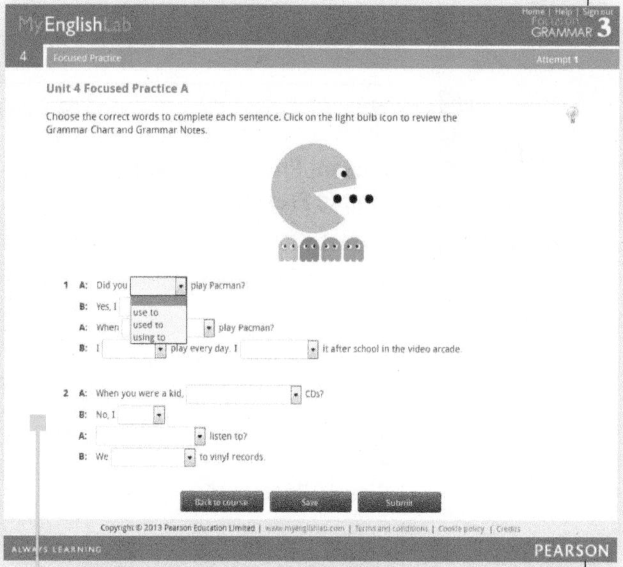

Grammar Coach videos give additional grammar presentations.

NEW!

MyEnglishLab provides students with:

- rich interactive practice in grammar, reading, listening, speaking, and writing
- immediate and meaningful feedback on wrong answers
- remediation activities
- grade reports that display performance and time on task

NEW!

MyEnglishLab delivers innovative teaching tools and useful resources to **teachers**.

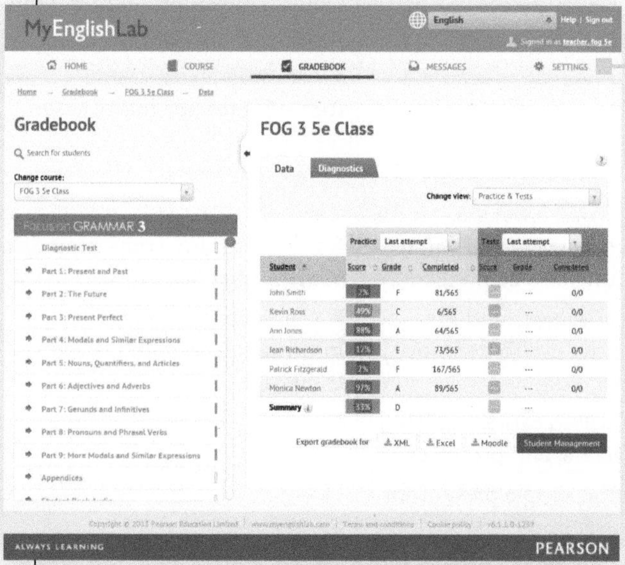

With **MyEnglishLab**, teachers can:

- view student scores by unit and activity
- monitor student progress on any activity or test
- analyze class data to determine steps for remediation and support

MyEnglishLab also provides teachers with:

- a digital copy of the student book for whole-class instruction
- downloadable assessments, including the placement test, that can be administered on MyEnglishLab or in print format
- printable resources including teaching notes, suggestions for teaching grammar, GSE mapping documents, answer keys, and audio scripts

Scope and Sequence

PART	UNIT	GRAMMAR	READING
PART **1** **Present and Past**	**1** **Present Progressive and Simple Present** Page 4 THEME Different Cultures	■ Can tell when to use the present progressive and the simple present to distinguish actions that are ongoing and actions that are habitual ■ Can use non-action verbs to describe states and situations PRONUNCIATION *What do you* and *What are you*	Information Article: *What's Your Cross-Cultural IQ?* ■ Can derive the meaning of unknown words in a simple text ■ Can recognize the main points in a straightforward text on a familiar topic
	2 **Simple Past** Page 18 THEME Poets	■ Can refer to past actions, states, or situations using regular and irregular past forms	Biography: *Matsuo Basho, 1644–1694* ■ Can follow chronological sequences in a short biography
	3 **Past Progressive and Simple Past** Page 33 THEME Reporting Events	■ Can use the past progressive to focus on the duration of a past action ■ Can use the past progressive with the simple past to describe an action interrupted by another action	Newspaper Article: *Disaster at Sea* ■ Can follow chronological sequences in a short news article
	4 ***Used to* and *Would*** Page 47 THEME Changes	■ Can use *used to* and *would* to refer to past habits and actions that are no longer happening and to convey contrast with the present	Information Article: *Dubai: Then and Now* ■ Can get the gist of a straightforward, familiar text about a popular location
	5 ***Wh-* Questions** Page 61 THEME In Court	■ Can ask *wh-* questions about the past	Court Transcript: *State of Illinois v. Harry M. Adams* ■ Can scan an interview transcript for key information
PART **2** **The Future**	**6** **Future** Page 74 THEME Space Travel	■ Can use *be going to* and *will* to refer to future facts or predictions ■ Can use *be going to* and the present progressive to describe future plans ■ Can use *will* to express quick decisions, offers, and promises ■ Can use the simple present for scheduled events PRONUNCIATION *Going to* or *gonna*	Radio Program Transcript: *Space Tourism: Not Just Science Fiction* ■ Can identify relevant information in an interview transcript

PART **2** CONTINUES ▼

LISTENING	SPEAKING	WRITING	VOCABULARY
Interviews with foreign students ■ Can distinguish a present action from a habitual activity in short interviews	■ Can express beliefs and opinions about cultural topics and identify the opinions of others	■ Can write a basic description of a new experience, using a model for support if needed	abroad culture AWL distance (n) event misunderstanding native (adj)
An interview with a poet ■ Can recognize the main points of an interview that addresses familiar topics	■ Can convey simple biographical information to others, emphasizing the most important point	■ Can write a basic description of some important life events, using a model for support if needed	admirer emotion journey (n) restless topic AWL
A witness's description of a traffic accident ■ Can identify the main points of a description of an unfamiliar event	■ Can ask or answer questions about an unfamiliar event	■ Can write a basic description of an unfamiliar past event	alarmed area AWL calm (adj) disaster sink (v) survivor AWL
A conversation about the changes in a small town ■ Can distinguish present events from past events in a conversation on familiar topics	■ Can describe one's past and present physical appearance and habits	■ Can write a description of a place and how it has changed	destination major (adj) AWL popular revenue AWL traditional AWL transformation AWL
A conversation about a court trial ■ Can identify the main point of a conversation	■ Can ask and answer basic interview questions	■ Can write a series of interview questions that elicit information about a past event	defendant frightened in a hurry indicate AWL record (n)
Conversations about current situations and future plans ■ Can recognize main points of conversations on familiar topics ■ Can distinguish between actions happening now and future plans	■ Can ask and answer questions about plans and intentions ■ Can make future arrangements and plans with reference to a diary or schedule	■ Can write a paragraph about a prediction	edge (n) experience (v) incredible purchase (v) AWL sold out takeoff (n)

AWL = Academic Word List item

UNIT	GRAMMAR	READING
▼ PART **2** CONTINUED		
7 **Future Time Clauses** Page 91 THEME Setting Goals	■ Can use a time clause to show the order between two future events ■ Can use time words such as *when* and *before* with the simple present to refer to future events	Information Article: *From Dream to Reality* ■ Can follow a sequence of two future events in a straightforward, factual text
PART **3** **Present Perfect**		
8 **Present Perfect: *Since* and *For*** Page 104 THEME Careers	■ Can use the present perfect with *since* or *for* to show that something began in the past and continues into the present	Biography: *King of Skate* ■ Can identify key details in a short biography
9 **Present Perfect: *Already*, *Yet*, and *Still*** Page 118 THEME Party Planning	■ Can use the present perfect with *already*, *yet*, or *still* to refer to things that happened or did not happen at some time in the past	Information Article: *It's Party Time!* ■ Can identify key details in an information article
10 **Present Perfect: Indefinite Past** Page 129 THEME Adventure Travel	■ Can use the present perfect to show that something happened at an indefinite time in the past ■ Can use the present perfect with adverbs of time and time expressions	Magazine Article: *Been There? Done That?* ■ Can recognize key details in a short magazine article on an everyday topic
11 **Present Perfect and Simple Past** Page 144 THEME Failure and Success	■ Can recognize when to use the present perfect and the simple past	Information Article: *Famous First-Time Failures* ■ Can recognize key details in a short, factual text that relates the core theme to everyday experiences
12 **Present Perfect Progressive and Present Perfect** Page 157 THEME Climate Change	■ Can use the present perfect progressive with *since/for* and time expressions ■ Can recognize the difference between the present perfect and the present perfect progressive	Scientific Article: *Global Warming: A Hot Topic* ■ Can follow a short, straightforward text on a scientific topic

LISTENING	SPEAKING	WRITING	VOCABULARY
A conversation about future plans ■ Can follow chronological sequences in extended informal speech at natural speed	■ Can describe future plans and intentions ■ Can discuss the order of future events using future time clauses	■ Can write a description of future plans and goals ■ Can show the time order of future events	achieve AWL catalog (n) goal AWL interview (n) path
A job interview ■ Can determine the length of time of events mentioned in an interview	■ Can carry out a prepared, structured interview with some spontaneous follow-up questions	■ Can write a paragraph about a person's experience and accomplishments	consider oneself dramatically AWL opportunity positive AWL residence AWL support oneself
A conversation about plans for a party ■ Can recognize and discuss tasks on a to-do list or plan	■ Can discuss what has or hasn't happened in everyday plans	■ Can write a paragraph about a goal and the steps needed to reach it	available AWL organized (adj) professional (adj) AWL specific AWL successful
A conversation with a travel agent ■ Can identify the main points of a conversation about travel plans	■ Can briefly give explanations and reasons for opinions ■ Can ask and answer questions about past activities	■ Can write a paragraph in response to a quote from literature	adventure affordable ancient annual AWL survey (n) AWL transportation AWL
An interview with two college professors ■ Can establish the time frame of important details in an interview	■ Can discuss past events and experiences and provide necessary details about them	■ Can write a paragraph about a personal experience of failure and success	attitude AWL award (n) create AWL discouraged (adj) reject (v) AWL
Conversations about recent finished and unfinished activities ■ Can determine the time frame of main events in short conversations	■ Can express opinions and attitudes and give reasons and explanations for them	■ Can write an email or letter that describes one's recent activities, both finished and unfinished	climate design (v) AWL develop energy AWL expert AWL trend AWL

AWL = Academic Word List item

	UNIT	GRAMMAR	READING
PART 4 **Modals and Similar Expressions**	**13** **Ability and Possibility: *Can, Could, Be able to*** Page 174 THEME Multilingualism	■ Can express ability and possibility in the present, future, and past with *can, could,* and *be able to*	Social Science Article: *Multilingualism* ■ Can follow a short, straightforward social science text
	14 **Permission: *Can, Could, May, Do you mind if*** Page 189 THEME Roommates	■ Can ask for, give, or deny permission with *can, could, may,* and *do you mind if*	Magazine Article: *Always Ask First* ■ Can skim a simple text about a day-to-day topic in order to identify key concepts
	15 **Requests: *Can, Could, Will, Would, Would you mind*** Page 202 THEME Messages	■ Can use *can, could, will, would,* and *would you mind* to make requests PRONUNCIATION *Could you, Would you, Will you, Can you*	Emails and Text Messages: *Messages 4 u!* ■ Can identify important details related to requests in emails and text messages
	16 **Advice: *Should, Ought to, Had better*** Page 214 THEME Internet Rules	■ Can use *should, ought to,* and *had better* to offer or ask for advice or suggestions PRONUNCIATION *Ought to* and *Had better*	Information Article: *Netiquette 101* ■ Can skim a text on rules and advice to identify key concepts
PART 5 **Nouns, Quantifiers, and Articles**	**17** **Nouns and Quantifiers** Page 230 THEME Time Capsules	■ Can use proper nouns and common nouns, count nouns and non-count nouns ■ Can use a range of basic quantifiers in affirmative and negative statements	Scientific Article: *Time in a Bottle* ■ Can identify the main points in a short, straightforward text on a scientific topic
	18 **Articles: Indefinite and Definite** Page 243 THEME Stories	■ Can use indefinite and definite articles to describe nouns ■ Can distinguish when to use definite articles, indefinite articles, or no article when describing nouns	Fable: *The Town Mouse and the Country Mouse* ■ Can skim a story to identify key concepts

LISTENING	SPEAKING	WRITING	VOCABULARY
A job interview ■ Can identify important details in a job interview	■ Can compare and contrast alternatives about plans and activities ■ Can effectively participate in a classroom discussion about an academic topic	■ Can write a paragraph in response to a question about progress and aspirations	adult AWL advantage field (n) majority AWL research (n) AWL retired
Short conversations asking and giving permission ■ Can distinguish between whether permission was granted or refused in a short conversation	■ Can come to a resolution with others by asking for permission to do something	■ Can write a short note or email that explains a day-to-day situation and asks or responds to a request for permission to do something	annoyed assume AWL establish AWL gain (v) guidelines AWL presentation
Short conversations making and answering requests ■ Can identify details related to a schedule in a short conversation	■ Can create and discuss a daily schedule that involves making requests of others	■ Can write and respond to a request in a text or email message	appreciate AWL deliver distribute AWL respond AWL urgent
An excerpt from a radio call-in show ■ Can evaluate statements of advice from radio and television shows	■ Can express opinions in regard to possible solutions and provide brief reasons and explanations for them	■ Can write a basic email or letter of complaint and request the recipient to take action	avoid behavior communication AWL identity AWL normal AWL protect

A discussion about a list of items ■ Can identify details in a conversation about day-to-day topics	■ Can use turn-taking to maintain a discussion, while emphasizing one's own points	■ Can write a note or letter that lists and describes quantities of items	civilization impressed intentional interpret AWL occasion (n) purpose
Short conversations about books and video games ■ Can understand and interpret important details in basic conversations about day-to-day activities	■ Can summarize and give opinions on the moral of a fable	■ Can write a paragraph about a personal experience that illustrates the meaning of a moral	enormous AWL famous honest immediately wonderful

AWL = Academic Word List item

	UNIT	GRAMMAR	READING
PART 6 **Adjectives and Adverbs**	**19** **Adjectives and Adverbs** Page 260 THEME Home	■ Can form basic adverbs by adding *-ly* to adjectives ■ Can use adverbs of manner, adverbs of degree, and one or several adjectives ■ Can form and use participial adjectives	Advertisement: *Wakefield House* ■ Can recognize significant points and arguments in an ad
	20 **Adjectives: Comparisons with *As . . . as* and *Than*** Page 276 THEME Food	■ Can use *as . . . as* with adjectives to express similarity ■ Can form comparative adjectives and use them with *than* to express difference ■ Can use two comparative adjectives to show an increase or decrease, or to show cause and effect	Newspaper Article: *A New Place for Pizza* ■ Can recognize significant points in a short newspaper article about local events
	21 **Adjectives: Superlatives** Page 290 THEME Cities	■ Can form the superlative with *-est* ■ Can form the superlative of longer regular adjectives with *most*	Travel Brochure: *A Superlative City* ■ Can identify key details in a short, informative text
	22 **Adverbs: *As . . . as*, Comparatives, Superlatives** Page 302 THEME Sports	■ Can use *as . . . as* with adverbs to express similarity ■ Can form comparative adverbs and use them with *than* to express difference ■ Can form the superlative with *-est* or *most* ■ Can use two comparative adverbs to show an increase or decrease, or to show cause and effect	Opinion Article: *Separation of the Sexes?* ■ Can recognize significant points and arguments in a straightforward opinion article on a familiar topic
PART 7 **Gerunds and Infinitives**	**23** **Gerunds: Subject and Object** Page 318 THEME Health Issues	■ Can use a range of common verbs followed by a gerund ■ Can use a gerund as the subject or the object of a verb	Information Article: *No Smoking Around the World from A to Z* ■ Can recognize significant points and ideas in an article about a common habit and trend

PART 7 CONTINUES ▼

LISTENING	SPEAKING	WRITING	VOCABULARY
A conversation about online apartment ads ■ Can identify speakers' opinions in a short conversation about day-to-day topics	■ Can use a range of adjectives and adverbs to compare and describe different options for an ideal home	■ Can write a description of one's ideal home	absolutely convenient ideal located in AWL peaceful satisfied
A conversation about opinions on food ■ Can recognize speakers' preferences and opinions in a short conversation	■ Can make simple, direct comparisons between two things using common adjectives ■ Can briefly give reasons and explanations for opinions	■ Can write a paragraph that compares and contrasts foods from different cities or countries	crowded delicious evident AWL relaxed AWL varied AWL
A conversation about travel plans ■ Can identify places and locations by their descriptions	■ Can give opinions and answer questions about cities	■ Can write a detailed description of one's hometown or city	continent (n) dynamic AWL feature (n) AWL financial AWL multicultural public (adj)
A debate ■ Can recognize the main ideas of and opinions in a debate about familiar topics	■ Can express and respond to opinions about controversial topics	■ Can write arguments for and against a statement about an everyday topic	compete debate (n) AWL insult (n) require AWL source (n) AWL value (n)
A conversation about health advice ■ Can determine whether an action is recommended or not recommended	■ Can discuss one's health and exercise habits ■ Can conduct a survey and discuss results ■ Can discuss and give one's opinion on a controversial topic	■ Can write a short opinion essay about a controversial topic	approve of ban (v) illegal AWL in favor of permit (v) prohibit AWL

AWL = Academic Word List item

UNIT	GRAMMAR	READING
▼ PART **7** CONTINUED		
24 **Infinitives After Certain Verbs** Page 330 THEME Happiness	■ Can use a wide range of verbs followed by an infinitive PRONUNCIATION *Want to* or *Wanna*	Psychology Article: *Can People Learn to Be Happy?* ■ Can identify statistics in a short, straightforward article and recognize how they support the author's ideas
25 **More Uses of Infinitives** Page 342 THEME Smart Devices	■ Can use an infinitive with *to* or *in order to* to express purpose and intention ■ Can make statements with the verb *be* plus an adjective / adverb followed by an infinitive ■ Can say something is possible or not possible, using *too* or *enough* with adjectives and adverbs	Information Article: *The World in Your Hand—or on Your Wrist* ■ Can identify important details and opinions in a short text with quotes
26 **Gerunds and Infinitives** Page 355 THEME Procrastination	■ Can use a range of common verbs followed by a gerund ■ Can use a range of common verbs followed by an infinitive ■ Can use a range of common verbs followed by a gerund or an infinitive	Magazine Article: *Stop Procrastinating—Now!* ■ Can recognize significant points and arguments in short articles about common habits

PART **8**
Pronouns and Phrasal Verbs

UNIT	GRAMMAR	READING
27 **Reflexive and Reciprocal Pronouns** Page 370 THEME Self-Talk	■ Can use *each other* and *one another*, and reflexive pronouns	Psychology Article: *Self-Talk* ■ Can identify the subject of a description or trait in a short, straightforward article
28 **Phrasal Verbs** Page 384 THEME Science	■ Can use a range of phrasal verbs ■ Can use phrasal verbs with separated objects	Scientific Article: *Planting Ideas* ■ Can identify key details in a straightforward article on a scientific topic

LISTENING	SPEAKING	WRITING	VOCABULARY
A casual conversation between two friends ■ Can recognize who is being asked to do an action in a conversation on an everyday topic	■ Can give an opinion in response to a literary quote ■ Can start and maintain a discussion about an abstract topic	■ Can write a paragraph on a personal topic using transition words to establish a time frame	appropriate (adj) AWL focus (v) AWL interact AWL participate in AWL significant (adj) AWL tend to
A TV ad ■ Can identify key details about products and recognize whether they are important or not	■ Can express and comment on ideas and suggestions in informal discussions about everyday objects	■ Can write a paragraph that weighs the pros and cons of a smart device	benefit (n) AWL combine (v) device AWL function (n) AWL multipurpose old-fashioned
An interview with a student about her study habits ■ Can identify key details in a recorded interview	■ Can give an opinion in response to a literary quote ■ Can express and comment on how to solve problems in an informal discussion	■ Can write several paragraphs that outline how to achieve one's goals	anxious discouraging (adj) project (n) AWL tactic task AWL universal
Workplace conversations ■ Can identify important information in everyday conversations	■ Can complete a questionnaire and discuss results ■ Can discuss illustrations using phrasal verbs	■ Can write an email or letter giving advice	fault (n) impact (v) AWL maintain AWL reaction AWL realize temporary AWL
Classroom conversations about a science class ■ Can recognize the main points of conversations and confirm their validity	■ Can express and comment on ideas and suggestions in informal discussions ■ Can discuss illustrations using phrasal verbs	■ Can write a paragraph in response to a specific question and support opinions with examples and observations	get by go on grow up pick out pick up take off

AWL = Academic Word List item

PART 9 More Modals and Similar Expressions

UNIT	GRAMMAR	READING
29 **Necessity: *Have (got) to, Must, Can't*** Page 398 THEME Rules and Regulations	■ Can use *have to, have got to,* and *must* to refer to or ask about necessity or obligation ■ Can use *don't/doesn't have to* to express absence of obligation and *must not* and *can't* to express prohibition PRONUNCIATION: *Have to* or *Hafta, Got to* or *Gotta*	Information Article: *Know Before You Go* ■ Can recognize significant points in an article to determine whether statements are true or false
30 **Expectations: *Be supposed to*** Page 414 THEME Manners	■ Can talk about expectations and obligations using *supposed to* and *not supposed to*	Article: *It Was Supposed to Be a Nice Evening* ■ Can recognize significant points in an article
31 **Future Possibility: *May, Might, Could*** Page 427 THEME Weather	■ Can use *may, might,* and *could* to express likelihood in the present and near future	News Transcript: *Weather Watch* ■ Can scan a news transcript for key information
32 **Present Conclusions: *Must, Have (got) to, May, Might, Could, Can't*** Page 438 THEME Mysteries	■ Can come to conclusions about present situations using *must, have (got) to, may, might, could,* and *can't*	Story Excerpt: *The Red-Headed League* ■ Can skim a simple text to identify key concepts

LISTENING	SPEAKING	WRITING	VOCABULARY
Conversations about driving ■ Can identify the main points of conversations about a familiar topic spoken in standard speech	■ Can recognize common signs and discuss their meaning ■ Can express personal obligations ■ Can discuss the rules and regulations of a public or private institution	■ Can write a paragraph describing rules or procedures for obtaining an official document	equipment AWL hassle (n) inspect AWL regulation AWL strict valid AWL
A radio show about etiquette and manners ■ Can identify details in recorded conversations	■ Can initiate and maintain a discussion about cultural customs	■ Can write a paragraph about a life event in a specific culture	definite AWL familiar issue (n) AWL norm AWL rude sense (v)
A weather forecast ■ Can understand the probability of a situation in a report about a familiar topic	■ Can give a short, rehearsed talk or presentation on a familiar topic ■ Can describe future plans and intentions in detail and give degrees of probability that something will happen	■ Can write short emails or letters that express the probability of future plans	affect (v) AWL exceed AWL forecast (n) local (adj) region AWL
A conversation about a mystery ■ Can recognize the key events in a short conversation and identify the certainty of each speaker about the events	■ Can draw conclusions about everyday objects and situations	■ Can write a paragraph about a short story and draw possible conclusions	advertisement amazed method AWL position (n) salary

AWL = Academic Word List item

About the Authors

Marjorie Fuchs has taught ESL at New York City Technical College and LaGuardia Community College of the City University of New York and EFL at Sprachstudio Lingua Nova in Munich, Germany. She has a master's degree in Applied English Linguistics and a certificate in TESOL from the University of Wisconsin-Madison. She has authored and co-authored many widely used books and multimedia materials, notably *Crossroads 4; Top Twenty ESL Word Games: Beginning Vocabulary Development; Families: Ten Card Games for Language Learners; Focus on Grammar 3* and *4* (editions 1–5); *Focus on Grammar 3* and *4, CD-ROM; Longman English Interactive 3* and *4; Grammar Express Basic; Grammar Express Basic CD-ROM; Grammar Express Intermediate; Future 1: English for Results; OPD Workplace Skills Builder*; workbooks for *Crossroads 1–4; The Oxford Picture Dictionary High Beginning* and *Low Intermediate*, (editions 1–3); *Focus on Grammar 3* and *4* (editions 1–5); and *Grammar Express Basic*.

Margaret Bonner has taught ESL at Hunter College and the Borough of Manhattan Community College of the City University of New York, at Taiwan National University in Taipei, and at Virginia Commonwealth University in Richmond. She holds a master's degree in library science from Columbia University, and she has done work toward a PhD in English literature at the Graduate Center of the City University of New York. She has authored and co-authored numerous ESL and EFL print and multimedia materials, including textbooks for the national school system of Oman; *Step into Writing: A Basic Writing Text; Focus on Grammar 3* and *4* (editions 1–5); *Focus on Grammar 4 Workbook* (editions 1–5); *Grammar Express Basic; Grammar Express Basic CD-ROM; Grammar Express Basic Workbook; Grammar Express Intermediate; Focus on Grammar 3* and *4, CD-ROM; Longman English Interactive 4*; and *The Oxford Picture Dictionary Low Intermediate Workbook* (editions 1–3).

Miriam Westheimer taught EFL at all levels of instruction in Haifa, Israel, for a period of six years. She has also taught ESL at Queens College, at LaGuardia Community College, and in the American Language Program of Columbia University. She holds a master's degree in TESOL and a doctorate in Curriculum and Teaching from Teachers College of Columbia University. She is the co-author of a communicative grammar program developed and widely used in Israel.

Acknowledgments

Before acknowledging the many people who have contributed to the fifth edition of *Focus on Grammar*, we wish to express our gratitude to the following people who worked on the previous editions and whose influence is still present in the new work: **Joanne Dresner**, who initiated the project and helped conceptualize the general approach of *Focus on Grammar*; our editors for the first four editions: **Nancy Perry**, **Penny Laporte**, **Louisa Hellegers**, **Joan Saslow**, **Laura LeDrean**, **Debbie Sistino**, and **Françoise Leffler**; and **Sharon Hilles**, our grammar consultant for the first edition.

In the fifth edition, *Focus on Grammar* has continued to evolve as we update materials and respond to valuable feedback from teachers and students who use the series. We are grateful to the following editors and colleagues:

- **Gosia Jaros-White** for overseeing with skill and sensitivity a complex series while never losing sight of the individual components or people involved in the project. She offered concrete and practical advice and was always mindful of learners' needs.
- **Bernard Seal**, of Page Designs International, who joined the *Focus on Grammar* team with a great deal of experience, expertise, energy, and enthusiasm. With his hands-on approach, he was involved in every aspect of the project. He read all manuscript, raising pertinent questions and offering sage advice.
- **Don Williams**, also of Page Designs International, for creating a fresh, new look, which is as user-friendly as it is attractive.
- **Françoise Leffler**, our editor *extraordinaire*, with whom we had the great fortune and pleasure of being able to continue our long collaboration. She provided both continuity and a fresh eye as she delved into another edition of the series, advising us on all things—from the small details to the big picture.
- Series co-authors **Irene Schoenberg** and **Jay Maurer** for their suggestions and support, and Irene for sharing her experience in teaching with earlier editions of this book.
- **Jane Curtis** for her advice founded in many years of teaching with the series.
- **Julie Schmidt** for her helpful presentation of information that was easy to understand and use.
- **Sharon Goldstein** for her insightful and practical suggestions, delivered with wisdom and wit.
- **Cindy Davis** for her classroom-based recommendations at the very beginning of this edition.

Special thanks to **Dr. Eloy Rodriguez** of Cornell University for generously providing us with photos to accompany the unit which features his research on zoopharmacognosy.

Finally, as always, Marjorie thanks **Rick Smith** for his unswerving support and excellent suggestions. He was a steadfast beacon of light as we navigated our way through our fifth *FOG*.

MF and MB

To the memory of my parents, Edith and Joseph Fuchs—MF

To my parents, Marie and Joseph Maus, and to my son, Luke Frances—MB

Reviewers

We are grateful to the following reviewers for their many helpful comments:

Susanna Aramyan, Glendale Community College, Glendale, CA; **Homeretta Ayala**, Baltimore Co. Schools, Baltimore, MD; **Barbara Barrett**, University of Miami, Miami, FL; **Rebecca Beck**, Irvine Valley College, Irvine, CA; **Crystal Bock Thiessen**, University of Nebraska-PIESL, Lincoln, NE; **Janna Brink**, Mt. San Antonio College, Walnut, CA; **Erin Butler**, University of California, Riverside, CA; **Joice Cain**, Fullerton College, Fullerton, CA; **Shannonine M. Caruana**, Hudson County Community College, Jersey City, NJ; **Tonya Cobb**, Cypress College, Cypress, CA; **David Cooke**, Mt. San Antonio College, Walnut, CA; **Lindsay Donigan**, Fullerton College, Fullerton, CA; **Mila Dragushanskya**, ASA College, New York, NY; **Jill Fox**, University of Nebraska, Lincoln, NE; **Katalin Gyurindak**, Mt. San Antonio College, Walnut, CA; **Karen Hamilton**, Glendale Community College, Glendale, CA; **Electra Jablons**, International English Language Institute, Hunter College, New York, NY; **Eva Kozlenko**, Hudson County Community College, Jersey City, NJ; **Esther Lee**, American Language Program, California State University, Fullerton, CA; **Yenlan Li**, American Language Program, California State University, Fullerton, CA; **Shirley Lundblade**, Mt. San Antonio College, Walnut, CA; **Thi Thi Ma**, Los Angeles City College, Los Angeles, CA; **Marilyn Martin**, Mt. San Antonio College, Walnut, CA; **Eve Mazereeuw**, University of Guelph English Language Programs, Guelph, Ontario, Canada; **Robert Mott**, Glendale Community College, Glendale, CA; **Wanda Murtha**, Glendale Community College, Glendale, CA; **Susan Niemeyer**, Los Angeles City College, Los Angeles, CA; **Wayne Pate**, Tarrant County College, Fort Worth, TX; **Genevieve Patthey-Chavez**, Los Angeles City College, Los Angeles, CA; **Robin Persiani**, Sierra College, Rocklin, CA; **Denise Phillips**, Hudson County Community College, Jersey City, NJ; **Anna Powell**, American Language Program, California State University, Fullerton, CA; **JoAnna Prado**, Sacramento City Community College, Sacramento, CA; **Mark Rau**, American River College, Sacramento, CA; **Madeleine Schamehorn**, University of California, Riverside, CA; **Richard Skinner**, Hudson County Community College, Jersey City, NJ; **Heather Snavely**, American Language Program, California State University, Fullerton, CA; **Gordana Sokic**, Douglas College, Westminster, British Columbia, Canada; **Lee Spencer**, International English Language Institute, Hunter College, New York, NY; **Heather Stern**, Irvine Valley College, Irvine, CA; **Susan Stern**, Irvine Valley College, Irvine, CA; **Andrea Sunnaa**, Mt. San Antonio College, Walnut, CA; **Margaret Teske**, Mt. San Antonio College, Walnut, CA; **Johanna Van Gendt**, Hudson County Community College, Jersey City, NJ; **Daniela C. Wagner-Loera**, University of Maryland, College Park, MD; **Tamara Williams**, University of Guelph, English Language Programs, Guelph, Ontario, Canada; **Saliha Yagoubi**, Hudson County Community College, Jersey City, NJ; **Pat Zayas**, Glendale Community College, Glendale, CA

Credits

PHOTO CREDITS

2–3: Peshkov/Fotolia, (background) Pixelrobot/Fotolia; **9:** Gold36/Fotolia; **10:** (bottom) Elnur/Fotolia, (center) Ake1150/Fotolia, (top) Jolopes/Fotolia; **11:** (bottom) Sumire8/Fotolia, (top) Sanjagrujic/Fotolia; **12:** Jasminko Ibrakovic/123RF; **15:** (center left) Kantver/Fotolia, (center right) Jedi Master/Fotolia, (left) Pathdoc/Fotolia, (right) Slasnyi/Fotolia; **18:** Picsfive/123RF; **18–19:** John Stevenson/Asian Art & Archaeology, Inc/Corbis Historical/Getty Images; **24:** Mary Evans Picture Library/Alamy Stock Photo; **26:** Betty Udesen/KRT/Newscom; **27:** Becker/Fotolia; **29:** (center left) Pictures From History/akg-images, (left) Adrian Sherratt/Alamy Stock Photo, (center right) Sueddeutsche Zeitung Photo/Alamy Stock Photo, (right) Eric Harlow/Keystone/Hulton Archive/Getty Images, (top) Picsfive/Fotolia; **30:** Warner Bros/Everett Collection; **33:** (left) Milosluz/Fotolia, (right) SZ Photo/Knorr + Hirth/Sueddeutsche Zeitung Photo/Alamy Stock Photo; **34:** Isonphoto/Fotolia; **38:** (right) Roman Samokhin/Fotolia, (left) Glopphy/Fotolia; **44:** AF Archive/Alamy Stock Photo; **47:** (bottom) Xavier Arnau/E+/Getty Images, (center) Bottleneck Studios/Alamy Stock Photo; **51:** Konstantin Stepanenko/123RF; **53:** MARKA/Mezzabarba/Alamy Stock Photo; **54:** Ritu Jethani/123RF; **55:** Yossarian6/Fotolia; **56:** Michael Shake/Shutterstock; **58:** (left) Tammie Arroyo/Hulton Archive/Getty Images, (right) Splash News/Newscom; **61:** Bikeriderlondon/Shutterstock; **66:** Spencer Grant/Art Directors & TRIP/Alamy Stock Photo; **68:** Goodween123/Fotolia; **69:** Michaeljung/Shutterstock; **72–73:** Maciek905/Fotolia; **74–75:** (bottom) Tsuneomp/Fotolia, (top) DM7/Fotolia; **80:** Tsuneo/123RF; **84:** Yossarian6/Fotolia; **85:** Arnau2098/Fotolia; **86:** Jakub Krechowicz/Fotolia; **88:** Syda Productions/Fotolia; **91:** Michaeljung/Fotolia; **95:** Salexander2/Fotolia; **96:** Archipoch/Fotolia; **99:** Africa Studio/Fotolia; **102–103:** Jan Will/123RF; **104:** Travis Rowan/Alamy Stock Photo; **109:** Lzf/Fotolia; **111:** (center) Zuzabax/Fotolia, (top) Rob/Fotolia; **112:** Lzf/Fotolia; **113:** Siraphol/Fotolia; **114:** (left) Suna/Fotolia, (right) David Gilder/123RF; **115:** Vlad_g/Fotolia; **118:** Shutterstock; **122:** Baibaz/Fotolia; **124:** (bottom) Chris Baker/123RF, (top) Donfiore/Fotolia; **125:** Sasajo/Fotolia; **129:** Anderm/Fotolia; **130:** (left) Cobalt/Fotolia, (right) Vetal1983/Fotolia; **134–135:** Pichugin Dmitry/Shutterstock; **136:** Onizu3d/Fotolia; **138:** JRB/Fotolia; **140–141:** Xbrchx/Fotolia; **144:** Superstock/Glow Images; **145:** Ray Mickshaw/WireImage/Getty Images; **148:** Tobias Hase/dpa/picture-alliance/Newscom; **149:** Katusha161107/Fotolia; **150:** Maksym Yemelyanov/Fotolia; **151:** Giuseppe Porzani/Fotolia; **152:** DragonImages/Fotolia; **154:** (bottom left) Robert Kaufman/Alamy Stock Photo, (bottom center) Susanna Saez/EFE/Newscom, (bottom right) Dennis Van Tine/LFI/Photoshot/Newscom, (top left) Adrian Sherratt/Alamy Stock Photo, (top center) Dennis Van Tine/UPI/Newscom, (top right) Richard Young/Ian Mcilgorm/REX/Newscom; **157:** Andrea Danti/Shutterstock; **164:** Bertrand Guay/AFP/Getty Images; **165:** Jesadaphorn/Fotolia; **166:** Markos86/Fotolia; **167:** (bottom left) Karmaknight/Fotolia, (bottom right) Tinx/Fotolia, (center left) Federico Rostagno/Fotolia, (center right) Alexey Stiop/Fotolia, (top left) Zigzagmtart/Fotolia, (top right) David_franklin/Fotolia; **168:** Jeffong/Fotolia; **169:** Jan Will/123RF; **172–173:** Angela Waye/Shutterstock; **174:** WENN Ltd/Alamy Stock Photo; **179:** Dpa picture alliance/Alamy Stock Photo; **179–180:** Flas100/Fotolia; **180:** PG/Splash News/Newscom; **182:** Sumire8/Fotolia; **185:** (bottom) Sumire8/Fotolia, (top) Stillfx/Fotolia; **194:** Roywylam/123RF; **197:** Roman Samokhin/Fotolia; **199:** Blaj Gabriel/123RF; **202:** Goodween123/Fotolia; **202–203:** (background) Denis_333/Fotolia, Vvoe/Fotolia; **203:** Alex/Fotolia; **211:** Aopsan/Fotolia; **214:** Elenarts/Fotolia; **214–215:** DigiClack/Fotolia; **215:** LuneWind/Fotolia; **219:** Digi Clack/Fotolia; **222:** Flashon Studio/123RF; **223:** Komi$ar/Fotolia; **224:** Phanuwatnandee/Fotolia; **228–229:** Reinhold Leitner/Shutterstock; **230:** Everett Collection/Newscom; **230–231:** C.E. Mitchell/BlackStar Photos/Newscom; **235:** (bottom) Alexzaitsev/Fotolia, (top) Tavarman/Fotolia; **236:** Sorincolac/Fotolia; **239:** (left) Tolgatezcan/Fotolia, (right) Picsfive/Fotolia; **240:** Okinawakasawa/Fotolia; **243:** 123dartist/Fotolia; **244:** 123dartist/Fotolia; **247:** Nexusseven/Fotolia; **248:** Shutterstock; **249:** (bottom) Olga Labusova/Fotolia, (top) Vladimir Tyutin/Fotolia; **250:** (bottom) Antiqueimages/Fotolia, (top) Dimashiper/Fotolia; **252:** Juan Carlos Rojas/Notimex/Newscom; **254:** Vladimir Prusakov/Fotolia; **258–259:** Quang Ho/Shutterstock; **260:** (bottom) Yossarian6/Fotolia, (background): rSnapshotPhotos/Shutterstock; **261:** (top) Yossarian6/Fotolia, (left) Pressmaster/Shutterstock, (center) AVAVA/Shutterstock, (right) S_I/Fotolia; **266:** Dragonstock/Fotolia; **267:** rSnapshotPhotos/Shutterstock; **269:** Ravennka/Fotolia; **270:** Jodie Johnson/Fotolia; **271:** Andy Dean/Fotolia; **272:** Ivonne Wierink/Shutterstock; **273:** Roman Bodnarchuk/Fotolia; **276:** (bottom) F9photos/Fotolia, (background) ki33/Fotolia; **277:** (left) Ki33/Fotolia, (right) Seamartini Graphics/Fotolia; **283:** (background) Peangdao/Fotolia, (bottom right) Raven/Fotolia, (center left) Volkovslava/Fotolia, (top) Gstudio Group/Fotolia; **284:** Rene Pi/Shutterstock; **285:** Alex/Fotolia; **287:** (bottom) Oly5/Fotolia, (top) Radoma/Fotolia; **290–291:** Stephanie Barbary/Shutterstock; **291:** Sumkinn/Fotolia; **294:** Earl Robbins/Fotolia; **295:** (top) Jacartoon/Fotolia, (top left) Pandavector/Fotolia, (center top) Pandavector/Fotolia, (center bottom) Skarin/Fotolia, (bottom left) Alek_maneewan/Fotolia, (bottom) Tackgalichstudio/Fotolia; **296:** Lisa Charbonneau/Shutterstock; **299:** Balaph/Fotolia; **302:** (background) Ki33/Fotolia, (bottom) Derek Shook/Splash News/Newscom; **303:** Ki33/Fotolia; **309:** Mezzotint/Shutterstock; **310:** Ron Sachs/UPI/Newscom; **311:** (left) Pathdoc/Shutterstock, (right) Wong Yu Liang/Fotolia; **312:** (bottom) Goir/Fotolia, (top) David Eulitt/MCT/Newscom; **313:** Nyul/Fotolia; **316–317:** Korn/Shutterstock; **318:** cartoonstock.com/Edgar Argo; **319:** Rob Epco/Fotolia; **322:** Ambassador806/Fotolia; **324:** Arek Malang/Shutterstock; **325:** Weedezign/Fotolia; **326:** Tyron Molteni/Fotolia; **330:** (background) Juri/Fotolia, (center) JHershPhoto/Shutterstock; **331:** Juri/Fotolia; **334:** Locotearts/Fotolia; **337:** Kaspars Grinvalds/Fotolia; **339:** Blaj Gabriel/Shutterstock; **342:** (bottom right) HektoR/Shutterstock, (top right) WavebreakMediaMicro/Fotolia, (top right) Pisit Santikulluk/123RF; **346:** Marc Dietrich/Shutterstock; **347:** (bottom) Antonio Diaz/Fotolia, (top left) Big-label/Fotolia, (top center) Vladimir Mucibabic/Fotolia, (center top) Alice_photo/Fotolia, (center bottom) Mario Beauregard/Fotolia, (bottom center) Adisa/Fotolia, (bottom left) Pavlo Burdyak/Fotolia, (top) Asierromero/Fotolia; **351:** Marisa Acocella Marchetto The New Yorker Collection/The Cartoon Bank; **352:** (bottom) Yeamake/Fotolia, (right) Alen Kadr/Fotolia, (left) Senkinv/Fotolia, (center left) Maxal Tamor/Fotolia, (right) Coprid/Fotolia, (top center right) Ilya Akinshin/Fotolia, (top center left) Vrisphuket/Fotolia, (top left) Vadidak/Fotolia, (top right) Coprid/Fotolia; **359:** Picsfive/Fotolia; **360:** Picsfive/Fotolia; **362:** Denchik/Fotolia; **364:** Joseph Helfenberger/Fotolia; **368–369:** Fikmik/123RF; **370:** Bikeriderlondon/Shutterstock; **370–371:** Weedezign/Fotolia; **371:** Andres Rodriguez/Fotolia; **374:** (bottom) Sari Gustafsson/REX/Newscom, (background) Siro46/Fotolia; **379:** Tortoon/Fotolia; **381:** (top right) Matthew Benoit/Fotolia, (background) Tolga Tezcan/Fotolia; **384:** Dr. Eloy Rodriguez; **385:** Dr. Eloy Rodriguez; **388:** Denchik/Fotolia; **389:** (bottom) Negoi Cristian/Fotolia, (background) Tanawatpontchour/Fotolia; **390:** TUNS/Picture Alliance/Arco Images G/Newscom; **396–397:** Aruba2000/Fotolia; **398:** (bottom) Eldad Carin/Fotolia, (top) Michael Jung/Fotolia; **404:** Sborisov/Fotolia; **405:** Elnur/Fotolia; **407:** Adimas/Fotolia; **411:** Andrey Kuzmin/Fotolia; **418:** (background) Paladin1212/Fotolia, (top) Patrisyu/Fotolia; **421:** Pathdoc/Fotolia; **424:** B Studio/Shutterstock; **427:** Semion/Fotolia; **432:** Picsfive/Fotolia; **434:** Mokee81/Fotolia; **435:** (background) Juri/Fotolia, (left) Leung Cho Pan/Fotolia, (right) Duckman76/Fotolia; **438:** (background) Pakhnyushchyy/Fotolia, (bottom) Franck Camhi/123RF; **439:** (bottom) Pakhnyushchyy/Fotolia, (top) Stillfx/Fotolia; **443:** (bottom) Aruba2000/Fotolia, (top) Pakhnyushchyy/Fotolia; **449:** (bottom center) Aleksandr Ugorenkov/Fotolia, (bottom left) Mercedes Fittipaldi/Fotolia, (bottom right) Mashe/Fotolia, (center top) Swisshippo/Fotolia, (right) Rob/Fotolia, (top center) My Portfolio/Shutterstock, (top left) Evgenia Tiplyashina/Fotolia; **450:** Scisetti Alfio/Fotolia

ILLUSTRATION CREDITS

Steve Attoe – pages 4, 5, 82, 83, 189, 225, 355, 423
Ron Chironna – page 25
Chi Chung – page 243
Jock MacRae – pages 43, 380, 414
Tom Newsom – pages 42, 137, 138, 376, 377
Dusan Petricic – page 251
Steve Schulman – pages 163, 365, 445 (left)
Gary Torrisi – pages 57, 126, 207, 255, 298, 445 (right)
Meryl Treatner – page 393

Present and Past

UNIT 1
Present Progressive and Simple Present
DIFFERENT CULTURES

UNIT 2
Simple Past
POETS

UNIT 3
Past Progressive and Simple Past
REPORTING EVENTS

UNIT 4
Used to and *Would*
CHANGES

UNIT 5
Wh- Questions
IN COURT

PART 1

OUTCOMES
- Describe actions that are happening now
- Describe actions, states, and situations that happen regularly, and unchanging facts
- Recognize the use of the present progressive and the simple present in reading and listening
- Express opinions about topics related to cross-cultural differences
- Write a description of a new experience

OUTCOMES
- Use the simple past with regular and irregular verbs
- Describe events, states, and situations in the past
- Identify the order of events in a reading and listening
- Discuss past events and situations
- Write about some important life events

OUTCOMES
- Describe past events or situations
- Use *when* or *while* to link clauses in the simple past and the past progressive
- Identify the order of events in a description of an accident
- Report on events that were interrupted by other events
- Write a description of a past event

OUTCOMES
- Describe past habits and situations, using *used to* and *would*
- Evaluate events and situations described in a reading and a listening
- Describe and discuss one's past and present physical appearance and habits
- Write a description of a place and how it has changed

OUTCOMES
- Ask questions about the past, using *wh-* words
- Identify important information in an interview transcript
- Identify the main point of a conversation
- Write a series of interview questions to get information about a past event

UNIT 1

Present Progressive and Simple Present

DIFFERENT CULTURES

OUTCOMES
- Describe actions that are happening now
- Describe actions, states, and situations that happen regularly, and unchanging facts
- Recognize the use of the present progressive and the simple present in reading and listening
- Express opinions about topics related to cross-cultural differences
- Write a description of a new experience

STEP 1 GRAMMAR IN CONTEXT

BEFORE YOU READ

Look at the cartoons. Discuss the questions.

1. What are the people doing?
2. How do they feel?

READ

01|01 **Read this article about cross-cultural communication.**

What's Your Cross-Cultural IQ?[1]

Are you living in your native country or in another country? Do you ever travel abroad? Do you understand the misunderstandings in these two situations?

Situation 1

Jason is standing at Dan's door. He thinks he's on time for the party, but he doesn't see any guests, and Dan is wearing shorts and a T-shirt! Dan looks surprised. In his culture, people never arrive at the exact start of a social event. They often come at least 30 minutes later.

1 *What's your cross-cultural IQ?:* How much do you know about other people's cultures?

Situation 2

Ina and Marty are talking. They are both feeling very uncomfortable. In Marty's culture, people usually stand quite close. This seems friendly to them. In Ina's culture, people prefer to have more distance between them. This doesn't mean they are unfriendly.

2 *What's the matter?:* What's wrong?
3 *perfume:* a liquid with a strong pleasant smell that you put on your skin

AFTER YOU READ

A VOCABULARY **Choose the word or phrase that is closest in meaning to the word in bold.**

1. Are you living in your **native** country?
   a. first b. new c. favorite
2. Do you ever travel **abroad**?
   a. by boat b. to foreign countries c. on expensive trips
3. What was the **misunderstanding** about?
   a. fight b. argument c. confusion
4. They come from different **cultures**.
   a. schools b. climates c. ways of life
5. They prefer to have more **distance** between them.
   a. streets b. space c. time
6. There are a lot of parties and other **events** at the Students' Club.
   a. members b. languages c. activities

B COMPREHENSION **Complete each statement with the correct name.**

1. ___Dan___ doesn't have shoes on.
2. ___Dan___ isn't expecting people to arrive at 8:00.
3. ___Jason___ thinks he's on time.
4. ___Marty___ is wearing perfume.
5. ___Ina___ wants to stand farther away.
6. ___Marty___ probably thinks the other person is a little unfriendly.

C DISCUSSION **Work with a partner. Compare your answers in B. Why did you choose each answer?**

STEP 2 GRAMMAR PRESENTATION

PRESENT PROGRESSIVE

Affirmative Statements

Subject	*Be*	Base Form of Verb + *-ing*	
I	**am**	**traveling**	now.
You	**are**		
He She It	**is**		
We You They	**are**		

Negative Statements

Subject	*Be*	*Not*	Base Form of Verb + *-ing*	
I	**am**	**not**	**traveling**	now.
He	**is**			
We	**are**			

***Yes/No* Questions**

Be	Subject	Base Form of Verb + *-ing*	
Is	he	**traveling**	now?

Short Answers

Yes,	he	**is.**
No,		**isn't.**

***Wh-* Questions**

Wh- Word	*Be*	Subject	Base Form of Verb + *-ing*	
Where	**are**	you	**traveling**	now?

SIMPLE PRESENT

Affirmative Statements

Subject		Verb
I	often	**travel.**
You		
He She It		**travels.**
We You They		**travel.**

Negative Statements

Subject	*Do*	*Not*	Base Form of Verb	
I	**do**	**not**	**travel**	often.
He	**does**			
We	**do**			

***Yes/No* Questions**

Do	Subject	Base Form of Verb	
Does	he	**travel**	often?

Short Answers

Yes,	he	**does.**
No,		**doesn't.**

***Wh-* Questions**

Wh- Word	*Do*	Subject		Base Form of Verb
Where	**do**	you	usually	**travel?**

GRAMMAR NOTES

1 Present Progressive

Use the present progressive to show that something is **happening now** or **in a longer present time**.

- **happening now**
  (*right now, at the moment*)

Diego **is speaking** English ***now***.
He**'s wearing** shorts ***at the moment***.

- **happening in a longer present time**
  (*this month, this year, these days, nowadays*), even if it's not happening now

We**'re studying** U.S. history ***this month***.
(But we aren't studying it now.)
Laura**'s studying** in France ***this year***.
Are you **studying** hard ***these days***?

2 Simple Present

Use the simple present to show that something **happens regularly** or for **unchanging facts**.

- **happens regularly**
  (*usually, often, every day, always*)

Diego ***usually*** **speaks** Spanish.
He **wears** jeans ***every day***.

- **unchanging facts**

Miguel **comes** from Oaxaca. Oaxaca **is** in Mexico.

BE CAREFUL! Remember to add *-s* or *-es* to third-person-singular (*he, she, it*) verbs. Also, remember to use ***does*** in questions and ***doesn't*** in negatives for third-person-singular verbs.

He **wears** jeans. He **doesn't wear** shorts.
NOT He ~~wear~~ jeans. He ~~don't~~ wear shorts.

3 Simple Present + Adverbs of Frequency

Use the simple present with adverbs of frequency to show **how often something happens**.

always — In Spain, women ***always*** **kiss** on both cheeks.
usually
often/frequently — In France, women ***often*** **kiss** on both cheeks.
sometimes
rarely/seldom — We ***rarely*** **stand** very close to each other.
hardly ever
never — In China, children ***never*** **call** adults by their first names.

Adverbs of frequency usually go **before the verb**. However, ***sometimes*** and ***usually*** can also go at the **beginning of the sentence**.

I ***sometimes*** **wear** shorts at home.
or
Sometimes I **wear** shorts at home.

BE CAREFUL! Adverbs of frequency usually go **after** the verb ***be***.

They **are** ***never*** late.
NOT They ~~never are~~ late.

4 Non-Action Verbs

Use non-action verbs to describe **states** or **situations**, but not actions.

Non-action verbs describe:	
• **emotions** (*like, love, hate, want, feel, fear, trust*)	We **like** Claude a lot. We **love** the stories he tells.
• **mental states** (*know, remember, believe, think, mean, understand, wonder*)	I **know** a lot of U.S. customs now. We **think** they're from Spain. What **do** you **mean**? I **don't understand**.
• **possession** (*have, own, possess, belong*)	Cesar **has** two brothers. Some students **own** cars.
• **senses** and **perceptions** (*hear, see, smell, taste, feel, notice, seem, look, be, appear, sound*)	I **hear** the telephone. Dina **looks** tired. They both **sound** sick.
BE CAREFUL! Use the **simple present** with most **non-action verbs**. Do not use the present progressive—even when the verb describes a situation that exists at the moment of speaking.	Jane **wants** to go home now. NOT Jane ~~is wanting~~ to go home now.
USAGE NOTE In **informal conversation**, some people use the **present progressive** with verbs of emotion (especially with ***like*** and ***love***) and with verbs of mental state. This often describes a **temporary feeling** or a change of feelings.	I'**m loving** this book! She'**s liking** him more and more. He'**s understanding** a lot better these days.

5 Non-Action and Action Verbs

Some verbs can have both a **non-action** and an **action** meaning.

	NON-ACTION	ACTION
• **sense and perception verbs** (*taste, smell, feel,* and *look*)	The soup **tastes** good. *(It's good.)*	He'**s tasting** the soup. *(He's trying it.)*
	His car **looks** great. *(It's beautiful.)*	I'**m looking** at his car. *(I'm examining it.)*
• ***have*** and ***think***	I **have** a new watch. *(I own a new watch.)*	I'**m having** fun. *(I'm experiencing fun.)*
	I **think** he's right. *(My opinion: He's right.)*	I'**m thinking** of going. *(I'm considering going.)*
USAGE NOTE We often use ***feel*** in the progressive form when it expresses an **emotion**. The **meaning is the same** as when we use the simple present form.	I **feel** very happy about this. or I'**m feeling** very happy about this.	

PRONUNCIATION NOTE

01|02 **Pronunciation of *What do you* and *What are you***

In informal American English conversation, people often pronounce ***What do you . . . ?*** and ***What are you . . . ?*** the same way: "whaddaya."	A: **What do you** do? *(whaddaya)* B: **What are you** doing? *(whaddaya)*

REFERENCE NOTES

For **spelling rules** on forming the **present progressive**, see Appendix 21 on page 462.

For **spelling rules** on forming the third-person singular of the **simple present**, see Appendix 20 on page 461.

For **pronunciation rules** for the **simple present**, see Appendix 29 on page 466.

For **contractions** of *I am, you are*, etc., see Appendix 26 on page 464.

For a list of **non-action verbs**, see Appendix 2 on page 454.

For the **present progressive** and the **simple present** to talk about the **future**, see Unit 6 on page 76.

STEP 3 FOCUSED PRACTICE

EXERCISE 1 DISCOVER THE GRAMMAR

GRAMMAR NOTES 1–5 **Read the postings by Brian, a Canadian student studying in Argentina. Underline all the verbs that describe what is happening now. Circle the verbs that describe what regularly happens.**

JUNE 30: 7:30 p.m. My host parents are still working. Carlos, my "father," works at home. My "little brother," Ricardo, is cute. He looks (and acts) a lot like Bobby. Right now, he's looking over my shoulder and trying to read my journal.

JULY 4: The weather is cold here in the summer. I usually spend the first weekend of July at the beach. Today, I'm walking around in a heavy sweater.

JULY 10: I'm sitting in the school cafeteria with some of my classmates. In Canada, I only drink tea, but at the moment I'm having a cup of strong coffee. It tastes great! The students here come from all over the world. Most of them don't speak English, so we're all speaking Spanish. It's a great way to learn!

AUGUST 6: I usually feel great in the evening, but tonight I feel really tired.

AUGUST 25: I'm feeling very comfortable here now—but it's almost time to go home! My host parents usually cook a light dinner, but tonight is a special event. They're preparing a big party for me to say goodbye. I miss them already!

EXERCISE 2 PRESENT PROGRESSIVE OR SIMPLE PRESENT

A GRAMMAR NOTES 1–5 **Some students are talking outside of a classroom. Circle the correct words to complete their conversations.**

Conversation 1

TARO: There's Miguel. He talks / (He's talking) to Luisa. (1.)

MARISA: Yes. They take / They're taking a class together this semester. (2.)

TARO: They stand / They're standing very close to each other. (3.) Do you think / Are you thinking (4.) that they date / they're dating? (5.)

MARISA: No. I don't think / I'm not thinking (6.) that it means / it's meaning (7.) anything special. I come / I'm coming (8.) from Costa Rica, and people usually stand / are standing (9.) that close to each other there.

Conversation 2

LI-WU: Hi, Paulo. What do you do / are you doing? (1.)

PAULO: Oh, I wait / I'm waiting (2.) for class to begin.

LI-WU: What's the matter? You seem / You're seeming (3.) a little down.

PAULO: I'm just tired. I work / I'm working (4.) evenings this semester. Hey, is that your teacher over there?

LI-WU: Yes. She talks / She's talking (5.) to a classmate.

PAULO: What's wrong? He doesn't look / He's not looking (6.) at her. He seems / He's seeming (7.) uncomfortable.

LI-WU: Oh. That doesn't mean / isn't meaning (8.) anything. In some countries, it's not polite to look directly at your teacher.

01|03 **B** LISTEN AND CHECK **Listen to the conversations and check your answers in A.**

EXERCISE 3 QUESTIONS AND STATEMENTS

A GRAMMAR NOTES 1–5 **Other students are talking outside of a classroom. Complete the conversations. Use the present progressive or the simple present form of the verbs in parentheses.**

Conversation 1

RASHA: There's Hans. Why ___is___ he ___walking___ (1. walk) so fast? Class ____________ (2. start) at 9:00. He still ____________ (3. have) 10 minutes!

CLAUDE: He always ____________ (4. walk) fast. I ____________ (5. think) Swiss people often ____________ (6. appear) to be in a hurry.

Conversation 2

IZUMI: Isn't that Sergio and Luis? Why ________ they ________ (1. shake) hands? They already ________ (2. know) each other!

LI-JING: In Brazil, men ________ (3. shake) hands every time they ________ (4. meet). It's normal in their culture.

IZUMI: ________ women ________ (5. shake) hands, too?

01|04 **B** LISTEN AND CHECK **Listen to the conversations and check your answers in A.**

EXERCISE 4 AFFIRMATIVE AND NEGATIVE STATEMENTS

GRAMMAR NOTES 1–2, 5 **Look at Brian's schedule in Argentina. He usually has a regular schedule, but today some things are different. Complete the sentences. Use the present progressive or the simple present. Choose between affirmative and negative.**

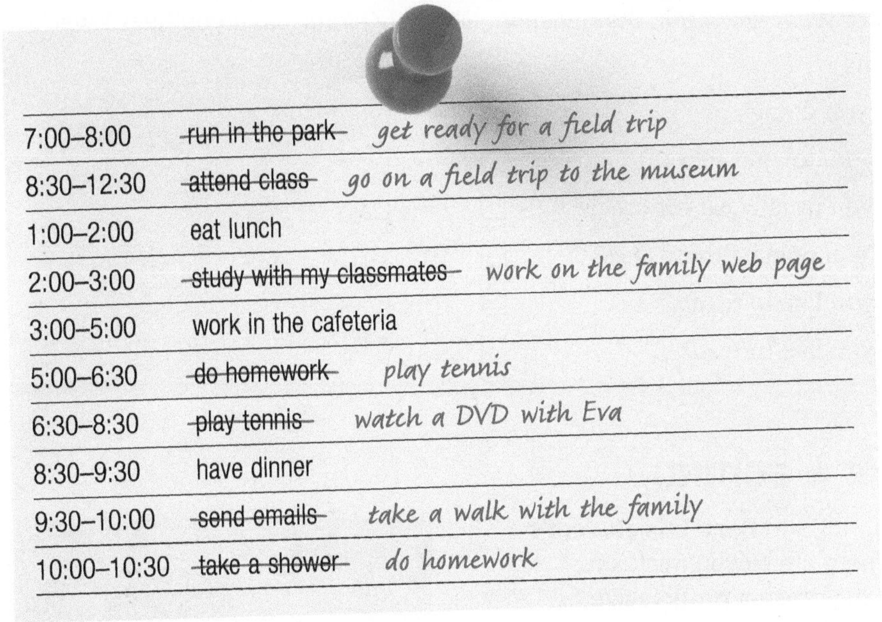

7:00–8:00	~~run in the park~~ *get ready for a field trip*
8:30–12:30	~~attend class~~ *go on a field trip to the museum*
1:00–2:00	eat lunch
2:00–3:00	~~study with my classmates~~ *work on the family web page*
3:00–5:00	work in the cafeteria
5:00–6:30	~~do homework~~ *play tennis*
6:30–8:30	~~play tennis~~ *watch a DVD with Eva*
8:30–9:30	have dinner
9:30–10:00	~~send emails~~ *take a walk with the family*
10:00–10:30	~~take a shower~~ *do homework*

1. Brian always *runs in the park* early in the morning, but today he *is getting ready for a field trip*.
2. Brian usually ________ between 8:30 and 12:30, but today he ________.
3. He always ________ between 1:00 and 2:00.
4. It's 1:30. He ________.
5. He normally ________ after lunch, but today he ________.
6. Every day from 3:00 to 5:00, he ________.

7. It's 5:15, but he ______________________________ now.
He ______________________________ instead.
8. It's 6:45, but he ______________________________.
He ______________________________.
9. It's 8:30. Brian ______________________________.
10. He always ______________________________ at 8:30.
11. After dinner, Brian usually ______________________________,
but tonight he ______________________________.
12. It's 10:15, but he ______________________________.
He ______________________________.

EXERCISE 5 *WHAT DO YOU, WHAT ARE YOU,* OR *WHADDAYA*

01|05 PRONUNCIATION NOTE Listen to the questions and answers. Check (✓) *Formal* if you hear *What do you* or *What are you* in the question. Check (✓) *Informal* if you hear *Whaddaya*.

	Formal	Informal
1. What are you doing?	☐	☑
2. What do you do after school?	☐	☐
3. What do you usually eat for lunch?	☐	☐
4. What are you reading these days?	☐	☐
5. What do you like to read?	☐	☐
6. What do you like to read?	☐	☐

EXERCISE 6 EDITING

GRAMMAR NOTES 1–5 **Read this student's blog entry. There are eleven mistakes in the use of the present progressive or simple present. The first mistake is already corrected. Find and correct ten more.**

It's 12:30 and ~~I sit~~ *I'm sitting* in the library right now. My classmates are eating lunch together, but I don't feel hungry yet. At home, we eat never this early. Today, our journal topic is culture shock (the strange feelings you have when you visit a foreign country for the first time). It's a good topic for me right now because I'm being pretty homesick. I miss speaking my native language with my friends. And I miss my old routine. At home, we always are eating a big meal at 2:00 in the afternoon. Then we rest. But here in Toronto, I'm having a 3:00 conversation class. Every day, I almost fall asleep in class, and my teacher ask me, "Are you bored?" Of course I'm not bored. I just need my afternoon nap! This class always is fun. This semester, we work on a project with videos. My team is filming groups of people from different cultures at social events. We are analyze "personal space." That is meaning how close to each other these people stand. According to my new watch, it's 12:55, and I have a 1:00 class. That's all for now. Teachers here really aren't liking lateness!

STEP 4 COMMUNICATION PRACTICE

EXERCISE 7 LISTENING

01|06 **A** You are going to listen to five short interviews of foreign students studying at a summer language program in the United States. Listen and check (✓) the things the students *Usually* do and the things they are doing *Now or These Days*. Then listen again and check your answers.

	Usually	Now or These Days
1. Ana		
a. speak English	☐	☑
b. speak Spanish	☐	☐
2. Mehmet		
a. live in a small town	☐	☐
b. live in a big city	☐	☐
3. Eva		
a. walk slowly	☐	☐
b. move quickly	☐	☐
4. Paulo		
a. wear a watch	☐	☐
b. ask other people for the time	☐	☐
5. Olga		
a. study grammar and pronunciation	☐	☐
b. study English literature	☐	☐

01|06 **B** **Work with a partner. Listen to each interview again. Discuss the questions.**

Interview 1
How does Ana feel? Why?
What does she find most difficult? Why?

EXAMPLE: A: Ana feels good.
B: Yes. Things are going well for her. She . . .

Interview 2
Does Mehmet like living in New York? Why or why not?

Interview 3
Is Eva experiencing culture shock?
What does she think about the "pace of life" in the United States?

Interview 4
What does Paulo do at home without a watch?
Why is Paulo upset?
Do *you* wear a watch? Why or why not?

Interview 5
How does Olga feel about her classes? Why?
What is she studying now?

EXERCISE 8 FIND SOMEONE WHO . . .

A GAME **Walk around your classroom. Ask your classmates questions and fill out the chart. The first person to finish wins.**

EXAMPLE: A: Tania, are you living in a dormitory?
B: No, I'm not. I'm living with a family.

Find someone who . . .	Name
isn't living in a dormitory	______________
likes visiting foreign countries	______________
speaks more than two languages	______________
is studying something in addition to English	______________
doesn't watch sports on TV	______________
is planning to travel abroad this year	______________
______________ (add your own)	______________

B **Report back to the class.**

EXAMPLE: Tania isn't living in a dormitory.

EXERCISE 9 WHAT'S HAPPENING?

PICTURE DISCUSSION **Work with a partner. Look at the photos. Describe them. What's happening? How do the people feel? Discuss possible explanations for each situation. Compare your answers with those of your classmates.**

EXAMPLE: A: She's pointing and she looks . . .
B: She also has a finger in front of her . . . Maybe she . . .

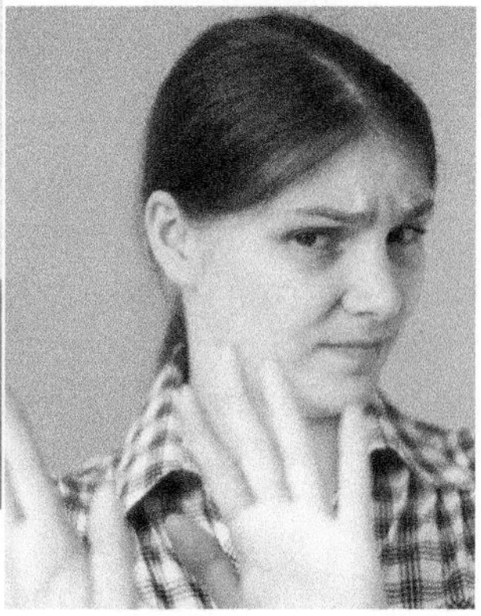

EXERCISE 10 IS IT OK IN YOUR CULTURE?

A CROSS-CULTURAL COMPARISON **Look at the questions. In your culture, which questions are appropriate to ask someone you just met? Check (✓) *OK*. Which questions are not appropriate? Check (✓) *NOT OK*.**

	Questions	OK	NOT OK
1.	Are you married?	☐	☐
2.	How much rent do you pay?	☐	☐
3.	How old are you?	☐	☐
4.	What are you studying?	☐	☐
5.	What do you do?	☐	☐
6.	Where do you live?	☐	☐

B **Work in a group. Compare your choices with those of your classmates.**

EXAMPLE: A: In my culture, it's OK to ask someone the question "Are you married?" What about in your culture?
B: It depends. It's OK for an older person to ask a young person this question. But, it's *not* OK for a man to ask a strange woman the question. What about in your culture?

C **What are other examples of inappropriate questions in your culture?**

EXAMPLE: A: In my culture, it's not OK to ask someone the questions "How tall are you?" or "What do you weigh?" What about in your culture?
B: . . .

FROM GRAMMAR TO WRITING

A BEFORE YOU WRITE **Think about a new experience you are having (for example, living in a new country, taking a new class, working at a new job). Complete the outline.**

____
(New Experience)

Usually	Now

B WRITE **Use your outline to write a paragraph about your new experience. How is it different from what you usually do? How do you feel in the new situation? Use *but* or *however* to contrast your usual experience with your new experience. Try to avoid the common mistakes in the chart.**

EXAMPLE: I usually live at home with my parents, but this month I'm living with my aunt and uncle. Everything seems different. My aunt always makes dinner at 6:00. However, at home we never eat before 8:00 p.m. . . .

Common Mistakes in Using the Present Progressive and Simple Present

Use the **simple present** with most **non-action verbs**. Do not use the present progressive.	I **think** my aunt's dinners are great. NOT I ~~am thinking~~ my aunt's dinners are great.
Put an **adverb of frequency before** the simple present verb. Do not put it after the verb.	We ***always*** **eat** at 6:00. NOT We ~~eat always~~ at 6:00.
Put an **adverb of frequency after** the verb *be*. Do not put it before *be*.	She **is *always*** on time. NOT She ~~always is~~ on time.

C CHECK YOUR WORK **Read your paragraph. Underline once the present progressive and underline twice the simple present forms. Circle the adverbs of frequency. Use the Editing Checklist to check your work.**

Editing Checklist

Did you use . . . ?

- ☐ the present progressive to describe something that is happening right now
- ☐ the simple present to describe what regularly happens
- ☐ the simple present with non-action verbs such as *be*, *like*, *seem*, and *want*
- ☐ adverbs of frequency in the correct position

D REVISE YOUR WORK **Read your paragraph again. Can you improve your writing? Make changes if necessary. Give your paragraph a title.**

UNIT 1 **REVIEW**

Test yourself on the grammar of the unit.

A Circle the correct words to complete the sentences.

1. What courses are you taking / do you take this semester?
2. I don't / I'm not understand this phrase. What's *culture shock*?
3. At home, we often speak / speak often Spanish.
4. Look! That's my teacher. He's talking / He talks to Andrea, one of my classmates.
5. Are / Do you feel better today?

B Complete the conversation with the present progressive or simple present form of the verbs in parentheses.

A: What ________ you ________ right now? (1. do)

B: Not much. I ________ just ________ a video game. Why? (2. play)

A: ________ you ________ to get some lunch? (3. want)

B: Sure. I usually ________ (4. not eat) this early, but I ________ (5. feel) pretty hungry right now.

A: Mmm, mushroom soup. It ________ (6. look) good.

B: It ________ (7. not taste) good, though. I had it yesterday.

A: Hey, there's Costa and Libby. Why ________ they ________ like that? (8. shout)

________ (9. be) they angry?

B: I don't think so. They always ________ (10. talk) like that. Let's go sit with them. They're fun.

C Find and correct five mistakes.

I live in Qatar, but right now I stay in Wisconsin. I'm studying English here. I have a good time this summer, but in some ways it's a pretty strange experience. Summer in Wisconsin feel like winter in Qatar! Every weekend, I go to the beach with some classmates, but I go never into the water—it's too cold! I'm enjoy my time here though, and my culture shock is going away fast.

Now check your answers on page 475.

UNIT

2 Simple Past
POETS

OUTCOMES
- Use the simple past with regular and irregular verbs
- Describe events, states, and situations in the past
- Identify the order of events in a reading and listening
- Discuss past events and situations
- Write about some important life events

STEP 1 GRAMMAR IN CONTEXT

BEFORE YOU READ

Look at the title of the reading and the handwritten text. Discuss the questions.

1. How long did Matsuo Basho live?
2. What did he do?

READ

02|01 **Read this short biography of Basho.**

Matsuo Basho, 1644–1694

Matsuo Basho wrote more than 1,000 *haiku* (three-line poems). He chose topics from nature, daily life, and human emotions. He became one of Japan's most famous poets, and his work established haiku as an important art form.

The old pond
A frog jumped in—
The sound of water
—Matsuo Basho

Basho was born Matsuo Munefusa near Kyoto in 1644. ("Basho" is the name he later used as a poet.) He did not want to become a samurai[1] like his father. Instead, he moved to Edo (present-day Tokyo) and studied poetry. Then he became a teacher, and by 1681 he had many students and admirers.

Basho, however, was restless. Starting in 1684, he traveled on foot and on horseback all over Japan. Sometimes his friends joined him, and they wrote poetry together. Travel was difficult in the seventeenth century, and Basho often got sick. He died in 1694 during a journey to Osaka. At that time, he had 2,000 students.

1 *samurai:* a member of the soldier class in Japan in past times

AFTER YOU READ

A VOCABULARY **Complete the sentences with the words from the box.**

admirers	emotions	journey	restless	topic

1. Basho wrote about everyday things. A frog is the ______________ of one of his most famous poems.
2. Basho's students and ______________ loved him and called him a great poet.
3. On his first ______________, Basho traveled a long way and visited his native village.
4. Basho became ______________ and did not want to stay in one place for very long.
5. Basho felt all kinds of strong ______________ in his travels, such as fear and happiness.

B COMPREHENSION **Check (✓) the boxes to complete the statements. Each statement has two correct answers.**

1. Basho lived _____.
   - ☐ from 1644 to 1694
   - ☐ in the sixteenth century
   - ☐ in the seventeenth century
2. Basho became a _____.
   - ☐ samurai
   - ☐ poet
   - ☐ traveler
3. In Edo, Basho _____.
   - ☐ studied poetry
   - ☐ became a teacher
   - ☐ became a samurai
4. On his journeys, he _____.
   - ☐ traveled in boats
   - ☐ walked
   - ☐ rode horses
5. At the end of his life, Basho _____.
   - ☐ had only a few students
   - ☐ traveled to Osaka
   - ☐ was famous

C DISCUSSION **Work with a partner. Compare your answers in B. Why did or didn't you check each answer?**

STEP 2 GRAMMAR PRESENTATION

SIMPLE PAST: *BE*

Affirmative Statements

Subject	*Be*	
I	**was**	famous.
You	**were**	
He She It	**was**	
We You They	**were**	

Negative Statements

Subject	*Be + Not*	
I	**wasn't**	famous.
You	**weren't**	
He She It	**wasn't**	
We You They	**weren't**	

***Yes/No* Questions**

Be	Subject	
Was	I	famous?
Were	you	
Was	he she it	
Were	we you they	

Short Answers

Affirmative		
Yes,	you	**were.**
	I	**was.**
	he she it	**was.**
	you we they	**were.**

Negative		
No,	you	**weren't.**
	I	**wasn't.**
	he she it	**wasn't.**
	you we they	**weren't.**

***Wh-* Questions**

Wh- Word	*Be*	Subject	
Where When Why	**was**	I	famous?
	were	you	
	was	he she it	
	were	we you they	

SIMPLE PAST: REGULAR AND IRREGULAR VERBS

Affirmative Statements

Subject	Verb	
I You He She It We You They	**moved** **traveled**	to Japan.
	came **left**	in 2012.

Negative Statements

Subject	*Did not*	Base Form of Verb	
I You He She It We You They	**didn't**	**move** **travel**	to Japan.
		come **leave**	in 2012.

Yes/No Questions

Did	Subject	Base Form of Verb	
Did	I you he she it we you they	**move** **travel**	to Japan?
		come **leave**	in 2012?

Short Answers

Affirmative		
Yes,	you I he she it you we they	**did.**

Negative		
No,	you I he she it you we they	**didn't.**

Wh- Questions

Wh- Word	*Did*	Subject	Base Form of Verb	
When Why	**did**	I you he she it we you they	**move** **travel**	to Japan?
			come? **leave**?	

GRAMMAR NOTES

1 Simple Past

Use the simple past to show that an action, state, or situation is **finished**.

Basho **lived** in the 17th century.
He **was** a poet. He **wrote** haiku.
He **didn't stay** in one place.
Where **did** he **travel**?

2 Simple Past + Past Time Expressions

We often use the simple past with past time expressions.

Some examples of **past time expressions** are:

- *yesterday*
- *last week*
- *300 years ago*
- *in the 17th century*
- *by 1681*

Yesterday, I **wrote** my first poem.
Last week, I **read** a poem by Basho.
He **died** more than ***300 years ago***.
He **lived** ***in the 17th century***.
By 1681, he **had** many students.

3 Regular Verbs

Form the simple past of regular verbs by **adding** ***-d*** or ***-ed*** to the base form of the verb.

- adding *-d*
- adding *-ed*

BASE FORM		SIMPLE PAST
live	→	live**d**
want	→	want**ed**

IN WRITING There are often **spelling changes** when you add ***-ed*** to the verb.

study	→	stud**ied**
plan	→	plan**ned**

4 Irregular Verbs

Many common verbs are irregular. Do not form their simple past by adding *-d* or *-ed* to the base form of the verb.

The list to the right includes the **most common irregular verbs**. They are especially common in conversation.

BASE FORM		SIMPLE PAST	BASE FORM		SIMPLE PAST
be	→	**was/were**	know	→	**knew**
come	→	**came**	make	→	**made**
get	→	**got**	mean	→	**meant**
give	→	**gave**	say	→	**said**
go	→	**went**	see	→	**saw**
have	→	**had**	think	→	**thought**

USAGE NOTE Some verbs have **two simple past forms**—one **regular** and one **irregular**. In conversation, the irregular past form is more common. There is one exception: for *dream*, the regular form is more common.

kneel	→	kneel**ed**/**knelt**
light	→	light**ed**/**lit**
dream	→	dream**ed**/**dreamt**

USAGE NOTE A few verbs have **two irregular simple past forms**.

forbid	→	**forbade/forbid**
sink	→	**sank/sunk**

REFERENCE NOTES

For **spelling rules** for the **simple past of regular verbs**, see Appendix 22 on page 462.
For **pronunciation rules** for the **simple past of regular verbs**, see Appendix 30 on page 467.
For a list of **irregular verbs**, see Appendix 1 on page 453.

STEP 3 FOCUSED PRACTICE

EXERCISE 1 DISCOVER THE GRAMMAR

GRAMMAR NOTES 1–4 **Read more about Basho. Underline all the regular simple past verbs. Circle all the irregular simple past verbs. Then complete the timeline on the right.**

As the son of a samurai, Basho (grew up) in the household of Todo Yoshitada, a young lord. After his father's death in 1656, Basho <u>stayed</u> in the Yoshitada household. He and Todo wrote poetry together, and in 1664, they published some poems. Two years later, Todo died suddenly. Basho left the area.

Basho was a restless young man, and he moved around for several years. In the 1670s, he went to Edo and stayed there. He found friendship and success once again. Basho judged poetry contests, published his own poetry, and taught students. His students built him a home outside the city in 1681. They planted a banana tree (*basho* in Japanese) in front and called his home "Basho Hut." That is how the poet got his name: Basho.

In spite of this success, Basho became unhappy. He often wrote about loneliness. He dreamed of traveling. His mother died in 1683, and he began his travels a year later. His trip to the northern part of Honshu in 1689 was difficult, but his travel diary about this journey, *Narrow Road to the Deep North*, became one of Japan's greatest works of literature.

As a famous poet, Basho had many visitors—too many, in fact. In 1693 he locked his gate for a month, stayed alone, and wrote. The following year, he took his final journey, to Osaka. He died there among his friends and admirers.

1644	Basho was born.
1656	Basho's father died.
1664	Basho (and Todo) published some poems.
1666	______
______	Students built the Basho Hut.
1683	______
1684	______
______	Basho traveled to northern Honshu.
______	Basho locked his gate to visitors.
1694	______

EXERCISE 2 AFFIRMATIVE STATEMENTS

GRAMMAR NOTES 1–4 **Complete this biography of American poet Emily Dickinson. Use the simple past form of the verbs in parentheses. See Appendix 1 on page 453 for help with the irregular verbs.**

Emily Dickinson, one of the most famous American poets, ___lived___ (1. live) from 1830 to 1886. Her favorite topics ________ (2. be) nature, time, and human emotions.

Dickinson ________ (3. lead) an unusual life. During the 1860s, she ________ (4. become) a recluse[1]—she almost never ________ (5. leave) her house in Amherst, Massachusetts, and she only ________ (6. wear) white. Dickinson ________ (7. allow) very few people to visit her, but she ________ (8. have) a lot of friends, and she ________ (9. write) them many letters.

1 *recluse:* someone who stays away from other people

EXERCISE 3 AFFIRMATIVE AND NEGATIVE STATEMENTS

GRAMMAR NOTES 1–4 **Complete this list of facts about Emily Dickinson. Use the simple past form of the verbs in parentheses. See Appendix 1 on page 453 for help with the irregular verbs.**

1. Dickinson ___wasn't___ (not be) only interested in poetry.
2. She also ________ (like) science.
3. She ________ (use) topics from science in many of her poems.
4. She never ________ (go) far from home, but she ________ (know) many people.
5. Dickinson ________ (not write) only poetry.
6. She ________ (send) her friends and admirers hundreds of letters.
7. Her letters ________ (be) full of jokes, recipes, cartoons, and poems.
8. But she ________ (not address) the envelopes—other people ________ (do) that for her.
9. Dickinson ________ (not own) a typewriter.
10. She ________ (write) the first drafts[1] of her poems on the back of old grocery lists.
11. During her lifetime, 7 of her 1,700 poems ________ (appear) in print.
12. She ________ (not know) about this, and no one ________ (ask) her permission.

1 *first drafts:* first copies of a piece of writing, with no corrections

EXERCISE 4 REGULAR AND IRREGULAR VERBS

A GRAMMAR NOTES 1–4 Complete the lines from a poem by Emily Dickinson. Use the simple past form of the verbs from the box. See Appendix 1 on page 453 for help with the irregular verbs.

bite	~~come~~	drink	eat	hop	not know

A bird ___came___ down the walk:
(1.)
He ____________ I saw;
(2.)
He ____________ an angle-worm in halves
(3.)
And ____________ the fellow raw.
(4.)

And then he ____________ a dew
(5.)
from a convenient grass,
And then ____________ sidewise to the wall
(6.)
To let a beetle pass.

02|02 **B** LISTEN AND CHECK Listen to the poem and check your answers in A.

EXERCISE 5 QUESTIONS AND ANSWERS

A GRAMMAR NOTES 1–4 Read the statements about Basho. Write questions about Emily Dickinson using the words in parentheses. Then answer your questions using the information from Exercises 2 and 3. Use short answers for *yes / no* questions and long answers for *wh-* questions.

1. Basho was a poet. (Dickinson / a poet)

   Q: *Was Dickinson a poet?*

   A: *Yes, she was.*

2. He was born in 1644. (when / she / born)

   Q: *When was she born?*

   A: *She was born in 1830.*

3. He lived in Japan. (where / she / live)

   Q: ____________________

   A: ____________________

4. He became famous during his lifetime. (she / become / famous during her lifetime)

   Q: ____________________

   A: ____________________

5. Basho's admirers often visited him. (Dickinson's admirers / often / visit her)

Q: ______________________________

A: ______________________________

6. He traveled a lot. (she / travel / a lot)

Q: ______________________________

A: ______________________________

7. Basho wrote more than 1,000 poems. (how many poems / Dickinson / write)

Q: ______________________________

A: ______________________________

8. He wrote about nature. (what / she / write about)

Q: ______________________________

A: ______________________________

9. He died in 1694. (when / she / die)

Q: ______________________________

A: ______________________________

02|03 **B** LISTEN AND CHECK **Listen to the Questions and Answers about Emily Dickinson and check your answers in A.**

EXERCISE 6 AFFIRMATIVE AND NEGATIVE STATEMENTS

A GRAMMAR NOTES 2–4 **Read this article about a modern writer.**

ANA CASTILLO is a modern poet, novelist, short story writer, and teacher. She was born in Chicago in 1953, and she lived there for 32 years. *Otro Canto*, her first book of poetry, appeared in 1977.

In her work, Castillo uses humor and a lively mixture of Spanish and English (Spanglish). She got her special writer's "voice" by living in a neighborhood with many different ethnic groups. She also thanks her father for her writing style. "He had an outgoing and easy personality, and this . . . sense of humor. I got a lot from him."

Castillo attended high school, college, and graduate school in Chicago. In the 1970s, she taught English and Mexican history. She received a PhD in American Studies from Bremen University in Germany in 1992. Her latest novel, *Give It to Me*, appeared in 2014.

Ⓑ **Read the statements. Write *That's right* or *That's wrong*. Correct the incorrect statements.**

1. Ana Castillo was born in Mexico City.

   That's wrong. She wasn't born in Mexico City. She was born in Chicago.

2. She lived in Chicago until 1977.

   ____

3. Her father was very shy.

   ____

4. She grew up among people of different cultures.

   ____

5. Castillo got most of her education in Chicago.

   ____

6. She taught Spanish in the 1970s.

   ____

7. She went to France for her PhD.

   ____

8. Her latest novel appeared in 2004.

   ____

EXERCISE 7 EDITING

GRAMMAR NOTES 1–4 **Read this student's journal. There are ten mistakes in the use of the simple past. The first mistake is already corrected. Find and correct nine more.**

Today in class, we read a poem by the American poet Robert Frost. I really ~~enjoy~~ *enjoyed* it. It was about a person who choosed between two roads in a forest. Many people believed the person were Frost. He thinked about his choice for a long time. The two roads didn't looked very different. Finally, he didn't took the road most people take. He took the one less traveled on. At that time, he didn't thought it was an important decision, but his choice change his life.

Sometimes I feel a little like Frost. As a child, I dreamed of traveling. Two years ago, I decide to move to a new country. It was a long journey and a big change. Did I made the right decision? I hope so.

STEP 4 COMMUNICATION PRACTICE

EXERCISE 8 LISTENING

02|04 **A** Read the statements. Then listen to the interview with a poet. Listen again and circle the correct information.

1. Murat came to the United States before / after his parents.
2. He had a wonderful life with his grandparents in Baltimore / Turkey.
3. In Baltimore, he had no friends, so he wrote poems / read books.
4. He wrote his first poem in English / Turkish.
5. In college, Murat studied farming / poetry.

02|04 **B** Read the information in the timeline. Then listen again to the interview and write the year for each event.

was born	parents left Turkey	moved to the U.S.	began to write poetry	graduated from college	won a poetry award	became a teacher
1970						

02|04 **C** Work with a partner. Listen again to the interview. Discuss these questions.

1. Why did Murat's parents go to the United States before Murat?

   EXAMPLE: A: They needed to find jobs.
   B: They also found a house.

2. Who did Murat live with when his parents left Turkey? How did he feel?
3. How did Murat feel when he first moved to the United States?
4. Why did he hate the city at first?
5. When did he write his first poem?
6. How did he learn to write poetry?

EXERCISE 9 BASHO AND DICKINSON

DISCUSSION Work in a group. Reread the information about Matsuo Basho (see pages 18 and 23) and Emily Dickinson (see page 24). In what ways were the two poets similar? How were they different? With your group, write as many ideas as you can. Compare your ideas with those of your classmates.

EXAMPLE: A: Both Basho and Dickinson were poets.
B: Basho lived in the seventeenth century. Dickinson lived in the nineteenth century.
C: Dickinson stayed at home, but Basho was restless and traveled a lot.

EXERCISE 10 RHYME TIME

02|05 **A** WORD PLAY In a poem, the last word in a line often rhymes[1] with the last word in another line. For example, read and listen to these lines of a famous poem called "Trees" by Joyce Kilmer. Notice that *see* rhymes with *tree* and *wear* rhymes with *hair*.

I think that I shall never see
A poem lovely as a tree

A tree that may in Summer wear
A nest of robins in her hair

B Work with a partner. See Appendix 1 on page 453. How many irregular past tense verbs rhyme with the verbs in the list? Write them. You have five minutes.

led *fed,* ____________________

bought ____________________

meant ____________________

drew ____________________

C Compare your answers with those of your classmates'. Who found the most pairs that rhyme?

1 *rhymes:* ends with the same sound as another word

EXERCISE 11 A TWENTIETH-CENTURY POET

A GROUP PROJECT Work in a group. Look at the photos of four twentieth-century poets. Choose one poet to research. Answer some of the questions below.

EXAMPLE: A: Maya Angelou was born in the United States in 1928. She grew up in Missouri and Arkansas.
B: She also spent time in California.
C: She became a poet. . . .
D: In addition to a poet, she . . .

Possible questions:

- When and where was he / she born?
- Where did he / she grow up?
- When did he / she write his / her first poem?
- What did he / she write about?
- Where did he / she attend school?
- When did he / she win a poetry prize?
- When and where did he / she travel?
- When and where did he / she die?
- What interesting fact(s) did you learn about this poet?

B Report back to your class. If your group chose the same poet as another group, do you have the same information about that poet? Compare answers.

EXAMPLE: A: Maya Angelou was born in the United States.
B: Right.
A: She grew up in Missouri.
B: She also grew up in Arkansas.
A: . . .

EXERCISE 12 CELEBRITY PROFILE

A INFORMATION GAP **Work with a partner. Student A will follow the instructions below. Student B will follow the instructions on page 485.**

STUDENT A

- **Read the profile of an actor who is also a poet, painter, and musician. Ask your partner questions to complete the missing information.**

  EXAMPLE: A: When was Viggo born?
  B: He was born on October 20, 1958.

- **Answer your partner's questions.**

  EXAMPLE: B: Where was Viggo born?
  A: He was born in New York.

- **If you don't know how to spell something, ask your partner.**

  EXAMPLE: A: How do you spell October?
  B: Capital *O, c, t, o, b, e, r.*

SCREEN-TIME PROFILE

Viggo Mortensen
actor, poet, painter, musician

Date of Birth: October 20, 1958

Place of Birth: New York

Mini Bio:

- lived in Argentina, Venezuela, and ____________ as a child
- attended school in Argentina
- learned to speak ____________
- returned to the United States in 19____
- became a movie actor in 1985
- first movie was *Witness*
- played the part of ____________ in *Lord of the Rings* (This movie made him famous.)
- finished his first ____________ in 1993 (The title was *Ten Last Night.*)
- created the paintings for the movie *A Perfect Murder* (He played the part of the artist.)
- wrote music for *Lord of the Rings*

B When you are finished, compare the profiles. Are they the same?

FROM GRAMMAR TO WRITING

A BEFORE YOU WRITE **Create a timeline like the one on page 28. Choose five important events in your life. Write the year of each event in the timeline and give a short description of the event above the year.**

Events: ______________ ______________ ______________ ______________ ______________

______________ ______________ ______________ ______________ ______________

Years: [ ] [ ] [ ] [ ] [ ]

B WRITE **Use your timeline to write a paragraph about some important events in your life. Include your feelings about the events. Try to avoid the common mistakes in the chart.**

EXAMPLE: I was born in the Dominican Republic in 1990. In 1999, I moved to Canada with my family. At first, I felt lonely and missed my country. My mother got a job as a cook in a restaurant. I loved to eat there. My father was an electrician and he found a job at a large school. That's where I met my future wife, Lidia. We didn't get married until 2015 and we had our first child a year later. It was the happiest time in my life.

Common Mistakes in Using the Simple Past

Use the **base form** of the verb **after *did*** or ***didn't***. Do not use the past form after *did* or *didn't*.	We didn't **get** married until 2015. NOT We didn't ~~got~~ married until 2015.
Use the **correct spelling** of **regular** simple past verbs. Do not forget that the spelling often changes when you add *-ed* to the base form.	I **studied** English. NOT I ~~studyed~~ English.
Use the **correct form** of **irregular** simple past verbs. Do not add *-d* or *-ed* to the base form.	He **found** a job at a school. NOT He ~~finded~~ a job at a school.

C CHECK YOUR WORK **Read your paragraph. Underline the regular simple past verbs and circle the irregular simple past verbs. Use the Editing Checklist to check your work.**

Editing Checklist

Did you use . . . ?

- ☐ the simple past for actions, states, or situations that are finished
- ☐ the correct spelling of regular simple past verbs
- ☐ the correct form of irregular simple past verbs

D REVISE YOUR WORK **Read your paragraph again. Can you improve your writing? Make changes if necessary. Give your paragraph a title.**

UNIT 2 **REVIEW**

Test yourself on the grammar of the unit.

A **Choose the correct answer to complete each sentence.**

1. Last night, I ____ a poem for my English class.
   a. write b. wrote c. written
2. It ____ about my childhood.
   a. be b. were c. was
3. At first, I didn't ____ what to write about.
   a. know b. knowing c. knew
4. My roommate ____ a good suggestion.
   a. makes b. did make c. made
5. Did you ____ a poem for your class?
   a. write b. writing c. wrote
6. I really ____ the experience.
   a. enjoy b. enjoys c. enjoyed

B **Complete the conversation with the simple past form of the verbs in parentheses and a short answer.**

A: I ____________ (1. call) you last night, but you ____________ (2. not answer). ____________ you ____________ (3. go) out?

B: ____________, I ____________ (4.). I ____________ (5. go) to the movies.

A: What ____________ you ____________ (6. see)?

B: I ____________ (7. see) *Dead Poets Society*. I ____________ (8. not like) it very much, though.

C **Find and correct six mistakes.**

The poet Elizabeth Alexander was born in New York City, but she didn't grew up there. Her father taked a job with the government, and her family moved to Washington, D.C. As a child, she have a loving family. Her parents were active in the civil rights movement, and Alexander gots interested in African-American history. In her first book, she wrote about important African leaders. She met Barack Obama at the University of Chicago. They both teached there in the 1990s. On January 20, 2009, she reads a poem at President Obama's inauguration.

Now check your answers on page 475.

UNIT 3

Past Progressive and Simple Past

REPORTING EVENTS

OUTCOMES
- Describe past events or situations
- Use *when* or *while* to link clauses in the simple past and the past progressive
- Identify the order of events in a description of an accident
- Report on events that were interrupted by other events
- Write a description of a past event

STEP 1 GRAMMAR IN CONTEXT

BEFORE YOU READ

Look at the picture. Discuss the questions.

1. What do you know about the *Titanic*?
2. What happened to the ship?

READ

03|01 **Read this newspaper article about a terrible event.**

VOL CCXII, NO 875 | Monday, April 15, 1912 | Price One Cent

DISASTER AT SEA

NEW YORK, April 15—It was a clear night. The sea was calm. The *Titanic*, the largest luxury ship[1] in the world, was sailing from Southhampton, England, to New York City. This was its first voyage,[2] and it was carrying more than 2,200 passengers and crew.[3] At around 11:30 p.m. crew member Frederick Fleet was looking at the sea when, suddenly, he saw a huge white

1 *luxury ship:* a boat that has many great things (beautiful rooms, swimming pools, restaurants, etc.)
2 *voyage:* a long trip, usually on a ship
3 *crew:* the people who work on a ship or airplane

form in front of the ship. When he saw it, Fleet immediately rang the ship's bell three times and shouted, "Iceberg ahead!" But it was too late. The great ship crashed into the mountain of ice.

When the *Titanic* hit the iceberg, people were sleeping, reading, and playing cards. Some passengers heard a loud noise, but they were not alarmed. They believed the ship was unsinkable.[4] But soon it became clear that the *Titanic* was in danger. There was a hole in the side of the ship. Water was entering fast, and it was starting to sink. There were lifeboats, but only 1,178 spaces for 2,224 people. In an attempt to keep everyone calm, the ship's band played a lively tune while people were getting into the boats.

The *Titanic* was not the only ship on the sea that night. There were several other ships in the area. The *Californian* was nearby, but it did not hear the *Titanic's* calls for help. And then there was the *Carpathia*. While the *Titanic* was sailing toward New York, the *Carpathia* was traveling from New York to the Mediterranean.

When it heard the *Titanic's* distress signals,[5] the *Carpathia* turned around and headed back toward the sinking ship. By the time the *Carpathia* arrived, the *Titanic* was already at the bottom of the sea, but there were 18 lifeboats full of cold and frightened survivors. Thanks to the *Carpathia*, more than 700 people lived to tell the story of that terrible night.

4 *unsinkable:* cannot go underwater
5 *distress signals:* calls for help

AFTER YOU READ

A VOCABULARY **Match the words with their definitions.**

_____ **1. disaster**	**a.** afraid
_____ **2. calm**	**b.** someone who continues to live after an accident
_____ **3. area**	**c.** to go underwater
_____ **4. survivor**	**d.** one part of a larger place
_____ **5. alarmed**	**e.** a terrible event
_____ **6. sink**	**f.** quiet

B COMPREHENSION **Number the events in order (1–7).**

_____ Water entered the *Titanic*.
_____ Frederick Fleet rang the ship's bell.
_____ The *Titanic* hit an iceberg.
_____ The *Carpathia* arrived and saved the survivors.
_____ The *Titanic* was sailing to New York.
_____ The *Titanic* sank.
_____ Frederick Fleet saw an iceberg.

C DISCUSSION **Work with a partner. Compare your answers in B. Are they the same? Explain your choices.**

STEP 2 GRAMMAR PRESENTATION

PAST PROGRESSIVE

Statements

Subject	*Was/Were*	*(Not)*	Base Form of Verb + *-ing*	
I	**was**	(not)	**reading** **eating** **sleeping**	yesterday at 11:30 p.m. when Anton called. while Mia was talking.
You	**were**			
He She	**was**			
We You They	**were**			

Yes/No Questions

Was/Were	Subject	Base Form of Verb + *-ing*	
Was	I	**reading** **eating** **sleeping**	yesterday at 11:30 p.m.? when Anton called? while Mia was talking?
Were	you		
Was	he she		
Were	we you they		

Short Answers

Affirmative		
Yes,	you	**were.**
	I	**was.**
	he she	**was.**
	you we they	**were.**

Negative		
No,	you	**weren't.**
	I	**wasn't.**
	he she	**wasn't.**
	you we they	**weren't.**

Wh- Questions

Wh- Word	*Was/Were*	Subject	Base Form of Verb + *-ing*	
Why	**was**	I	**reading** **eating** **sleeping**	yesterday at 11:30 p.m.? when Anton called? while Mia was talking?
	were	you		
	was	he she		
	were	we you they		

GRAMMAR NOTES

1 Past Progressive

Use the past progressive to focus on the **duration of a past action**, not its completion.

Paul **was reading** a book last night.
(We don't know if he finished it.)

USAGE NOTE We often use the past progressive with a **specific time in the past**.

He **was reading** a book ***at 11:30 p.m.***

2 Simple Past

Use the simple past to focus on the **completion of a past action**.

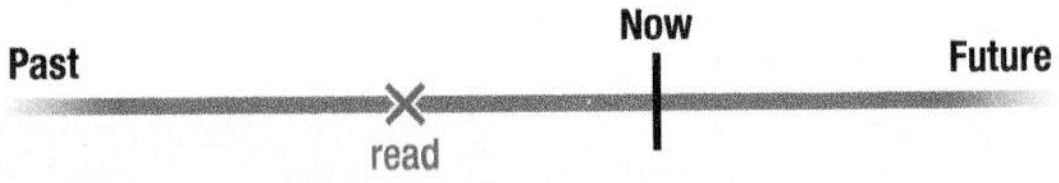

Paul **read** a book last night.
(He finished it.)

BE CAREFUL! Use the **simple past** with most **non-action verbs**. Do not use the past progressive.

She **heard** about the disaster.
NOT She ~~was hearing~~ about the disaster.

3 Past Progressive + Simple Past

Use the past progressive with the simple past to show that **one action interrupted another action in progress in the past**. Use the simple past for the interrupting action.

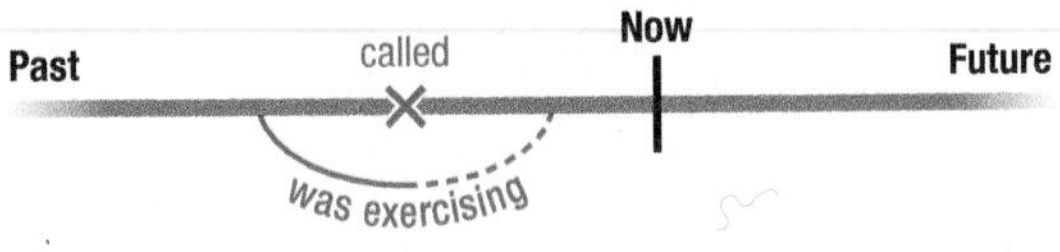

I **was exercising** when he **called.**
(I was exercising. The phone rang and interrupted my exercises.)

Use *when* or *while* to introduce one of the actions:

- ***when*** for the action in the **simple past**
- ***while*** for the action in the **past progressive**

He was running ***when*** he **fell.**
While he **was running**, he fell.

USAGE NOTE We can also use ***when*** to introduce the action in the past progressive.

When he **was running**, he fell.

4 Past Progressive + *While* or *When*

Use the past progressive with *while* or *when* to show **two actions in progress at the same time in the past**. Use the past progressive in both clauses.

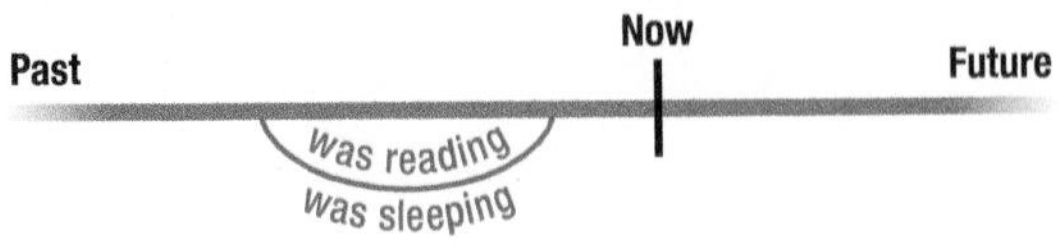

While I **was reading**, Amy **was sleeping.**
When I **was reading**, Amy **was sleeping.**
(I was reading. At the same time, Amy was sleeping.)

5 Simple Past + Simple Past or Simple Past + Past Progressive

A sentence with both clauses in the simple past has a very **different meaning** from a sentence with one clause in the simple past and one clause in the past progressive.

- both clauses in the **simple past**

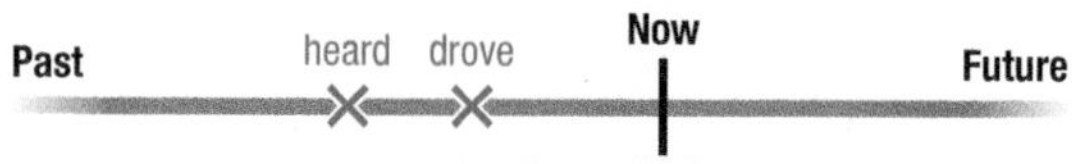

When she **heard** the news, she **drove** home.
(First she heard the news; then she drove home.)

- one clause is in the **simple past**, the other clause in the **past progressive**

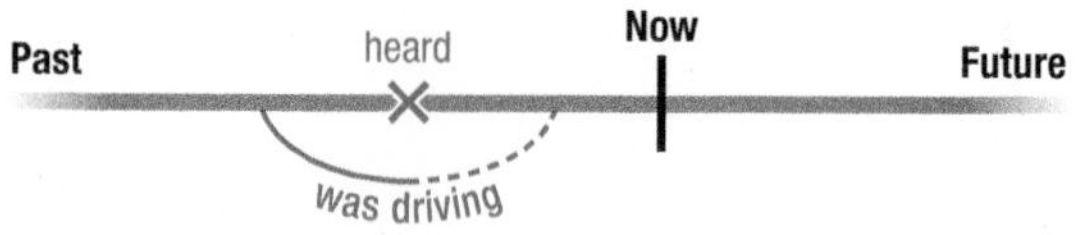

When she **heard** the news, she **was driving** home.
(First she was driving home; then she heard the news.)

6 Position of the Time Clause

The **time clause** (the part of the sentence with ***when*** or ***while***) can come at **the beginning or the end** of the sentence. The meaning is the same.

- at the **beginning** — ***When* you called,** I was eating.
- at the **end** — I was eating ***when* you called.**

IN WRITING Use a **comma after the time clause** when it comes at the **beginning** of the sentence. Do not use a comma after the main clause when the main clause comes first.

***While* she was sleeping,** I was reading.
I was reading ***while* she was sleeping.**
NOT I was reading, while she was sleeping.

REFERENCE NOTES

For **spelling rules** on forming the **past progressive**, see Appendix 21 on page 462.
For a list of **non-action verbs**, see Appendix 2 on page 454.

STEP 3 FOCUSED PRACTICE

EXERCISE 1 DISCOVER THE GRAMMAR

GRAMMAR NOTES 1–6 **Read each question. Then choose the correct sentence (*a* or *b*). In one item, both answers are correct.**

1. In which sentence did the passengers arrive before the ship left?

a. When the passengers arrived, the ship was leaving.
(b.) When the passengers arrived, the ship left.

2. Which sentence tells us that the ship reached New York?

a. It was sailing to New York.
b. It sailed to New York.

3. In which sentence do we know that the ship went completely underwater?
   a. It was sinking.
   b. It sank.

4. In which sentence did the man fall asleep during the movie *Titanic*?
   a. He fell asleep while he was watching *Titanic*.
   b. While he was watching *Titanic*, he fell asleep.

5. Which sentence talks about two actions that were in progress at the same time?
   a. While the ship was sinking, passengers were getting into lifeboats.
   b. When the ship sank, passengers got into lifeboats.

6. In which sentence was the phone call interrupted?
   a. When he heard the news, he called me.
   b. When he heard the news, he was calling me.

7. In which sentence did the woman leave after the phone call?
   a. When he called her, she left the house.
   b. When he called her, she was leaving the house.

EXERCISE 2
PAST PROGRESSIVE STATEMENTS

GRAMMAR NOTE 1 **Douglas is sailing to Europe on the SS *Atlantic*. Look at his schedule for yesterday. Complete the sentences. Use the past progressive form of the verbs in parentheses. Choose between affirmative and negative.**

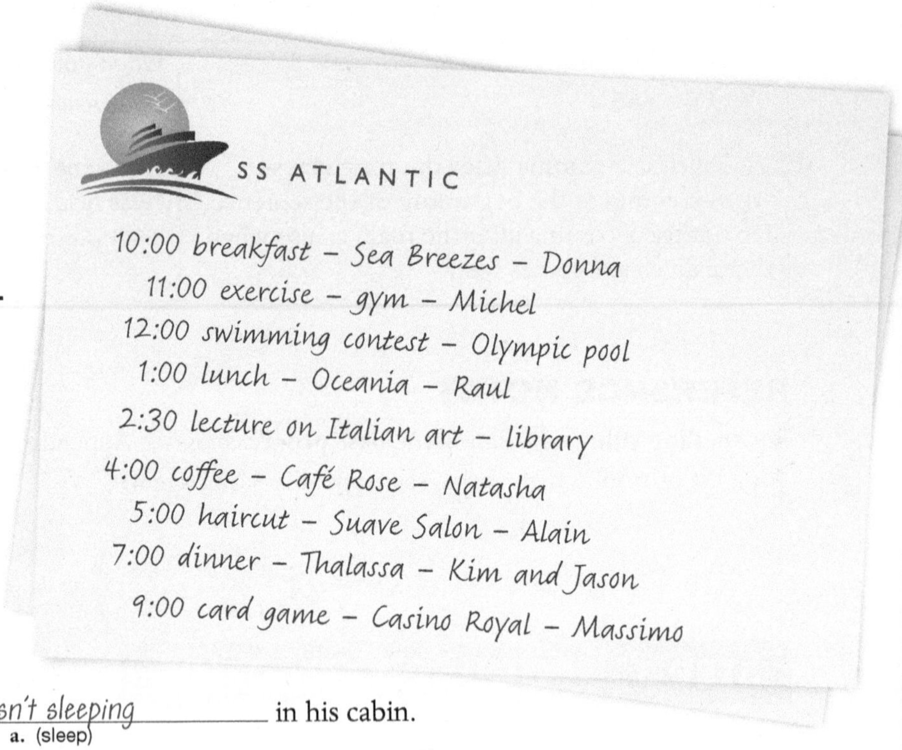

1. At 10:15, Douglas ______wasn't sleeping______ in his cabin.
   a. (sleep)

   He ______was having______ breakfast at Sea Breezes with Donna.
   b. (have)

2. At 11:05, he ______________________ in the ship's gym with Michel.
   a. (exercise)

   He ______________________ in the pool.
   b. (swim)

3. At 1:10, he ______________________ coffee at Café Rose.
   a. (drink)

   He ______________________ lunch at Oceania with Raul.
   b. (eat)

4. At 2:40, he ______________________ for a book in the ship's library.
   a. (look)

   He ______________________ to a lecture on Italian art.
   b. (listen)

5. At 4:05, he ____________________ a haircut at the Suave Salon.
a. (get)

He ____________________ coffee at Café Rose with Natasha.
b. (have)

6. At 7:10, he ____________________ in his room.
a. (rest)

He ____________________ dinner at Thalassa with Kim and Jason.
b. (enjoy)

7. At 9:15, he ____________________ cards at the Casino Royal with Massimo.
a. (play)

He ____________________ with Donna at the Discothèque.
b. (dance)

EXERCISE 3 PAST PROGRESSIVE OR SIMPLE PAST

GRAMMAR NOTES 1–5 **Complete the information about the *Titanic* disaster. Use the past progressive or simple past form of the verbs in parentheses. See Appendix 1 on page 453 for help with irregular verbs.**

Eyewitness Accounts[1]

According to eyewitness Lawrence Beesley, when the ship ___hit___ (1. hit) the iceberg, the engines ______ (2. stop). Minutes later, when Professor Beesley ______ (3. go) on deck, he ______ (4. find) only a few other passengers there. Everyone was calm. A few people ______ (5. play) cards in the smoking room. When he ______ (6. look) out the window, he ______ (7. see) an iceberg at the side of the ship.

Another survivor, Washington Dodge, said that it ______ (8. be) 11:30 p.m. when the crash ______ (9. happen). He ______ (10. decide) to go on deck. While the ship ______ (11. sink), the band ______ (12. play) a lively tune. At 1:55 a.m., the ship ______ (13. sink) completely into the sea.

While passenger Elizabeth Shutes ______ (14. eat) a chicken sandwich in her cabin, she "______ (15. feel) a shudder[2] travel through the ship." Shortly after, she ______ (16. sit) in a lifeboat in the middle of the ocean with thirty-four other people. Hours later, someone shouted "A light, a ship!" When Shutes ______ (17. look), she ______ (18. see) a ship with bright lights coming toward them. It was the *Carpathia*—the only ship in the area that came to help.

When Harold Bride, one of the ship's two radio operators, ______ (19. notice) some lights in the distance, he ______ (20. know) it was a steamship. It ______ (21. come) to rescue them. When the *Carpathia* ______ (22. arrive), it ______ (23. pick up) all of the survivors—including Mr. Bride.

1 *eyewitness accounts:* reports by people who saw an accident or crime
2 *shudder:* a quick shaking movement

EXERCISE 4 *YES/NO* AND *WH-* QUESTIONS

A GRAMMAR NOTES 1–5 **A newspaper is interviewing a *Titanic* passenger. Read the passenger's answers. Write the interviewer's questions. Use the words in parentheses and the past progressive or simple past.**

1. INTERVIEWER: *What were you doing Sunday night?*
(what / you / do / Sunday night)
PASSENGER: As I was saying, I was playing cards with some other passengers.

2. INTERVIEWER: ______________________________
(your wife / play / with you)
PASSENGER: No, she wasn't. My wife wasn't with me at the time.

3. INTERVIEWER: ______________________________
(what / she / do / while you / play cards)
PASSENGER: She was reading in our room.

4. INTERVIEWER: ______________________________
(you / feel / the crash)
PASSENGER: Not really. But I heard a very loud noise.

5. INTERVIEWER: ______________________________
(what / you / do / when you / hear the noise)
PASSENGER: At first, we all continued to play. We weren't alarmed. Everyone stayed calm.

6. INTERVIEWER: ______________________________
(what / you / do / when the lights / go out)
PASSENGER: I tried to find my wife.

7. INTERVIEWER: ______________________________
(what / she / do / while you / look for her)
PASSENGER: She was looking for *me*. Thank goodness we found each other!

8. INTERVIEWER: ______________________________
(what / you / do / when you / find her)
PASSENGER: We tried to get into a lifeboat.

03|02 **B** LISTEN AND CHECK **Listen to the interview and check your answers in A.**

EXERCISE 5 STATEMENTS WITH *WHEN* AND *WHILE*

GRAMMAR NOTES 1–6 **Combine the pairs of sentences. Use the past progressive or the simple past form of the verb. Keep the order of the two sentences. Remember to use commas when necessary.**

1. The storm started. Mr. Taylor attended a party.
When *the storm started, Mr. Taylor was attending a party.*

2. The electricity went out. The wind began to blow.
______________________ when ______________________

3. He drove home. He listened to his car radio.
While ______________________________

4. He pulled over to the side of the road. He couldn't see anything.

_______________ when _______________

5. He listened to the news. He heard about a car crash near his home.

While _______________

6. It stopped raining. Mr. Taylor drove home in a hurry.

When _______________

EXERCISE 6 EDITING

GRAMMAR NOTES 1–6 **Read this blog post. There are ten mistakes in the use of the past progressive and the simple past. The first mistake is already corrected. Find and correct nine more. Remember to look at punctuation!**

Julio Delgado 6:15 p.m. April 15

This afternoon I ~~was going~~ *went* to a movie at school. It was *Titanic*. They were showing it because it was the anniversary of the 1912 disaster. What a beautiful and sad film! Jack (Leonardo DiCaprio) was meeting Rose (Kate Winslet) while they both sailed on the huge ship. It was the *Titanic*'s first voyage.

Rose was from a very rich family; Jack was from a poor family. They fell in love, but Rose's mother wasn't happy about it. When the ship was hitting the iceberg, the two lovers were together, but then they got separated. Rose was finding Jack while the ship was sinking. Seconds before the ship went under, they held hands and were jumping into the water. Rose survived, but Jack didn't. It was so sad. When I left the theater, I still was having tears in my eyes.

That wasn't my only adventure of the day. When the movie was over I left the school auditorium. While I walked home, I saw an accident between two pedestrians and a car. I was the only one in the area, so while I saw the accident, I immediately called the police. When the police got there, they asked me a lot of questions—there were no other witnesses. I'm glad to say that the accident had a happier ending than the movie!

STEP 4 COMMUNICATION PRACTICE

EXERCISE 7 LISTENING

A You're going to hear a witness describe a traffic accident. Before you listen, look at the pictures. The pictures show three versions of what happened. Work with a partner and describe what happened in each of the three stories.

1.

2.

3.

03|03 **B** Listen to the witness describe the traffic accident. According to the witness, which set of pictures is the most accurate? Circle the number.

03|03 **C** **Work with a partner. Listen to the conversation again. Discuss the questions.**

1. What was the witness doing when the accident happened?

   EXAMPLE: A: What was the witness doing when the accident happened?
   B: She was walking down the street.
   A: That's right. She was walking down the street when she heard a car honking its horn.

2. How was the man driving?
3. What were the two friends doing?
4. When did the driver honk his horn?
5. Who was responsible for the accident? Why?

EXERCISE 8 ARE YOU A GOOD WITNESS?

A GAME **Look at the picture for 30 seconds. Then close your book and write down what was happening. Make a list of all the details you can remember: What were the people doing? What were they wearing? Was anything unusual going on?**

EXAMPLE: *A man and a woman were standing by the fireplace.*
The woman was wearing . . .

B **When you are finished, compare your list with those of your classmates. Who remembered the most?**

EXERCISE 9 ALIBI[1]

A ROLE PLAY **There was a bank robbery yesterday at 2:15 p.m. Work in a group of three to six. Some students are police officers; some are witnesses; and some are suspects.[2] The police are questioning the witnesses and the suspects. Use your imagination to ask and answer questions.**

EXAMPLE: OFFICER: What were you doing when the robbery took place?
WITNESS 1: I was standing in line at the bank.
WITNESS 2: I was crossing the street in front of the bank. I saw everything.
OFFICER: What was happening in the bank? . . .

EXAMPLE: OFFICER: Where were you yesterday at 2:15 p.m.?
SUSPECT 1: At 2:15? I was sitting in class.
SUSPECT 2: I was at home. I was watching TV.
OFFICER: Were there other people with you?

B **Discuss these questions with your group.**

EXAMPLE: A: So, what happened at the bank?
B: There was a robbery.
C: What were the witnesses doing?
D: Well, one woman . . .

1. What happened at the bank?
2. What were the witnesses doing?
3. Do the suspects have good alibis?
4. What were they doing when the robbery occurred?
5. Do you believe their alibis?

1 *alibi:* the proof that someone was not at the location of a crime at the time of the crime
2 *suspects:* people who may be guilty of a crime

FROM GRAMMAR TO WRITING

A BEFORE YOU WRITE **Think about a past event you witnessed. Answer these questions.**

1. What was the event? ______________________________
2. When and where did it happen? ______________________________
3. What happened? ______________________________
4. What were you doing when it happened? ______________________________
5. What did you do while it was happening? ______________________________
6. How did you feel after it happened? ______________________________

B WRITE **Use your answers to write a paragraph about the event. Use the past progressive and simple past to describe what was happening and what happened during the event. Use *when* and *while*. Try to avoid the common mistakes in the chart.**

EXAMPLE: While I was going to lunch today, I saw a wedding party. People were waiting for the bride and groom outside City Hall. When they saw the couple, they . . .

Common Mistakes in Using the Past Progressive and Simple Past

Use the **past progressive** when an action was **interrupted**. Do not use the simple past.	While I **was driving** home, I saw an accident. NOT While I ~~drove~~ home, I saw an accident.
Use the **simple past** with most **non-action verbs**. Do not use the past progressive.	I **saw** an accident. NOT I ~~was seeing~~ an accident.
Use a **comma after the time clause** when it comes **first**. Do not use a comma after the main clause when the main clause comes first.	***When*** **I saw the accident,** I called the police. NOT I called the police, when I saw the accident.

C CHECK YOUR WORK **Read your paragraph. Underline the past progressive verbs and circle the simple past verbs. Use the Editing Checklist to check your work.**

Editing Checklist

Did you use . . . ?

- ☐ the past progressive to show the duration of a past action
- ☐ the simple past to show the completion of a past action
- ☐ the simple past with non-action verbs
- ☐ *while* with a past progressive action
- ☐ *when* with a simple past action
- ☐ commas after time clauses at the beginning of a sentence

D REVISE YOUR WORK **Read your paragraph again. Can you improve your writing? Make changes if necessary. Give your paragraph a title.**

UNIT 3 **REVIEW**

Test yourself on the grammar of the unit.

A **Complete the conversation with the past progressive or simple past form of the verbs in parentheses.**

A: ________________ you ________________ about the big storm last night?
                                        1. (hear)

B: Yes, I ________________ the pictures when I ________________ on the news.
               2. (see)   3. (turn)

________________ you ________________ home during the storm?
                                        4. (drive)

A: No. At 6:00, I ________________ in my office. So while it ________________ really hard,
                          5. (work)   6. (rain)

I ________________ a report. And just when I ________________ work, the rain
       7. (finish)   8. (leave)

________________!
       9. (stop)

B: I'm glad. Those pictures on the news ________________ pretty bad. There were a lot of
                                                          10. (look)

accidents because of the storm.

B **Combine the sentences. Use the past progressive or simple past form of the verbs.**

1. While ____.
(Danielle watched TV. At the same time, I studied.)

2. ________________________ when ________________________.
(I closed my book. The show *Dr. Davis* came on.)

3. ________________________ when ________________________.
(Dr. Davis talked to his patient. The electricity went off.)

4. When ____.
(The electricity went off. We lit some candles.)

5. ________________________ while ________________________.
(We talked about a lot of things. We waited for the lights to come on.)

C **Find and correct five mistakes.**

When I turned on the TV for the first episode of *Dr. Davis*, I unpacked boxes in my freshman dorm room. I stopped and watched for an hour. After that, I wasn't missing a single show while I was attending school. While I was solving math problems, Dr. Davis was solving medical mysteries. And *just* while my dumb boyfriend broke up with me, the beautiful Dr. Grace left Davis for the third time. I even watched the show from the hospital when I was breaking my leg. The show just ended. I was sad when I was seeing the last episode, but I think it's time for some real life!

Now check your answers on page 475.

UNIT

4

Used to and *Would*

CHANGES

OUTCOMES
- Describe past habits and situations, using *used to* and *would*
- Evaluate events and situations described in a reading and a listening
- Describe and discuss one's past and present physical appearance and habits
- Write a description of a place and how it has changed

STEP 1 GRAMMAR IN CONTEXT

BEFORE YOU READ

Look at the photos. Discuss the questions.

1. What part of the world is Dubai in?
2. What was Dubai like before 1966? What is it like now?

READ

04|01 Read this article about an amazing change.

Dubai: Then and Now

Cities change, but usually not as much or as fast as Dubai. This exciting city in the United Arab Emirates used to be a small town in the desert. Today, it is a large international center with towering[1] skyscrapers. Not very long ago, people used to ride camels to get from place to place, and they would do most of their shopping at outdoor markets. Today, they drive expensive foreign sports cars and shop at huge indoor malls filled with luxury stores.[2]

How did this amazing transformation happen? The answer is oil. After its discovery in 1966, oil provided 60 percent of the city's revenue. The government used the money to build roads, ports,[3] and

1 *towering:* very tall
2 *luxury stores:* stores selling expensive, high-quality items
3 *ports:* places where ships can load and unload people or things

skyscrapers. Today, a large part of the city's money comes from tourism. Tourism? People never used to think of Dubai as a popular vacation destination. But today, tourists come from around the world to view the sights from the Burj Khalifa, the tallest building in the world. They also come to ski indoors when it's 120°F (49°C) outside and to dance under the stars on artificial[4] islands in the shape of palm trees.

The city planners did an amazing job in changing Dubai from a sleepy town to a major international city. Not everyone, however, believes that all the changes are good. For example, because of heavy traffic, a trip that used to take only 10 minutes now takes much longer. And some people believe that Dubai lost a lot of its charm[5] when the skyscrapers went up. They miss the small, traditional houses and markets. But love the changes or not, one thing everyone agrees on: Dubai is not the same city it used to be.

---

4 *artificial:* not natural, made by people
5 *charm:* the special quality that makes people like something or someone

AFTER YOU READ

A VOCABULARY **Choose the word or phrase that best completes each sentence.**

1. If a city is **popular**, ____.
   a. it's very large b. it's poor c. many people like it
2. A **destination** is a place people ____.
   a. live in b. travel to c. don't like
3. A **transformation** is a ____.
   a. way to travel b. city c. change
4. A **traditional** house has a(n) ____ style.
   a. old b. modern c. amazing
5. A **major** city is usually ____.
   a. important b. small c. not very big
6. **Revenue** is ____ that a government gets.
   a. a review b. information c. money

B COMPREHENSION **Read the statements. Check (✓) *True* or *False*.**

	True	False
1. Dubai is a small town in the desert.	☐	☐
2. In the past, camels were a common form of transportation.	☐	☐
3. Today, most people shop at outdoor markets.	☐	☐
4. In the past, Dubai was a popular tourist destination.	☐	☐
5. Today, traffic is a problem in Dubai.	☐	☐
6. Dubai today is very different from Dubai in the past.	☐	☐

C DISCUSSION **Work with a partner. Compare your answers in B. Why did you check *True* or *False*?**

STEP 2 GRAMMAR PRESENTATION

USED TO

Statements

Subject	*Used to / Did not use to*	Base Form of Verb	
I You He She It We You They	**used to** **didn't use to**	**be**	popular.

***Yes/No* Questions**

Did	Subject	*Use to*	Base Form of Verb	
Did	you it they	**use to**	**be**	popular?

Short Answers

Affirmative		
Yes,	I it they	**did.**

Negative		
No,	I it they	**didn't.**

***Wh-* Questions**

Wh- Word	*Did*	Subject	*Use to*	Base Form of Verb	
When	**did**	you it they	**use to**	be	popular?

WOULD

Statements

Subject	*Would*	Base Form of Verb	
I He They	**would**	**shop**	all day.

Contractions*

I would	=	I**'d**
He would	=	He**'d**
They would	=	They**'d**

*The contraction for *would* is the same for all subjects.

GRAMMAR NOTES

1 *Used to* for Past Habits and Situations

Use ***used to*** + **base form** of the verb for past habits (repeated activities) and situations that are no longer happening or true in the present.

- **past habits**

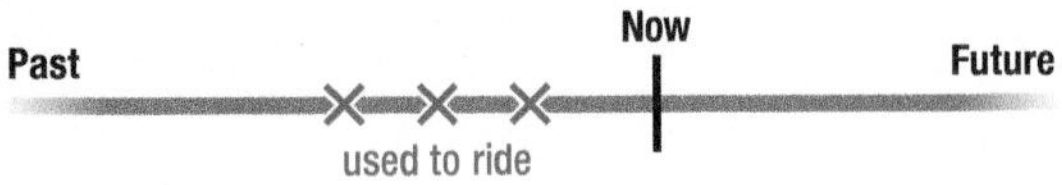

When my father was a teenager, he **used to ride** a camel.
(He rode a camel many times in the past, but he doesn't ride one now.)

- **past situations**

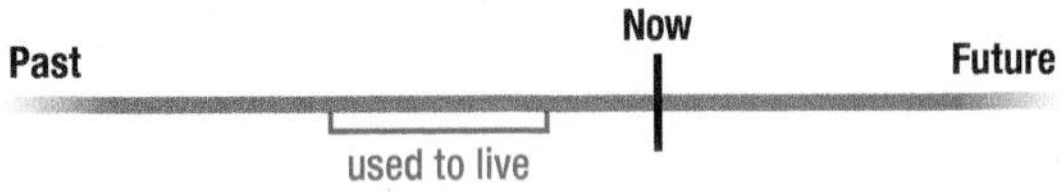

We **used to live** in Dubai.
(We lived in Dubai for a period of time, but we don't live there any longer.)

USAGE NOTE We often use ***used to*** in order to contrast the past and the present. **Time expressions** such as ***now***, ***no longer***, and ***not anymore*** emphasize the contrast.

He **used to ride** his camel every day, but ***now*** he drives a car.
They **used to shop** at an outdoor market, but they do***n't*** shop there ***anymore***.

BE CAREFUL! Use the **simple past** for a one-time past activity. Do not use *used to.*

He **drove** to the mall ***yesterday***.
NOT He ~~used to drive~~ to the mall yesterday.

BE CAREFUL! Use the **simple past** in a time clause with ***when***. Do not use *used to.*

When I **lived** in Dubai, I used to ride a camel.
NOT When I ~~used to live~~ in Dubai, . . .

2 Forms of *Used to*

Used to always refers to the **past**. There is no present or future forms.

She **used to** ski when she was younger.
NOT She ~~uses~~ to ski every winter.
NOT She ~~will use~~ to ski next month.

IN WRITING The form ***use to*** often comes after ***did*** in **negative statements** or **questions**, but people sometimes write *used to.* Some people, including many English teachers, think this is not correct in American English. However, other people think it is correct. In conversation, ***use to*** and ***used to*** sound the same: /ˈyustə/

He ***didn't*** **use to** live there.
or
He ***didn't*** **used to** live there.

Did you **use to** have long hair?
or
Did you **used to** have long hair?

USAGE NOTE In **negative statements**, ***never*** + ***used to*** is much more common than *didn't use(d) to.*

He ***never*** **used to** study. *(more common)*
He ***didn't*** **use(d) to** study. *(less common)*

USAGE NOTE In **questions**, the **simple past** is more common than *did* + *use(d) to.*

Did you **have** long hair then? *(more common)*
Did you **use(d) to** have long hair then? *(less common)*

3 *Would* for Past Habits

You can also use ***would* + base form** of the verb for past habits (repeated activities) that no longer happen in the present.

- **past habits**

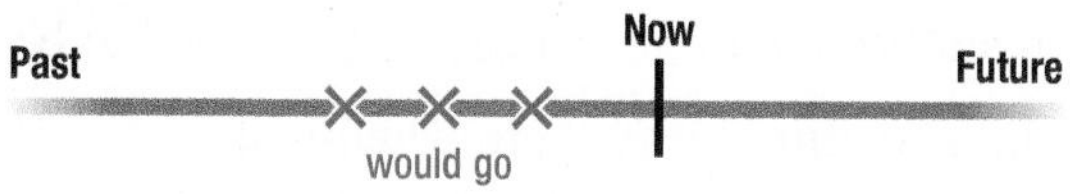

When I was a teenager, I **would go** to the mall every Saturday afternoon.
(I went to the mall every Saturday afternoon, but I no longer do that.)

BE CAREFUL! Do not use ***would*** for past situations. Use ***used to***.

I **used to live** in Dubai.
NOT I ~~would live~~ in Dubai.

USAGE NOTE When we reminisce (tell stories) about the past, we often begin with ***used to*** and then continue with ***would*** to give more details or examples.

When I was a kid, I **used to ride** my bike everywhere. I **would ride** it to school during the week, and I **would take** it to the park on weekends.

BE CAREFUL! When we use ***would***, it must already be clear that we are talking about the past. Do not begin a story with ***would***.

I hear you got a new bike! I **used to** ride my bike everywhere. I would ride it to school . . .
NOT I hear you got a new bike! I ~~would~~ ride my bike everywhere. I would ride it to school . . .

STEP 3 FOCUSED PRACTICE

EXERCISE 1 DISCOVER THE GRAMMAR

GRAMMAR NOTES 1–3 **Read this tourist's email. Underline the expressions that refer to past habits and situations that are no longer true.**

Greetings from Dubai!

Every time I return here, I'm absolutely amazed at all the changes! Today, I did some typical tourist things. First, I went to the top of the Burj Khalifa—the tallest building in the world. (As I'm sure you know, our CN Tower back home in Canada used to be the tallest. Oh, well. Things change.) Today, from the observation deck, I had a bird's-eye view of the city. It's hard to believe that Dubai used to be just a small town! The transformation is really amazing.

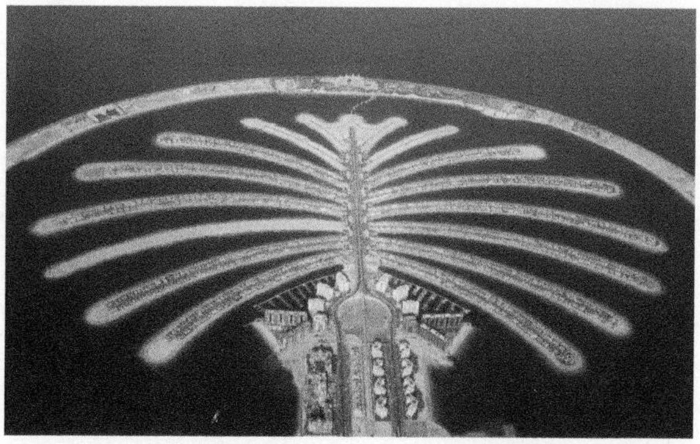

This afternoon, I walked around for hours. I also visited one of the Palm Islands. They're islands built in the early 2000s in the Persian Gulf. They are artificial, but the builders used only natural sand and rock. Amazing—as you can see from the photo. By the way, I used that new travel app on my smartphone. Thanks for telling me about it! It was really helpful—especially the maps. I used to get lost a lot!

After all my sightseeing, I was tired, so right now I'm sitting in an Internet café. There used to be a small hotel right across the street on the corner. I would sometimes stay there when I came here on business. Now there's another huge skyscraper in its place. So many changes! Prices have changed, too. This cup of tea didn't use to cost so much!

Wish you were here. I think you would like it.

Dania

EXERCISE 2 FORMS OF *USED TO*

GRAMMAR NOTE 2 **Complete the Questions and Answers (Q & A) about Dubai. Use the correct form of *used to* and the words in parentheses.**

Q: What are some of the major tourist attractions in Dubai?

A: Well, there are many, of course, but the Burj Khalifa is probably the most famous one. It's the tallest building in the world. That title ___used to belong___ (1. belong) to the CN Tower in Canada.

Q: What's the population of Dubai?

A: It ______________ (2. be) just about 60,000. And that was only fifty years ago! Today, it's over two million.

Q: Do many foreigners live in Dubai?

A: Yes. Very few foreigners ______________ (3. live) here, but now a large percentage of Dubai's population is foreign born. Many of them are workers from other countries.

Q: ______________ there always ______________ (4. be) so much traffic?

A: No, not at all. Traffic is much worse these days. Remember, not too long ago many people ______________ (5. ride) camels.

Q: How are the roads?

A: Dubai ______________ (6. not have) many roads. In fact, there was only one major road. Today, of course, there are many more and they are very good. The famous Sheikh Zayed Road, for example, ______________ (7. have) just one lane. Today, it has twelve.

Q: Where ______________ people ______________ (8. shop) before all the big malls?

A: They ______________ to outdoor marketplaces. These traditional *souks* still exist, but
9. (go)
there are fewer of them.

Q: Do a lot of tourists visit Dubai?

A: Yes! Dubai never ______________ a tourist destination, but today it is very, very popular.
10. (be)

EXERCISE 3 *USED TO* OR *WOULD*

GRAMMAR NOTES 1–3 **Just like cities, people's lives can change a lot. Read this online newsletter. Circle *used to* or *would* to complete the article. Sometimes only *used to* is possible. Sometimes both *used to* and *would* are possible.**

David Beckham (used to) / would (1.) live in London, England. Today, he owns homes around the world, including on one of the Palm Islands in Dubai. Born in 1975, Beckham grew up in a family that loved football,[1] and he used to / would (2.) often play in London's Ridgeway Park. His family used to / would (3.) frequently travel to see their team, Manchester United, compete. Beckham used to / would (4.) love those trips, and he knew even then that he wanted to play football professionally. When his teachers used to / would (5.) ask the young Beckham the typical "What do you want to be when you grow up?" question, his answer was always the same: "I want to be a footballer." Beckham, who is now retired, went on to become one of the greatest football players in the world.

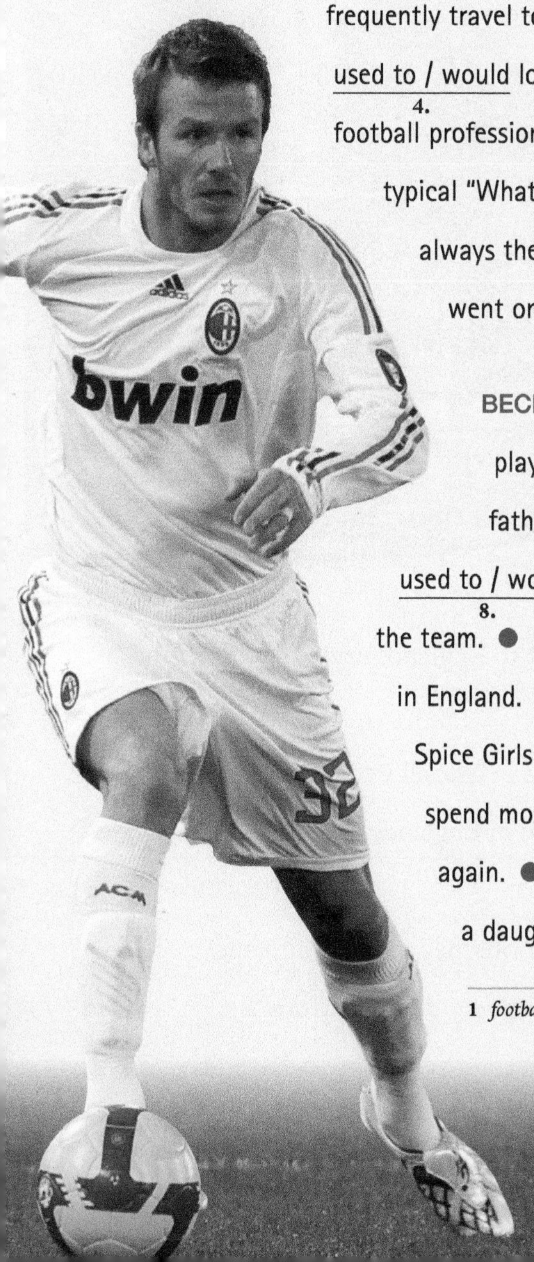

BECKHAM BIO BYTES ● He used to / would (6.) be a famous football player, but now he's retired. ● When he was a child, Beckham and his father used to / would (7.) play football together for hours. ● They also used to / would (8.) watch Manchester United compete. ● Later, Beckham joined the team. ● He didn't use to / wouldn't (9.) be rich, but he became the richest athlete in England. ● He used to / would (10.) be single, but now he's married to famous Spice Girls singer Victoria Adams. ● In the past, the couple used to / would (11.) spend most of their time in the United States, but now they live in England again. ● They used to / would (12.) have all boys, but now they also have a daughter.

1 *football:* the sport called "soccer" in the United States

EXERCISE 4 *USED TO* OR *WOULD*

GRAMMAR NOTES 1–3 **Complete the conversation between two travelers at Dubai International airport. Use *used to* or *would* and the correct verb from the box. Use *would* when possible. You will use one verb more than once.**

be	buy	eat	live	make	take	watch

A: This is a beautiful airport. And it's huge!

B: Yes. I remember when it ___used to be___ (1.) just a small airport with only a few flights a week and there were often delays. It really ______________ (2.) a long time to get anywhere.

A: I remember that, too, of course. And there ______________ (3. (negative)) so many stores or restaurants.

B: That's right. We ______________ (4.) cheese sandwiches at home and then we ______________ (5.) them right here in the terminal.

A: Flying from here ______________ (6. (negative)) much fun. Now, there are more than eighty places to get something to eat or drink.

B: Oh, look. Isn't that David and Victoria Beckham over there?

A: Yes! I read that they own a house on one of the Palm Islands.

B: But don't they live in California?

A: No. They ______________ (7.) there, but they moved back to England. And now they come here sometimes, too.

B: I'm a big football fan. When I was younger, I ______________ (8.) all Beckham's games on TV. And I ______________ (9.) tickets every time he played in England.

A: Oh, wait. There's an announcement. . . . Our flight is delayed.

B: Well, you know that old saying: "The more things change, the more they remain the same!"

A: But not in Dubai! Things are *always* changing here, and life seems very different from the way it ______________ (10.).

EXERCISE 5 EDITING

GRAMMAR NOTES 1–3 Read these online posts from foreigners visiting or living in Dubai. There are seven mistakes in the use of *used to* and *would*. The first mistake is already corrected. Find and correct six more.

Jason Smith, USA: I come here often for business. It's a great city, but driving in Dubai is difficult. The traffic is really heavy. It used to ~~took~~ *take* me just 20 minutes to drive from the airport to my hotel. Now, it sometimes takes me almost an hour. Also, the police are very strict. I was only going a little over the speed limit, but I got a ticket last week on the way to my hotel. I was upset at first, but at least these days you can pay the ticket online. You used to have to pay in person. It would took forever!

Lynda Davis, Australia: I love Dubai. It's so international. The population never would be so diverse. Now, more than 85 percent of the people living here are foreign born (including me)! It's all very exciting. And there is so much to do. Today, I used to visit the Burj Khalifa. Afterwards, I walked around for hours. I love all the malls and theaters. When I first came here, there didn't use to be that many things to do in the evening. After work, I would just go home. Now, I can choose from many different activities and events.

Wolfgang Meyer, Germany: There are still these wonderful traditional *souks* (marketplaces), but there used to be many more of them. When I lived here twenty years ago, I would stop at one or more of them on my way home from work. I would buy some fresh fish and vegetables and maybe some interesting spices. Then I would went home and cook a great meal for my family.

Graham Scott, UK: This is my first time back in fifteen years. People look really different from before. For one thing, you used to saw more people wearing traditional clothing. Men would wearing *kanduras* (long white robes). Women would wear the *abaya* (a full-length black piece of clothing they wear over other clothes). Today, you see more Western-style clothing.

STEP 4 COMMUNICATION PRACTICE

EXERCISE 6 LISTENING

04|02 **A** Listen to the conversation between two friends. Decide if the woman is talking about something that was true in the past or that is true now. Then listen again and check (✓) *Past* or *Now*.

	Past	Now
1. a lot of small family-owned stores	☑	☐
2. a lot of banks	☐	☐
3. big shopping malls outside of town	☐	☐
4. people hanging out on the street	☐	☐
5. some break-ins[1]	☐	☐
6. clean streets	☐	☐
7. garbage on the street	☐	☐
8. free parking	☐	☐
9. pay parking	☐	☐
10. large movie theaters outside of town	☐	☐
11. small neighborhood movie theaters	☐	☐
12. a lot of restaurants	☐	☐

1 *break-ins:* crimes in which criminals enter buildings in order to steal things

04|02 **B** Listen to the conversation again. Then work with a partner. Do you think the changes in the woman's town are good or bad? Would *you* like to live there? Why or why not? Discuss your answers.

EXAMPLE: A: There used to be a lot of small stores. Now, there are a lot of banks. I don't think that's a good thing.
B: I agree. It's nicer to shop in your neighborhood. And how many banks does a town need? But, . . .

EXERCISE 7 THINGS CHANGE

A PICTURE COMPARISON **Work with a partner. Look at the pictures. What changes do you notice? Discuss them with your partner.**

EXAMPLE: A: The street used to be called First Avenue. Now it's called Park Avenue.
B: Right. And there didn't use to be many trees. Now there are a lot of trees.

B **Compare your answers with those of your classmates. Who noticed the most changes?**

EXERCISE 8 A PLACE YOU KNOW WELL

CONVERSATION **Work in a group. Talk about changes in a place you know well. Don't forget to use *used to* and *would*.**

EXAMPLE: A: Last month, I went back to the town I grew up in. It was very different. I used to know a lot of people there. I would see them every day.
B: Oh. What happened to them? Did they move?
A: Yes. Many of them used to have jobs in the local factory, but the factory closed and they left town to look for work.

EXERCISE 9 PEOPLE CHANGE

PICTURE COMPARISON Work with a partner. Look at the photos of Jennifer Lopez and read the information about her. Discuss the changes in her appearance and in her life. Use *used to* to describe her past and the simple present to describe her present.

EXAMPLE: A: She used to be very pretty.
B: What do you mean "used to be"? She still is!

- was called Jennifer Lopez
- lived in New York City
- shared a small apartment with her family
- didn't have a lot of money
- took singing and dancing lessons
- dreamed of becoming a movie star
- was single
- wasn't a star

- people call her J. Lo
- divides her time between Los Angeles and New York
- owns several mansions[1]
- earns millions of dollars a year
- sings and dances professionally
- is a world-famous actress
- is divorced from singer Marc Anthony
- performs all over the world (including Dubai!)

1 *mansions:* very large houses

EXERCISE 10 WHAT ABOUT YOU?

CONVERSATION Work in a group. Talk about how you used to be and how you are now. Answer the questions below. Use *used to* and *would*. If you have a picture of yourself from that time, you can bring it to class and show it to your group.

EXAMPLE: A: I used to have very long hair. Now I wear my hair short.
B: Anton, did you use to have long hair?
C: Everybody used to have long hair back then. I wouldn't get a haircut for months and months!

1. How did you use to look?
2. What type of things would you do?
3. How did you use to dress?

FROM GRAMMAR TO WRITING

A BEFORE YOU WRITE Think of a place you know that has changed. You can choose, for example, a country, city, neighborhood, school, or workplace. Complete the outline. List four changes.

______________________________: **Then and Now**
(Name of Place)

	Then	Now
1.	______________________	______________________
2.	______________________	______________________
3.	______________________	______________________
4.	______________________	______________________

B WRITE Use your outline to write a paragraph about the changes. Contrast how the place was in the past and how it is now. Use *used to* and *would*. You can use *Today, however,* or *Now, however,* to introduce the contrasts. Try to avoid the common mistakes in the chart.

EXAMPLE: Greenville is very different from the way it used to be. People used to shop in local stores. They would buy their vegetables at the corner grocery store and their clothes at a neighborhood shop. Today, however, they drive to big shopping malls in the suburbs . . .

Common Mistakes in Using *Used to* and *Would*

Use the **base form** of the verb after ***used to*** or ***would***. Do not use the verb + *-ing* and do not add *-s* to the base form after *he*, *she*, or *it*.	She **used to shop** every day. NOT She used to ~~shopping~~ every day. She **would buy** fresh fruit and vegetables. NOT She would ~~buys~~ fresh fruit and vegetables.
Use ***used to*** to describe **past situations**. Do not use *would*.	I **used to** live in Dubai. NOT I ~~would~~ live in Dubai.
Use ***used to*** to show that you are writing about the past. Then, you can change to ***would*** for **past habits**. Do not begin your writing with *would*.	I **used to** ride my bike every day. I **would** spend hours in the park. NOT I ~~would~~ ride my bike every day . . .

C CHECK YOUR WORK Read your paragraph. Underline *used to* and circle *would*. Use the Editing Checklist to check your work.

Editing Checklist

Did you use . . . ?

- ☐ *used to* + base form of the verb to write about past situations or habits
- ☐ *would* + base form of the verb to write about past habits (but not situations)
- ☐ *used to* and then change to *would* to write about past habits

D REVISE YOUR WORK Read your paragraph again. Can you improve your writing? Make changes if necessary. Give your paragraph a title.

UNIT 4 **REVIEW**

Test yourself on the grammar of the unit.

A **Circle the correct words to complete the sentences.**

1. What did / would you use to like to do when you were a kid?
2. I used to / would love hanging out at the mall.
3. Do / Did you use to go to concerts?
4. My sister would plays / play video games for hours.
5. I never used to / would like video games before, but now I love them.
6. My life used to / would be so different back then.

B **Complete the conversations with *used to* or *would* and the verb in parentheses. Use *would* when possible.**

1. IAN: Hey, is that Jorge? He ______________ (a. look) very different. I almost didn't recognize him!
   BEN: Yes. He ______________ (b. have) long hair, but he cut it last month.
   IAN: I ______________ (c. wear) my hair very long, too, especially in the summer.
   BEN: Me too. Sometimes I ______________ (d. not get) a haircut for a whole year!
2. MIA: I ______________ (a. play) the guitar. I'm sorry I quit.
   LEE: I had a guitar, too. I ______________ (b. practice) for hours.
   MIA: ______________ you ______________ (c. go) to concerts when you were a student?
   LEE: Yes. I ______________ (d. love) the free concerts in the park. Once, I even heard J. Lo!

C **Find and correct six mistakes.**

1. As a little girl, Yi Ling would live in Singapore.
2. In 1998, her family used to move to England.
3. Singapore used to being a part of Malaysia. Today, it is a separate country.
4. The Singapore River used to had hundreds of small boats on it.
5. The water would be very dirty.
6. In the past, flights from England to Singapore would took several days. Planes used to make many stops to refuel.

Now check your answers on page 475.

UNIT

5

Wh- Questions

IN COURT

OUTCOMES

- Ask questions about the past, using *wh-* words
- Identify important information in an interview transcript
- Identify the main point of a conversation
- Write a series of interview questions to get information about a past event

STEP 1 GRAMMAR IN CONTEXT

BEFORE YOU READ

A lawyer is questioning a crime witness in court. Look at the photo. Discuss the questions.

1. Who is the lawyer? The judge? The witness?
2. What do you think the lawyer is asking?

READ

05|01 **Read this excerpt from a court transcript.**

State of Illinois vs.[1] Harry M. Adams

March 30, 2015

LAWYER: What happened on the night of May 12, 2014? Please tell the court.[2]

WITNESS: I went to Al's Grill.

LAWYER: Who did you see there?

WITNESS: I saw one of the defendants.

LAWYER: Which one did you see?

WITNESS: It was that man. *[The witness is pointing to Mr. Adams.]*

1 *vs.:* against (*vs.* is the written abbreviation of *versus*)

2 *court:* the people (judge, lawyers, jury) who decide if someone is guilty of a crime

LAWYER: Let the record show that the witness is indicating the defendant, Harry Adams. OK, you saw Mr. Adams. Did he see you?
WITNESS: No, no, he didn't see me.
LAWYER: But somebody saw you. Who saw you?
WITNESS: A woman. He was talking to a woman. She saw me.
LAWYER: OK. What happened next?
WITNESS: The woman gave him a box.
LAWYER: A box! What did it look like?
WITNESS: It was about this long...
LAWYER: So, about a foot and a half. What did Mr. Adams do then?
WITNESS: He took the box. He looked frightened.
LAWYER: Why did he look frightened? What was in the box?
WITNESS: I don't know. He didn't open it. He just took it and left in a hurry.
LAWYER: Where did he go?
WITNESS: Toward the parking lot.
LAWYER: When did the woman leave?
WITNESS: I don't know. She was still there when we heard his car speed away.

AFTER YOU READ

A VOCABULARY **Choose the word or phrase that best completes each sentence.**

1. A **defendant** is someone that ____.
   a. saw a crime   b. possibly broke a law   c. works in the court
2. If something is for the **record**, you can find it in a ____.
   a. music CD   b. box   c. written report
3. If you are **frightened**, you are ____.
   a. dangerous   b. afraid   c. unhappy
4. If you leave **in a hurry**, you leave ____.
   a. quickly   b. in a storm   c. by bus
5. The witness **indicated** Harry Adams by ____ him.
   a. laughing at   b. speaking about   c. pointing to

B COMPREHENSION **Match the questions and answers.**

____ 1. Where does the reading take place?   a. Harry Adams.
____ 2. When did the events take place?   b. In court.
____ 3. Where did the witness go that night?   c. A box.
____ 4. Who did the witness see there?   d. Toward the parking lot.
____ 5. Who saw the witness?   e. May 12, 2014.
____ 6. What did the woman give Mr. Adams?   f. Al's Grill.
____ 7. Where did Mr. Adams go?   g. A woman.

C DISCUSSION **Work with a partner. Compare your answers in B. Why did you choose each answer?**

STEP 2 GRAMMAR PRESENTATION

WH- QUESTIONS: *WHO, WHAT*

Questions About the Subject

Wh- Word Subject	Verb	Object
Who	saw	Harry?
		the box?

Answers

Subject	Verb	Object
Marta	saw	him.
		it.

Questions About the Object

Wh- Word Object	Auxiliary Verb	Subject	Main Verb
Who	did	Marta	see?
What			

Answers

Subject	Verb	Object
She	saw	Harry.
		the box.

WH- QUESTIONS: *WHICH, WHOSE, HOW MANY*

Questions About the Subject

Wh- Word + Noun	Verb	Object
Which witness	saw	you?
Whose lawyer		
How many people		

Answers

Subject	Verb	Object
Mr. Ho	saw	me.
Harry's lawyer		
Five people		

Questions About the Object

Wh- Word + Noun	Auxiliary Verb	Subject	Main Verb
Which witness	did	you	see?
Whose lawyer			
How many people			

Answers

Subject	Verb	Object
I	saw	the first witness.
		Harry's lawyer.
		five people.

WH- QUESTIONS: *WHEN, WHERE, WHY*

Questions

Wh- Word	Auxiliary Verb	Subject	Main Verb
When	did	Marta	go?
Where			
Why			

Answers

Subject	Verb	Time/Place/Reason
She	went	yesterday.
		to the police.
		because she was frightened.

GRAMMAR NOTES

1 *Wh-* Questions and *Wh-* Words

Use ***wh-* questions** (also called **information questions**) to ask for specific information.

Wh- questions begin with ***wh-* words** such as: *who, what, when, where, why, which, whose, how, how many, how much,* and *how long.*	A: **Who** did you see at Al's Grill? B: Harry Adams. A: **When** did you go there? B: On May 12, 2014. A: **How many** people saw you? B: Two.
USAGE NOTE In conversation, **answers** to *wh-* questions are usually **short**. They just give the requested information.	A: How long did you stay there? B: **Three hours.** *(more common)* I stayed there three hours. *(less common)*

2 *Wh-* Questions with *Who* and *What*

Use ***who*** to ask for information about **people**. Use ***what*** to ask for information about **things**.

For **questions about the subject**, use ***who*** or ***what*** in place of the subject, and use statement word order: ***wh-* word (= subject) + verb**	SUBJECT Someone saw you. **Who** saw you?	SUBJECT Something happened. **What** happened?
For **questions about the object**, use ***who*** or ***what*** and question word order: ***wh-* word + auxiliary + subject + verb**	OBJECT You saw someone. **Who** did you see?	OBJECT He said something. **What** did he say?
Remember that an **auxiliary verb** is a verb such as ***do*** *(does, did)*, ***have*** *(has, had)*, ***can***, or ***will***. ***Be*** can be an auxiliary too.	What ***does*** he **do**? Who ***will*** she **defend**? What ***is*** he **doing**?	
BE CAREFUL! Do not use an auxiliary verb in questions about the **subject**.	Who **saw** you there? NOT Who ~~did see~~ you there?	
USAGE NOTE In very formal English, we sometimes use ***whom*** instead of *who* in questions about the **object**.	**Whom** did you see? *(very formal)* **Who** did you see? *(more common)*	

3 *Wh-* Questions with *Which*, *Whose*, and *How many*

You can also use ***which***, ***whose***, and ***how many*** to ask for information about **people** and **things**.

• ***which*** **+ noun** (to ask about a choice) • ***whose*** **+ noun** (to ask about possessions) • ***how many*** **+ noun** (to ask about quantities)	***Which*** **witness** told the truth? ***Whose*** **lawyer** do you believe? ***How many*** **questions** did the lawyer ask?
For **questions about the subject**, use the word order: ***wh-* word + noun + verb**	***Which*** **defendant answered** best?
For **questions about the object**, use the word order: ***wh-* word + noun + auxiliary + subject + verb**	***Which*** **defendant did you trust** more?

4 *Wh-* Questions with *Where*, *Why*, and *When*

Use ***where***, ***why***, and ***when*** to ask about **place**, **reason**, and **time**.	
• ***where*** (to ask about place) • ***why*** (to ask about reason) • ***when*** (to ask about time)	**Where** will she go? **Why** does she want to defend him? **When** did she arrive?
Use the word order: ***wh*-** **word** + **auxiliary** + **subject** + **verb**	***Where* did they travel?**

5 *Wh-* Questions with *Be*

When the **main verb** is a form of ***be*** (*am, is, are, was, were*), it goes directly after the *wh-* question word or *wh-* question word + noun combination.	
• ***wh*- word + *be***	***Who* is** the witness? ***What* was** the best answer? ***Where* are** the lawyers?
• ***wh*- word + noun + *be***	***Which* witnesses are** in court? ***How many* people were** in the room?

STEP 3 FOCUSED PRACTICE

EXERCISE 1 DISCOVER THE GRAMMAR

GRAMMAR NOTES 1–5 **Match the questions and answers.**

__h__ **1.** Where were you?
____ **2.** Who did you see?
____ **3.** Who saw you?
____ **4.** What hit her?
____ **5.** Why did he leave?
____ **6.** What did she hit?
____ **7.** Which man did you give the money to?
____ **8.** Which man gave you the money?
____ **9.** How many witnesses were there?

a. His wife saw me.
b. She hit a car.
c. I gave the money to Harry.
d. A car hit her.
e. Six.
f. Harry gave me the money.
g. I saw the defendant.
~~**h.**~~ At Al's Grill.
i. Because he wanted to meet Harry.

EXERCISE 2 *WH-* QUESTIONS

A GRAMMAR NOTES 1–5 **Complete the cross-examination. Write the lawyer's questions. Use the words in parentheses and make any necessary changes.**

1. LAWYER: *What time did you return home?*
(what time / you / return home)
WITNESS: I returned home just before midnight.

2. LAWYER: ______________________________
(how / you / get home)
WITNESS: Someone gave me a ride. I was in a hurry.

3. LAWYER: ______________________________
(who / give you / a ride)
WITNESS: A friend from work.

4. LAWYER: ______________________________
(what / happen / next)
WITNESS: I opened my door and saw someone on my living room floor.

5. LAWYER: ______________________________
(who / you / see)
WITNESS: Deborah Collins.

6. LAWYER: For the record, ______________________________
(who / be / Deborah Collins)
WITNESS: She's my wife's boss. I mean, she *was* my wife's boss. She's dead now.

7. LAWYER: ______________________________
(what / you / do)
WITNESS: I called the police.

8. LAWYER: ______________________________
(when / the police / arrive)
WITNESS: In about 10 minutes.

9. LAWYER: ______________________________
(what / they / ask you)
WITNESS: They asked me to describe the crime scene.

10. LAWYER: ______________________________
(how many police officers / come)

WITNESS: I don't remember. Why?

LAWYER: I'm asking the questions here. Please just answer.

05|02 **B** LISTEN AND CHECK **Listen to the cross-examination and check your answers in A.**

EXERCISE 3 *WH-* QUESTIONS

GRAMMAR NOTES 1–5 **Read the answers. Then ask questions about the underlined words or phrases.**

1. Court begins at 9:00 a.m.
   When does court begin?
2. Something horrible happened.
   ____
3. Five witnesses described the crime.
   ____
4. The witness indicated Harry Adams.
   ____
5. The witness indicated Harry Adams.
   ____
6. The lawyer questioned the restaurant manager.
   ____
7. The manager looked frightened.
   ____
8. The judge spoke to the jury.
   ____
9. The verdict was "guilty."
   ____
10. The jury found Adams guilty because he didn't have an alibi.
    ____
11. The trial[1] lasted two weeks.
    ____
12. Adams paid his lawyer $2,000.
    ____

1 *trial:* a legal process in a court of law that decides if someone is guilty of a crime

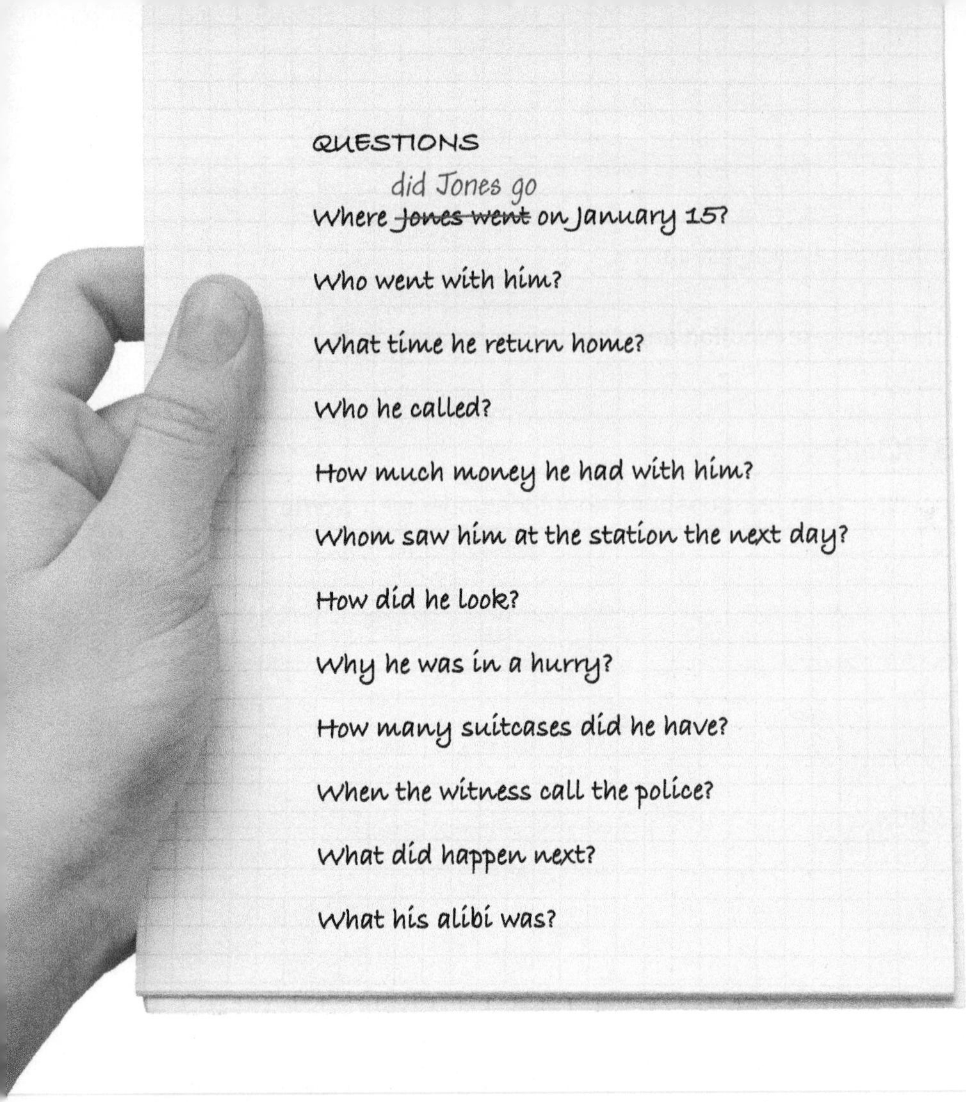

EXERCISE 4 EDITING

GRAMMAR NOTES 1–5

Read a reporter's notes. There are nine mistakes in the use of *wh-* questions. The first mistake is already corrected. Find and correct eight more.

STEP 4 COMMUNICATION PRACTICE

EXERCISE 5 LISTENING

05|03 **A** Listen to the conversation between two reporters who are covering a trial. Check (✓) the questions you hear.

- [x] **1.** Where were you?
- [ ] **2.** What happened to you?
- [ ] **3.** What did they say?
- [ ] **4.** What did they do?
- [ ] **5.** Who did they see at the movies?
- [ ] **6.** Who saw them at the movies?
- [ ] **7.** What happened after the movie?
- [ ] **8.** Why did they go?
- [ ] **9.** What did her boss say?
- [ ] **10.** Who did you believe?
- [ ] **11.** Who believed you?
- [ ] **12.** Who did the jury believe?

05|03 **B** Listen to the conversation again. Then work with a partner. Discuss your answers. Did you check the same questions? Explain why you didn't check a question.

EXAMPLE: A: Well, number 1 is already checked. What about number 2? I checked it. Did you?
B: No. I didn't because the woman didn't ask, "What happened to you?" She asked, "What happened here?"
A: You're right. What about question 3 . . . ?

EXERCISE 6 ON THE WITNESS STAND

ROLE PLAY **Work with a partner. Look at the excerpt from a court transcript on page 61 again. Read it aloud. Then continue the lawyer's questioning of the witness. Ask at least six more questions.**

EXAMPLE: LAWYER: When did the woman leave?
WITNESS: She was still there when we heard his car speed away.
LAWYER: What happened next?
WITNESS: I saw . . .

EXERCISE 7 TO TELL THE TRUTH

A GAME **Work in a group of three. Each student tells the group an interesting fact about his or her life. The fact can *only* be true for this student.**

EXAMPLE: A: I play three musical instruments.
B: I speak four languages.
C: I have five pets.

B **The group chooses a fact and goes to the front of the class. Each student states the same fact, but remember: Only one student is telling the truth.**

EXAMPLE:

C **The class asks the three students *wh-* questions to find out who is telling the truth.**

EXAMPLE: THEA: Cezar, which four languages do you speak?
CEZAR: I speak Russian, French, Spanish, and English.

LEV: Cezar, where did you learn Russian?
CEZAR: I was born in Russia.

MEI: Cezar, who taught you French?
CEZAR: My grandmother is French. I learned it from her.

JOSÉ: Cezar, how do you say "witness" in Spanish?
CEZAR: . . .

FROM GRAMMAR TO WRITING

A BEFORE YOU WRITE **Work with a partner. Your partner will tell you about something exciting he or she once saw. Write a list of questions to ask your partner in order to get more information. Then interview your partner and take notes on the answers.**

EXAMPLE: A: I once saw a bad car accident.
B: When did the accident happen?
A: About two years ago.
B: Where . . . ?

Questions to Ask

When ______	How much/How many ______
Where ______	Why ______
Who ______	*Other:* ______
What ______	______

B WRITE **Use your notes to write up the interview. Try to avoid the common mistakes in the chart.**

EXAMPLE: TANIA: I once saw a bad car accident.
OMARI: When did the accident happen?
TANIA: About two years ago.
OMARI: Where . . . ?

Common Mistakes in Using *Wh-* Questions

Use the **auxiliary *do*** in questions about the **object**. Do not leave it out.	What **did** he say? NOT What ~~he say~~?
Use **question word order** with an auxiliary verb. Do not use statement word order.	Who **did you see**? NOT Who ~~you saw~~?

C CHECK YOUR WORK **Read your interview. Circle the *wh-* words and underline the *wh-* questions. Use the Editing Checklist to check your work.**

Editing Checklist

Did you use . . . ?
- ☐ the correct *wh-* words
- ☐ the correct word order
- ☐ auxiliary verbs in questions about the object
- ☐ auxiliary verbs in questions beginning with *when*, *where*, and *why*

D REVISE YOUR WORK **Read your interview again. Can you improve your writing? Make changes if necessary.**

UNIT 5 **REVIEW**

Test yourself on the grammar of the unit.

A Match the questions and answers.

_____ **1.** Where did Feng go Wednesday night?	**a.** *Night Court 2*
_____ **2.** When was the movie over?	**b.** It got great reviews.
_____ **3.** How long was it?	**c.** Feng's.
_____ **4.** Which movie did he see?	**d.** At 11:00.
_____ **5.** How many people went?	**e.** Laurel and Xavier.
_____ **6.** Who went with him?	**f.** Two and a half hours.
_____ **7.** Whose car did they use?	**g.** Three.
_____ **8.** Why did they choose that movie?	**h.** To the movies.

B Circle the correct words to complete the sentences.

1. Which court does Shari work / works at now?

2. How did she / she did find that job?

3. Who did tell / told Shari about it?

4. Why she left / did she leave her old job?

5. When did she start / started to work there?

6. Who is her boss / her boss is?

7. What did / does she do at her new job?

C Find and correct five mistakes.

A: What did you did with my law book? I can't find it.

B: Nothing. Where you saw it last?

A: In the living room. I was watching *Judge Judy* on TV. What Zack's phone number?

B: I'm not sure. Why you want to know?

A: He took the course last year. I'll call him. Maybe he still has his book.

B: Good idea. What time does he gets out of work?

Now check your answers on page 476.

The Future

UNIT 6
Future
SPACE TRAVEL

UNIT 7
Future Time Clauses
SETTING GOALS

PART 2

OUTCOMES

- Discuss future facts, predictions, plans, and scheduled events
- Express quick decisions, offers, and promises
- Identify important information in an interview transcript
- Identify actions happening now and future plans in a conversation
- Write a paragraph about a prediction

OUTCOMES

- Describe the order between future events, using a future time clause
- Follow the sequence of two future events in a reading
- Follow the time order of events in a conversation
- Discuss future plans and goals
- Write a description of future plans and goals

UNIT 6

Future
SPACE TRAVEL

OUTCOMES
- Discuss future facts, predictions, plans, and scheduled events
- Express quick decisions, offers, and promises
- Identify important information in an interview transcript
- Identify actions happening now and future plans in a conversation
- Write a paragraph about a prediction

STEP 1 GRAMMAR IN CONTEXT

BEFORE YOU READ

Look at the photo. Discuss the questions.

1. Where do you think the first space tourists will travel?
2. Why do people want to travel into space? Would *you* like to?

READ

06|01 **Read this transcript of a radio program about space tourism.**

Space Tourism: Not Just Science Fiction[1]

ROHAN: Good evening, and welcome to *The Future Today*. I'm Enid Rohan, and tonight Dr. Richard Starr, president of YourSpace, Inc., is going to talk to us about space tourism. Dr. Starr, is space really going to become a popular tourist destination?

STARR: Yes, it is, Enid. We're already building the space planes. And we're selling tickets and planning our first trips now. In fact, our training program for passengers is starting next January.

ROHAN: Where will these tours go? Will they travel to the Moon? Mars?

STARR: No, they won't. The first space tourists aren't going to go that far. They're only going to travel about 110 kilometers, or 68 miles above the Earth. That's the edge of space. A trip will last about two and a half hours.

ROHAN: Tickets cost $250,000. Who's going to pay that much for just a few hours?

STARR: Hundreds of people are purchasing tickets and are waiting for takeoff. It's going to be an incredible trip. And tickets won't always be so expensive. Costs are going to fall a lot.

ROHAN: What will a trip be like?

1 *science fiction:* stories about the future, often about space travel and scientific discoveries

STARR: First of all, you'll experience zero gravity.[2] That means you will float freely in the cabin. And you'll get a bird's-eye view[3] of the Earth from space. You won't believe your eyes! You're going to think about the Earth in a whole new way.

ROHAN: Sounds great. I think I'll ask my boss to send me on a trip. When does the next flight leave?

STARR: January 1, two years from now. But you won't be on that one—our next three flights are already sold out!

2 *gravity:* the force that makes things fall to the ground. (In zero gravity, things do not stay on the ground.)
3 *bird's-eye view:* a view from a very high place

AFTER YOU READ

A VOCABULARY **Complete the sentences with the words from the box.**

edge	experience	incredible	purchase	sold out	takeoff

1. I want to go on this trip. How can I ______________ a ticket?
2. There are no more tickets for the space tour. It's ______________.
3. I was so excited watching *Gravity 3* that I was at the ______________ of my seat!
4. I was only scared at ______________—when the space plane left the ground.
5. Sy took ______________ photos from the spacecraft. He saw some amazing sights.
6. In space, people ______________ a lot of feelings—amazement, excitement, fear, and much more.

B COMPREHENSION **Read the statements. Which of the statements are true right now? Which will be true only in the future? Check (✓) *Now* or *Future*.**

	Now	Future
1. Tourists are buying tickets.	☐	☐
2. A training program for passengers is starting.	☐	☐
3. Space tours travel about 110 km (68 miles) above the Earth.	☐	☐
4. Tickets are very expensive.	☐	☐
5. The next flight is ready to leave.	☐	☐
6. A trip lasts about two and a half hours.	☐	☐

C DISCUSSION **Work with a partner. Compare your answers in B. Why did you check *Now* or *Future*?**

STEP 2 GRAMMAR PRESENTATION

BE GOING TO FOR THE FUTURE

Statements

Subject	*Be*	*(Not) Going to*	Base Form of Verb	
I	**am**	(**not**) **going to**	**leave**	soon.
You	**are**			
He She It	**is**			
We You They	**are**			

***Yes/No* Questions**

Be	Subject	*Going to*	Base Form of Verb	
Am	I	**going to**	**leave**	soon?
Are	you			
Is	he she it			
Are	we you they			

Short Answers

Affirmative			Negative		
Yes,	you	**are.**	**No,**	you**'re**	**not.**
	I	**am.**		I**'m**	
	he she it	**is.**		he**'s** she**'s** it**'s**	
	you we they	**are.**		you**'re** we**'re** they**'re**	

***Wh-* Questions**

Wh- Word	*Be*	Subject	*Going to*	Base Form of Verb
When Why	**are**	you	**going to**	**leave**?

WILL FOR THE FUTURE

Statements

Subject	*Will (not)*	Base Form of Verb	
I You He She It We You They	**will (not)**	**leave**	soon.

***Yes/No* Questions**

Will	Subject	Base Form of Verb	
Will	I you he she it we you they	**leave**	soon?

Short Answers

Affirmative		
Yes,	you I he she it you we they	**will.**

Negative		
No,	you I he she it you we they	**won't.**

***Wh-* Questions**

Wh- Word	*Will*	Subject	Base Form of Verb
When	**will**	you	**leave**?

PRESENT PROGRESSIVE FOR THE FUTURE

Statements

Subject + *Be*	*(Not)* + Base Form + *-ing*	
We**'re**	**(not) leaving**	soon.
It**'s**		

SIMPLE PRESENT FOR THE FUTURE

Statements

Subject	Verb	
We	**leave**	Monday at 6:45 a.m.
It	**leaves**	

GRAMMAR NOTES

1 Referring to Future Events

There are **several ways to refer to future events**. Sometimes only one form is appropriate, but in many cases more than one form is possible.

- *be going to*
- *will*
- **present progressive**
- **simple present**

They**'re going to have** a meeting.
I think I**'ll go**. **Will** you **be** there?
It**'s taking** place next week.
It **starts** at 9:00 a.m. on Monday.

2 Future Facts

For facts or events that you are **certain will happen in the future**, you can use ***be going to*** or ***will***.

- *be going to*
- *will*

The sun **is going to rise** at 6:43 tomorrow.
The sun **will rise** at 6:43 tomorrow.

3 Predictions

For predictions about things you are **quite sure will happen in the future**, you can also use ***be going to*** or ***will***.

- *be going to*
- *will*

I think a lot of people **are going to travel** to space.
I think a lot of people **will travel** to space.

USAGE NOTE We often use ***I think*** before a prediction.

I think tickets **are going to get** cheaper.

IN WRITING We use ***will*** more in **formal writing** and ***be going to*** more in **conversation**.

Prices **will drop** in time. *(formal writing)*
Prices **are going to drop** in time. *(conversation)*

BE CAREFUL! Do not use ***will*** when something you notice right now makes you almost certain that an event is going to happen. Use ***be going to***.

A: Look at that car!
B: Oh, no. It**'s going to crash**!
NOT It~~'ll crash~~.

4 Future Plans

For plans or things that are **already decided**, use ***be going to*** or the **present progressive**.

- *be going to*
- **present progressive**

I**'m going to fly** to Chicago next week.
I**'m flying** to Chicago next week.
NOT ~~I'll fly~~ to Chicago next week.

USAGE NOTE We often use the **present progressive** for plans that are already arranged.

I**'m flying** to Chicago next week. I already have a ticket.

USAGE NOTE When the main verb is *go*, it is more common to use the **present progressive** (*be going*) than *be going to go*.

I**'m going** to Paris tomorrow. *(more common)*
I**'m going to go** to Paris tomorrow. *(less common)*

5 Quick Decisions, Offers, and Promises

For decisions that you make quickly while you are speaking, or to make offers or promises, use ***will***.

• **quick decision**	A: The Space Show is opening next week. B: Really? Sounds interesting. I think **I'll go**.
• **offer**	A: I'd like to go too, but I don't have a ride. B: **I'll drive** you. But I'd like to leave by 7:00.
• **promise**	A: No problem. **I'll be** ready.

6 Future Scheduled Events

For scheduled future events such as **timetables**, **programs**, and **schedules**, you can use the **simple present**.

• **simple present**	The shuttle **leaves** at 9:00 a.m. Dr. Starr **speaks** Tuesday afternoon.
USAGE NOTE We often use verbs such as ***begin***, ***start***, ***leave***, ***arrive***, ***last***, and ***end*** for scheduled future events.	The conference **begins** May 11. Registration **lasts** until May 10.
USAGE NOTE You can also use ***be going to*** and ***will*** for scheduled future events.	Registration **is going to last** until May 10. Registration **will last** until May 10.

PRONUNCIATION NOTE

06|02

Pronunciation of *Going to*

In **informal conversation**, we often pronounce ***going to*** as "gonna."	A: What time are you **going to** be home? *(gonna)* B: I'm **going to** get home late. *(gonna)*
IN WRITING Sometimes people use ***gonna*** in **informal notes**, **text messages**, and **email** to friends.	Hi Lyn, I'm **gonna** be late. *(email)*
BE CAREFUL! Do not use ***gonna*** when you write to people you have a formal relationship with.	Professor, I'm **going to** be late. *(email)* NOT Professor, I'm ~~gonna~~ be late.
Also do not use ***gonna*** in formal writing.	According to scientists, Mars is **going to** become a tourist destination. *(paper)* NOT According to scientists, Mars is ~~gonna~~ become a tourist destination.

REFERENCE NOTES

For **contractions** of *I am, you are, I will, you will,* etc., see Appendix 26, page 464.
For the **present progressive** and **simple present** forms, see Unit 1, page 4.
For ***will*** for **making a request**, see Unit 15 on page 204.

STEP 3 FOCUSED PRACTICE

EXERCISE 1 DISCOVER THE GRAMMAR

A GRAMMAR NOTES 1–6 **Read this transcript of an interview with a future space tourist. There are thirteen forms of the future. The first form is already underlined. Find and underline twelve more.**

Out of This World

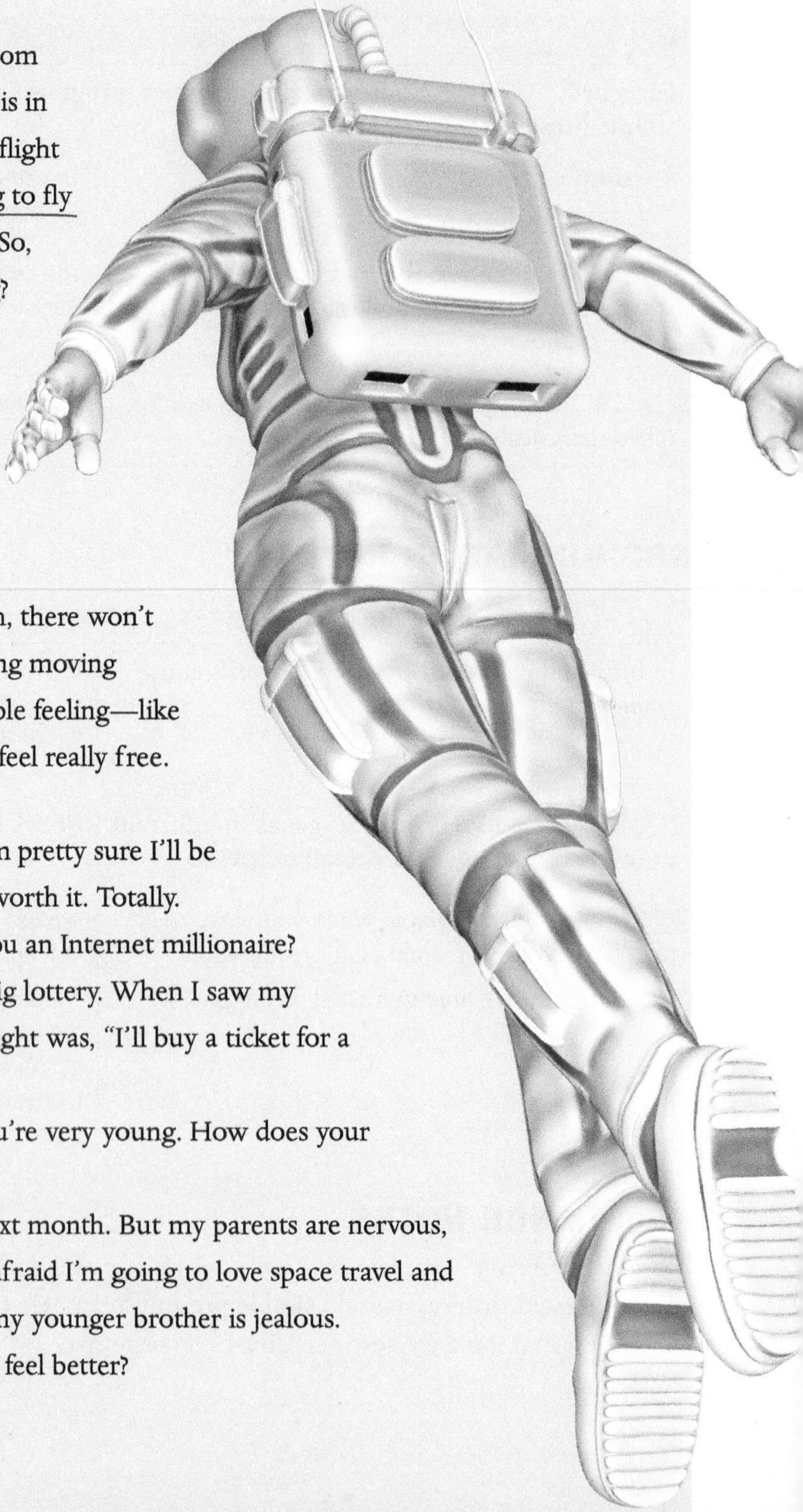

ROHAN: This is Enid Rohan, reporting from Spaceport America. Lyn Filipov is in the training program here for a flight with YourSpace, Inc. She's going to fly to the edge of space very soon. So, Lyn, which flight are you taking?

FILIPOV: The one that leaves on March 30. By the time I purchased my ticket, the earlier flights were all sold out.

ROHAN: What's the training like?

FILIPOV: Well, at 110 kilometers—that's 68 miles—above the Earth, there won't be any gravity, so we're practicing moving around in zero-g. It's an incredible feeling—like floating in water, or flying. You feel really free.

ROHAN: Aren't you even a little scared?

FILIPOV: Right now, I can't wait to go. I'm pretty sure I'll be terrified on takeoff, but it'll be worth it. Totally.

ROHAN: How can you afford this? Are you an Internet millionaire?

FILIPOV: No, I'm not. Actually, I won a big lottery. When I saw my winning numbers, my first thought was, "I'll buy a ticket for a space tour."

ROHAN: What an amazing story! But you're very young. How does your family feel about this?

FILIPOV: I'm not that young. I'll be 23 next month. But my parents are nervous, of course. My mother is really afraid I'm going to love space travel and I'll want to keep doing it. And my younger brother is jealous.

ROHAN: What do you say to make them feel better?

FILIPOV: I tell my mother, "Listen, Mom, this is an incredible once-in-a-lifetime thing. I won't make a habit of space travel, I promise." My brother? He wants a career in space travel, so he's going to study a lot harder from now on. That's what he says, anyway.

ROHAN: Thanks for the interview, Lyn. And good luck!

FILIPOV: Thanks. I'll send you photos.

B Complete the chart. List the thirteen future verb forms. Then check (✓) the correct column for each form.

	Facts	Predictions	Plans	Quick Decisions	Promises	Schedules
1. 's going to fly			✓			
2.						
3.						
4.						
5.						
6.						
7.						
8.						
9.						
10.						
11.						
12.						
13.						

EXERCISE 2 *WILL* FOR FACTS AND PREDICTIONS

A GRAMMAR NOTES 1–2 **It is the year 2020, and an international group of space tourists is getting ready for its space flight. Part of the training program includes a Question and Answer (Q & A) session. Complete the questions and answers. Use the verbs in parentheses with *will* or *won't*.**

Q: ___Will___ it ___take___ a long time to get used to zero gravity?
1. (take)

A: No, it ___won't___. Every day you ________ more comfortable, and after
2. 3. (feel)

three days you ________ used to being in space.
4. (become)

Q: ________ I ________ sick?
5. (feel)

A: Yes, you might feel sick for a little while. But it ________ long.
6. (last)

Q: I'm a runner. How __________ I __________ **7.** (stay) in shape in space?

A: Actually, all space tourists, or "spaceflight participants," as they prefer to be called, __________ **8.** (do) exercises during the flight. There __________ **9.** (be) at least one stationary bike on board, for example.

Q: __________ I __________ **10.** (look) the same?

A: Actually, you __________ **11.** (look) the same at all. Your face and eyes __________ **12.** (get) puffy. The first time you look in a mirror, you probably __________ **13.** (recognize) yourself.

Q: __________ I __________ **14.** (float) in my sleep?

A: Yes, if you are not tied down. And then you should be careful because you __________ **15.** (bump) into things all night long. Trust me. You can get hurt!

Q: I like salt and pepper on my food. Can I still use them in zero gravity?

A: Yes, you __________ still __________ **16.** (have) salt and pepper, but not like you do on Earth. You __________ **17.** (use) small, squeezable bottles with salt water and pepper water so the grains don't float away. You just squeeze it on your food. Don't worry about it. It __________ **18.** (be) great!

06|03 **B** LISTEN AND CHECK **Listen to the Question and Answer session and check your answers in A.**

EXERCISE 3 *BE GOING TO* FOR PREDICTION

GRAMMAR NOTE 3 **Look at the pictures. They show future events in the life of Professor Starr. Write predictions or guesses. Use the words from the box and a form of *be going to* or *not be going to*. Choose between affirmative and negative.**

answer the phone	get out of bed	give a speech	rain	~~take a trip~~
drive	get very wet	have dinner	sleep	watch TV

1. *He's going to take a trip.*
2. __________

3. ______________________________

4. ______________________________

5. ______________________________

6. ______________________________

7. ______________________________

8. ______________________________

9. ______________________________

10. ______________________________

EXERCISE 4 PRESENT PROGRESSIVE FOR PLANS

GRAMMAR NOTE 4 **Write about Professor Starr's plans for next week. Use the information from his calendar and the present progressive.**

	MONDAY	TUESDAY	WEDNESDAY	THURSDAY	FRIDAY	SATURDAY
A.M.	Teach my science class	Take the train to Chicago	Do the interview for *The Space Show*	Work on the Space Future website	Go to an exercise class	Answer emails from the Space Future website
P.M.		Meet friends from England for dinner	Answer questions from the online chat	↓	Fly to New York for the Space Transportation Conference	Write a speech for the next space travel conference

1. On Monday morning, *he's teaching his science class*.
2. On Tuesday morning, ________________.
3. On Tuesday evening, ________________.
4. On Wednesday morning, ________________.
5. On Wednesday afternoon, ________________.
6. All day Thursday, ________________.
7. On Friday morning, ________________.
8. On Friday evening, ________________.
9. On Saturday morning, ________________.
10. On Saturday afternoon, ________________.

EXERCISE 5 SIMPLE PRESENT FOR SCHEDULES

GRAMMAR NOTE 6 **It is June 2050. You and a friend are planning a trip to the Moon. Your friend just got the schedule, and you are deciding which shuttle to take. Use the words in parentheses to ask questions and look at the schedule to write the answers. Use the simple present.**

2050 SHUTTLE SERVICE TO THE MOON

Fall Schedule • All times given in Earth's Eastern Standard Time

SEPTEMBER				OCTOBER				NOVEMBER			
Leave Earth		Arrive Moon		Leave Earth		Arrive Moon		Leave Earth		Arrive Moon	
9/4	7:00 a.m.	9/7	6:00 a.m.	10/15	4:00 a.m.	10/18	3:00 a.m.	11/4	1:00 a.m.	11/8	12:00 a.m.
9/20	10:00 a.m.	9/23	9:00 a.m.	10/27	11:00 a.m.	10/30	10:00 a.m.	11/19	6:00 a.m.	11/23	5:00 a.m.

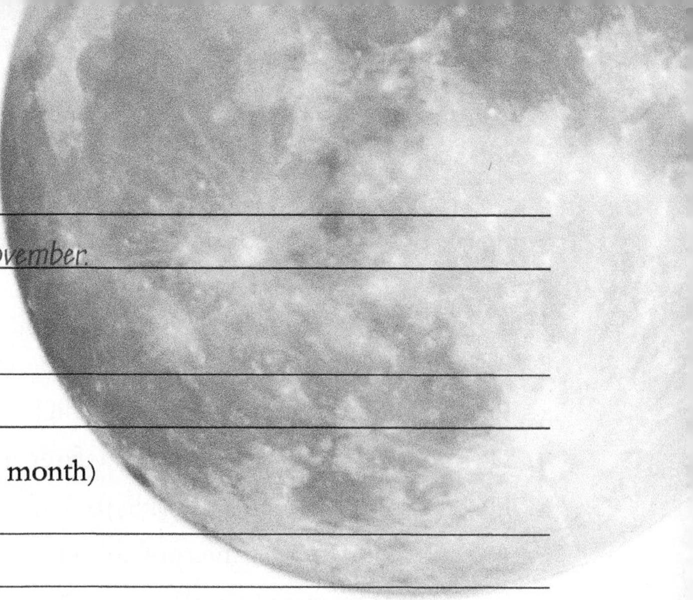

1. (when / the shuttle / fly to the Moon this fall)

   A: *When does the shuttle fly to the Moon this fall?*

   B: *It flies to the Moon in September, October, and November.*

2. (how many / shuttle flights / leave this fall)

   A: ______________________________

   B: ______________________________

3. (how often / the shuttle / depart for the Moon each month)

   A: ______________________________

   B: ______________________________

4. (when / the October 27 flight / arrive on the Moon)

   A: ______________________________

   B: ______________________________

5. (how long / the November 19 flight / last)

   A: ______________________________

   B: ______________________________

EXERCISE 6 FORMS OF THE FUTURE

A GRAMMAR NOTES 1–6 **Two people are having a cup of coffee and planning their trip to the Space Conference. Circle the correct words to complete their conversation.**

JASON: I just heard the weather report. It's raining / It's going to rain (1.) tomorrow.

ARIEL: Oh no. I hate driving in the rain. And it's a long drive to the conference.

JASON: Wait! I have an idea. We'll take / We're going to take (2.) the train instead!

ARIEL: Good idea! Do you have a train schedule?

JASON: Yes. Here's one. There's a train that will leave / leaves (3.) at 7:00 a.m.

ARIEL: What about lunch? Oh, I know. I'll make / I'm making (4.) some sandwiches for us.

JASON: Good idea! You know, it's a long trip. What are we doing / are we going to do (5.) all those hours?

ARIEL: Don't worry. We'll think / We're thinking (6.) of something.

JASON: Maybe I'll bring / I'm bringing (7.) my laptop, and we can watch a movie.

ARIEL: Great. Hey, Jason, your cup will fall / is going to fall (8.)! It's right at the edge of the table.

JASON: Got it! You know, we have to get up really early. I think I'm going / I'll go (9.) home now.

ARIEL: OK. In that case, I'm seeing / I'll see (10.) you tomorrow. Good night.

06|04 **B** LISTEN AND CHECK **Listen to the conversation and check your answers in A.**

EXERCISE 7 *GOING TO* OR *GONNA*

06|05 PRONUNCIATION NOTE Listen to the sentences. Check (✓) *More Formal* if you hear ***be going to***. Check (✓) *Less Formal* if you hear ***gonna***.

	More Formal	Less Formal
1. Takeoff is going to be soon.	☐	☑
2. It's going to be full.	☐	☐
3. Professor Starr is going to be on the flight.	☐	☐
4. He's going to speak at the space conference.	☐	☐
5. He believes that people are going to fly to the moon.	☐	☐
6. Are you going to be at the conference?	☐	☐
7. It's going to be very interesting.	☐	☐

EXERCISE 8 EDITING

GRAMMAR NOTES 1–6 Read this student's report on space travel. There are eleven mistakes in the use of the future. The first mistake is already corrected. Find and correct ten more.

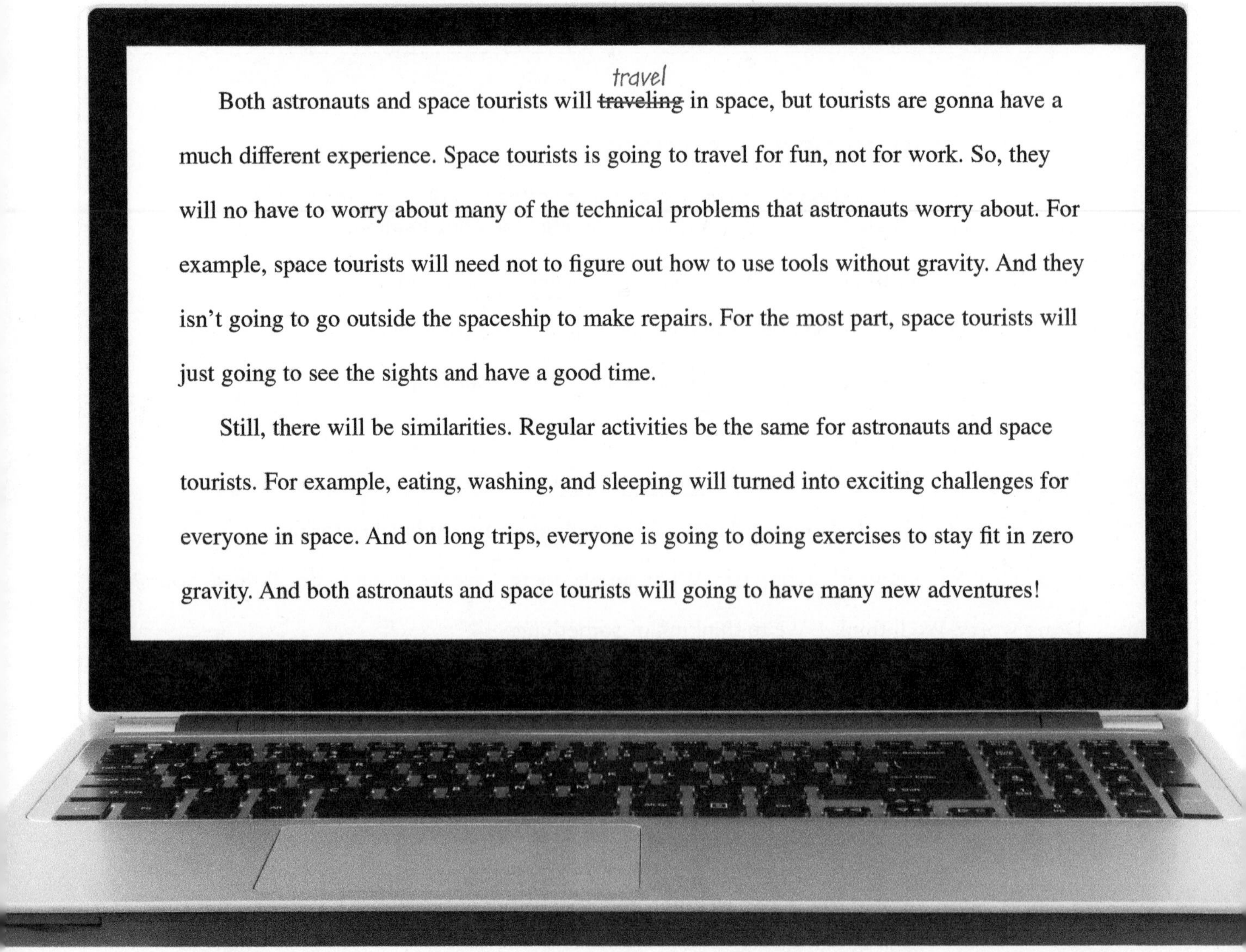

Both astronauts and space tourists will ~~traveling~~ travel in space, but tourists are gonna have a much different experience. Space tourists is going to travel for fun, not for work. So, they will no have to worry about many of the technical problems that astronauts worry about. For example, space tourists will need not to figure out how to use tools without gravity. And they isn't going to go outside the spaceship to make repairs. For the most part, space tourists will just going to see the sights and have a good time.

Still, there will be similarities. Regular activities be the same for astronauts and space tourists. For example, eating, washing, and sleeping will turned into exciting challenges for everyone in space. And on long trips, everyone is going to doing exercises to stay fit in zero gravity. And both astronauts and space tourists will going to have many new adventures!

STEP 4 COMMUNICATION PRACTICE

EXERCISE 9 LISTENING

06|06 **A** Listen to six short conversations. Decide if the people are talking about something happening now or in the future. Then listen again and check (✓) *Now* or *Future*.

	Now	Future		Now	Future		Now	Future
1.	☐	☑	3.	☐	☐	5.	☐	☐
2.	☐	☐	4.	☐	☐	6.	☐	☐

06|06 **B** Listen to each conversation again. Then work with a partner and decide if each statement below is *True* or *False*. If there isn't enough information to decide, check (✓) *Don't Know*. Discuss your answers. Give a reason for each answer.

EXAMPLE: A: Is the woman going out with friends tonight?
B: No she's not. That's false. She says she's staying home and watching TV.

	True	False	Don't Know
1. The woman is going out with friends tonight.	☐	☑	☐
2. The woman will probably watch the rest of the TV show.	☐	☐	☐
3. Professor Starr won't take the call.	☐	☐	☐
4. The lecture is about traveling to Mars.	☐	☐	☐
5. The man is going to meet his parents at the airport.	☐	☐	☐
6. The train to Chicago left five minutes ago.	☐	☐	☐

EXERCISE 10 DO YOU HAVE PLANS FOR THE WEEKEND?

A MAKING PLANS Before you make plans, complete your weekend schedule. If you have no plans, write *free*.

	SATURDAY	SUNDAY
12:00 p.m.		
1:00 p.m.		
2:00 p.m.		
3:00 p.m.		
4:00 p.m.		
5:00 p.m.		
6:00 p.m.		
7:00 p.m.		
8:00 p.m.		
9:00 p.m.		

B Work with a partner. Ask questions to decide on a time when you are both free to do something together.

EXAMPLE: A: What are you doing Saturday afternoon? Do you want to go to the movies?
B: I'm going to the library. How about Saturday night? Are you doing anything then?

EXERCISE 11 DO YOU WANT TO . . . ?

REACHING AGREEMENT **Work with a partner. Look at the weekend schedule of events. Then look at your schedules from Exercise 10. Decide which events to attend and when.**

EXAMPLE: A: What are you doing Sunday? Do you want to see *Zero G* at 3:00 p.m.?
B: Hmm. I'd like to go, but I can't. I'm meeting my sister on Sunday afternoon.
A: There's also a show at 6:00 p.m. Could you make that show?
B: Yes! Great! Are you going to get the tickets?
A: Yes, I'll get them online. See you Sunday!

WEEKEND EVENTS IN RIVERSIDE
June 20 and 21

EVENTS	WHERE AND WHEN
Art in the Park Painting, photography, jewelry, and more! Support our local artists.	River Park, all day Saturday and Sunday
International Food Festival Moussaka, pad thai, spaetzle—you'll find plenty of interesting tastes here. International music and dance, too.	Conference Center, Saturday, 1:00 p.m.–7:00 p.m.
Walking Event 5 kilometers for Jay Street Clinic. Join us and help the city's only free clinic.	Start at River Park, Sunday, 11:00 a.m. End at the clinic, 10 W. Jay St.
Zero G Experience space travel in this new film. On the big IMAX screen, it'll feel like you're really there. Purchase tickets online.	Science Museum, starts Sunday Show times: 3:00 p.m. and 6:00 p.m.
Dancing with the Stars Free concert, with plenty of room for dancing. Bring a picnic and your own chairs.	Brown's Beach, Sunday 7:00 p.m.–Midnight

EXERCISE 12 WHAT DO YOU THINK?

DISCUSSION **Work in a group. Discuss these questions.**

1. Do you think space tourism will become really popular? Why or why not?

   EXAMPLE: A: I don't think space tourism will become really popular. Only very rich people will be able to afford a ticket.
   B: Oh, I don't know about that. In time, prices will come down.
   C: Yeah, but they're never going to be low enough for most people.

2. How will space tourism change the world? Think about positive and negative changes.
3. Do you think you will ever fly to the moon? What about your children?

FROM GRAMMAR TO WRITING

A BEFORE YOU WRITE **Choose one of the ideas below to write a paragraph about the future of space travel. Then list three reasons for your idea.**

- Space travel is going to become very popular.
- Space travel will change the world.
- One day, I am going to travel to space.
- Space travel won't help people.

Reason 1: ______________________________

Reason 2: ______________________________

Reason 3: ______________________________

B WRITE **Use your list of reasons to write a paragraph about the future of space travel. Put your most important reason last. Connect your reasons with *To begin with, In addition*, and *Most importantly*. Try to avoid the common mistakes in the chart.**

EXAMPLE: I don't think space travel is going to become very popular in the near future. To begin with, it is much too expensive. I don't believe prices will fall very much. Only extremely wealthy people will have enough money to purchase tickets. In addition, . . .

Common Mistakes in Using the Future

Use the **base form** of the verb after ***will***. Do not add *-s* to the base form after *he, she,* or *it*.	My son **will travel** to space one day. NOT My son will ~~travels~~ to space one day.
Use ***will*** or ***be going to*** in formal writing. Do not use *gonna*.	I'm **going to** look for a job in space tourism. NOT I'm ~~gonna~~ look for a job. . . .

C CHECK YOUR WORK **Read your paragraph. Underline *be going to* + base form of the verb and circle *will* + base form of the verb. Use the Editing Checklist to check your work.**

Editing Checklist

Did you use . . . ?

☐ *will* or *be going to* for predictions and facts

☐ *be going to* or the present progressive for plans

☐ the base form of the verb after *will* and *be going to*

D REVISE YOUR WORK **Read your paragraph again. Can you improve your writing? Make changes if necessary. Give your paragraph a title.**

UNIT 6 **REVIEW**

Test yourself on the grammar of the unit.

A Circle the correct words to complete the sentences.

1. We'll go / We're going to Dr. Starr's lecture tomorrow night. I already have the tickets.
2. Great! I'll meet / I'm going to meet you after school.
3. Take your umbrella. It'll rain / It's going to rain.
4. Sara gives / is giving a party after the lecture. Why don't we go?
5. Oh! Look out! That vase will fall / is going to fall off the shelf!

B Complete the sentences about the future with the correct form of the verbs in parentheses. Sometimes there may be more than one correct answer.

1. It's almost 9:00. What time ______________ our flight ______________ (leave)?
2. Don't eat so much. You ______________ (feel) sick during the flight.
3. The plane ______________ (land) in a few minutes.
4. Our taxi driver ______________ (get) a speeding ticket. The police are right behind us.
5. Put your wallet away. I ______________ (pay).
6. Look at those clouds. I think it ______________ (rain).
7. What time ______________ the lecture ______________ (start)?
8. ______________ Dr. Starr ______________ (call) back this afternoon?
9. Don't worry. He ______________ (not forget) to call you.
10. Bye. I ______________ (speak) to you next week.

C Find and correct five mistakes.

1. When will Dr. Starr gets home tomorrow?
2. His lecture starts at 7:00, so I think I go.
3. Do you want to go with me, or are you study tonight?
4. What you are going to do next weekend?
5. I'm going be home all day.

Now check your answers on page 476.

UNIT 7

Future Time Clauses
SETTING GOALS

OUTCOMES
- Describe the order between future events, using a future time clause
- Follow the sequence of two future events in a reading
- Follow the time order of events in a conversation
- Discuss future plans and goals
- Write a description of future plans and goals

STEP 1 GRAMMAR IN CONTEXT

BEFORE YOU READ

Look at the photo and at the title of the article. Discuss the questions.

1. The girl wants to become a businesswoman. What do you think she will do to reach her goal?
2. What are some other typical goals that people have?
3. What's one of *your* goals?

READ

07|01 **Read this article.**

From Dream to Reality

We all have dreams, but how can we make them a reality? We change them into goals and make an action plan. Read about how one student, Latoya Jones, turned *her* dreams into goals and made an action plan.

PUT YOUR DREAMS ON PAPER. After you write a dream down, it will start to become a goal. Your path will then be a lot clearer.

Latoya Jones wrote this:
- Before I turn 30, I'm going to be a successful businessperson.

LIST YOUR REASONS. When things get difficult, you can read this list to yourself and it will help you go on.

This is what Latoya put at the top of her list:
- My parents will be proud of me when I'm a successful businessperson.

WRITE AN ACTION PLAN. Once you know what your goal is and why you want to achieve it, you must write an action plan.

This is Latoya's action plan:

- I'm going to go to business school as soon as I save enough money to pay for it.
- When I graduate, I'll get a job with a big company.
- After I get some experience, I'll find a better job.

TAKE YOUR FIRST STEPS TODAY. Don't wait. As soon as you have an action plan, take steps to achieve it.

Here are the first steps Latoya is going to take:

- Before I apply to schools, I'm going to download some catalogs.
- After I apply, I'll prepare carefully for interviews.

You can do exactly what Latoya did to achieve your goals and turn them into reality. It's not always easy, but remember: The longest journey starts with the first step!

AFTER YOU READ

A VOCABULARY **Choose the word or phrase that best completes each sentence.**

1. When you **achieve** something, you get it ____.
a. as a gift **b.** after hard work **c.** from your family

2. Sam got a college **catalog** because he wanted to ____.
a. pay his bill **b.** do his homework **c.** learn about classes

3. A **goal** is something you ____.
a. don't want very much **b.** plan and work for **c.** buy at a store

4. A **path** is a way to ____ your goals.
a. reach **b.** buy **c.** choose

5. At a college **interview**, someone ____.
a. asks you questions **b.** shows you the school **c.** gives you a job

B COMPREHENSION **For each pair of statements about Latoya's action plan, choose the action (*a* or *b*) that comes first.**

1. a. She will download school catalogs.
b. She will apply to schools.

2. a. She will save money.
b. She will go to business school.

3. a. She will get a job with a big company.
b. She will graduate.

4. a. She will find a better job.
b. She will get some experience.

5. a. She will turn 30.
b. She will become a successful businesswoman.

C DISCUSSION **Work with a partner. Compare your answers in B. Explain why you think your answers are correct.**

STEP 2 GRAMMAR PRESENTATION

FUTURE TIME CLAUSES

Statements

Main Clause		Time Clause	
I **will** I **am going to**	**get** a job	**when**	I **graduate**.
She **will** She **is going to**			she **graduates**.
They **will** They **are going to**			they **graduate**.

***Yes/No* Questions**

Main Clause		Time Clause	
Will you **Are** you **going to**	**get** a job	**when**	you **graduate**?

Short Answers

Affirmative			Negative		
Yes,	I	**will.** **am.**	**No,**	I	**won't.** **'m not.**

***Wh-* Questions**

Main Clause			Time Clause	
Where	**will** you **are** you **going to**	**get** a job	**when**	you **graduate**?

GRAMMAR NOTES

1 Function of a Future Time Clause

Use a future time clause to show the **time order between two future events**.

A future time clause begins with a **time expression** such as ***when***, ***after***, ***as soon as***, ***before***, ***until***, or ***while***.

MAIN CLAUSE TIME CLAUSE
He**'s going to move** ***after*** he **graduates**.
(First he'll graduate. Then he'll move.)

The time expression shows which of two future events **will happen first**.

MAIN CLAUSE TIME CLAUSE
We**'ll visit** him ***before*** he **leaves**.
(First we'll visit him. Then he'll leave.)

BE CAREFUL! A **future time clause** is about a **future event**, but its verb is in the **simple present**. Do not use *be going to* or *will* in a future time clause. Use the simple present.

He's going to move after he **graduates**.
NOT after he ~~is going to graduate~~
We'll miss him when he **leaves**.
NOT when he~~'ll leave~~

2 Position of the Future Time Clause

The **time clause** can come **at the beginning or the end** of the sentence. The meaning is the same.

- at the **beginning**
- at the **end**

***Before* she applies,** she'll visit schools.
She'll visit schools ***before* she applies.**

IN WRITING Use a **comma after the time clause** when it comes at the **beginning** of the sentence. Do not use a comma after the main clause when the main clause comes first.

***After* he graduates,** he'll look for a job.
He'll look for a job ***after* he graduates.**
NOT He'll look for a job, after he graduates.

USAGE NOTE In **conversation**, we often answer a *when* question with **just the time clause**.

A: When will she visit schools?
B: ***Before* she applies.**

3 Time Words for the First Event

When, ***after***, and ***as soon as*** introduce the **first event**.

***When* I graduate,** I'll look for a job.
I'll look for a job ***after* I graduate.**
(First I'll graduate. Then I'll look for a job.)

USAGE NOTE Use ***as soon as*** to emphasize that the second event will happen immediately after the first event.

***As soon as* I graduate,** I'll look for a job.
(First I'll graduate. Immediately after that, I'll look for a job.)

4 Time Words for the Second Event

Before and ***until*** introduce the **second event**.

***Before* I get a job,** I'll finish school.
(First I'll finish school. Then I'll get a job.)

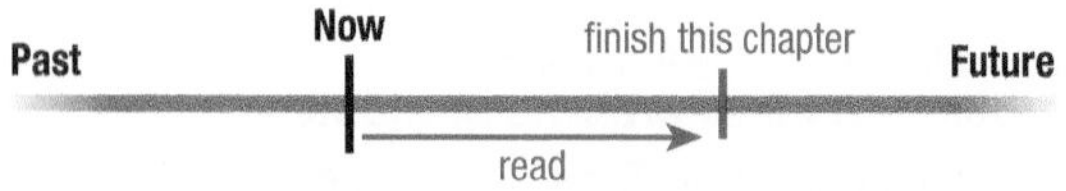

I'll read ***until* I finish this chapter.**
(I'll keep reading, but only up to the time that I finish this chapter. Then I'll stop.)

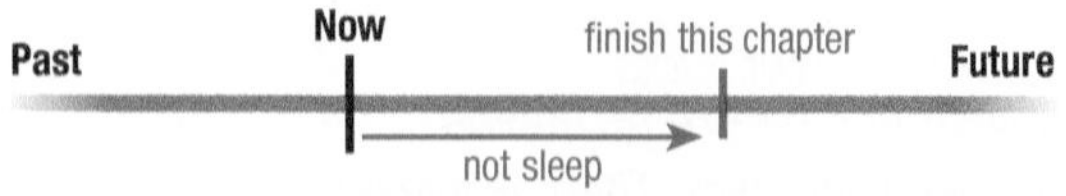

I won't sleep ***until* I finish this chapter.**
(I'll stay awake, but only up to the time that I finish this chapter. Then I'll go to sleep.)

5 *While* for Same-Time Events

While introduces an event that will happen **at the same time** as another event.

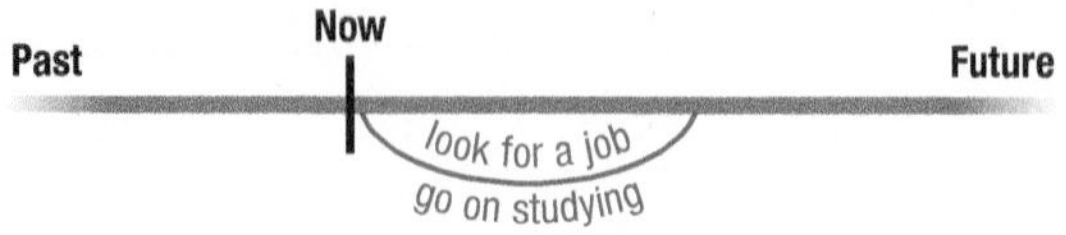

Notice that you can use the **simple present** or **present progressive** with an action verb after ***while***.

***While* I look for a job,** I'll go on studying.
or
***While* I'm looking for a job,** I'll go on studying.
(I'll look for a job and study at the same time.)

STEP 3 FOCUSED PRACTICE

EXERCISE 1 DISCOVER THE GRAMMAR

GRAMMAR NOTES 1–5 **Read the numbered sentence. Then choose the pair of sentences that has a similar meaning.**

1. Amber will open her own business when she finishes school.
   - **a.** Amber will open her own business. Then she'll finish school.
   - ⓑ Amber will finish school. Then she'll open her own business.
2. Denzell won't quit until he finds another job.
   - **a.** Denzell will find another job. Then he'll quit.
   - **b.** Denzell will quit. Then he'll find another job.
3. Jake is going to retire as soon as he turns 60.
   - **a.** Jake is going to retire. Then he'll turn 60.
   - **b.** Jake is going to turn 60. Then he'll retire.
4. After the Morrisons sell their house, they'll move to Florida.
   - **a.** The Morrisons will sell their house. Then they'll move to Florida.
   - **b.** The Morrisons will move to Florida. Then they'll sell their house.
5. Marisa will call you when she gets home.
   - **a.** Marisa will call you. Then she'll get home.
   - **b.** Marisa will get home. Then she'll call you.
6. Dimitri is going to live with his parents until he gets married.
   - **a.** Dimitri is going to get married. Then he'll live with his parents.
   - **b.** Dimitri will live with his parents. Then he'll get married.
7. While Li-jing is in school, she's going to work part-time.
   - **a.** Li-jing will finish school. Then she's going to get a part-time job.
   - **b.** Li-jing will go to school. At the same time, she's going to have a part-time job.
8. Marta will have her degree before she turns twenty-one.
   - **a.** Marta will get her degree. Then she'll turn twenty-one.
   - **b.** Marta will turn twenty-one. Then she'll get her degree.
9. Adel and Farah won't buy a house until their son is two years old.
   - **a.** They'll buy a house. Then their son will turn two.
   - **b.** Their son will turn two. Then they'll buy a house.
10. Ina will live in Paris while she's studying French cooking.
    - **a.** First she'll study French cooking. Then she's moving to Paris.
    - **b.** She'll study French cooking. At the same time, she'll live in Paris.

EXERCISE 2 SIMPLE PRESENT OR FUTURE

GRAMMAR NOTES 1–3 **Complete this student's worksheet. Use the correct form of the verbs in parentheses.**

GOAL PLANNING WORKSHEET

A. What is your most important goal?

- To find a job after graduation.

B. List the reasons you want to achieve this goal.

- When I ___get___ (1. get) a job, I ___'ll have___ (2. have) more money.
- When I ________ (3. save) enough money, I ________ (4. buy) a used car.
- I ________ (5. feel) happier when I ________ (6. be) employed.
- I ________ (7. learn) new skills while I ________ (8. work).

C. What is your action plan? What path will you take to reach your goal?

- Every morning when I ________ (9. get up), I ________ (10. check) online for employment ads.
- When I ________ (11. talk) to my friends, I ________ (12. ask) them if they know of any jobs.
- I ________ (13. download) information about résumé writing before I ________ (14. write) a new résumé.
- While I ________ (15. try) to find a job, I ________ (16. improve) my computer skills.
- Before I ________ (17. go) on an interview, I ________ (18. know) how to use Excel and PowerPoint.

D. What are the steps you will take right away?

- Before I ________ (19. do) anything else, I ________ (20. write) a list of people to contact for help.
- As soon as I ________ (21. contact) all the people on my list, I ________ (22. work) on fixing up my résumé.

EXERCISE 3 ORDER OF EVENTS

GRAMMAR NOTES 1–5 **Combine each pair of sentences. Use the future or the simple present form of the verb. Decide which sentence goes first. Remember to use commas when necessary.**

1. Sandy and Jeff will get married. Then Sandy will graduate.

   Sandy and Jeff will get married before *Sandy graduates*.

2. Jeff is going to get a raise. Then they are going to move to a larger apartment.

   ______________________ as soon as ______________________.

3. They're going to move to a larger apartment. Then they're going to have a baby.

   After ______________________.

4. They'll have their first child. Then Sandy will get a part-time job.

   ______________________ after ______________________.

5. Sandy will work part-time. Then their child will be two years old.

   ______________________ until ______________________.

6. Jeff will go to school. At the same time, Sandy will work full-time.

   ______________________ while ______________________.

7. Sandy and Jeff will achieve their goals. Then they'll feel very proud.

   When ______________________.

EXERCISE 4 EDITING

GRAMMAR NOTES 1–5 **Read this student's blog. There are eight mistakes in the use of future time clauses. The first mistake is already corrected. Find and correct seven more.**

Graduation is next month! I need to make some plans now because when exams ~~will start~~ *start*, I don't have any free time. What am I going to do when I'll finish school? What path will I take? My roommate is going to take a vacation before she'll look for a job. I can't do that because I need to earn some money soon. I think that after I'll graduate, I'm going to take a desktop publishing class. As soon as I learned the software, I look for a job with a business publisher. It's hard to find full-time jobs, though. Part-time jobs are easier to find. Maybe I'll take a part-time job until I'll find a good full-time one. Or maybe I'll take a workshop in making decisions before I do anything!

STEP 4 COMMUNICATION PRACTICE

EXERCISE 5 LISTENING

07|02 **A** Two classmates are discussing Ela's future plans. Listen to their conversation. Listen again and number the steps in order.

Ela is going to:

_____ **a.** go back to Turkey

_____ **b.** take a course in German

_____ **c.** take some more English classes

_____ **d.** return to the United States

_____ **e.** take a degree program in hotel management

__1__ **f.** get a part-time job

07|02 **B** Listen again to the conversation. Then work with a partner and discuss your answers to the questions.

1. Why is Ela going to get a part-time job after she finishes her English class?

   EXAMPLE: A: So, why is Ela going to get a part-time job after she finishes her class?
   B: She wants to save enough money to return to Turkey. She misses her family.

2. Will she return to Turkey before or after she takes another English course?
3. Why is she going to study German while she's back in Turkey?
4. What else will Ela do while she's in Turkey?
5. After she returns to the United States, what step will she take to reach her goal?
6. Why does Ela's friend say, "You'll need to check into a hotel for a vacation!"?

EXERCISE 6 WHAT ABOUT YOU?

A SURVEY Complete the notes with information about yourself.

1. I'm going to continue studying English until ______________________.
2. While I'm in this class, ______________________.
3. When I finish this class, ______________________.
4. I'll stay in this country until ______________________.
5. As soon as ______________________, I'll ______________________.
6. I'm not going to ______________________ until ______________________.
7. I'm going to feel a lot better after ______________________.
8. Before ______________________, ______________________.

Ⓑ **Work in a group. Compare your answers with those of your classmates. How many different answers are there?**

EXAMPLE: A: I'm going to study English until I pass the TOEFL exam. What about you?
B: I'm going to continue studying until I get a job.
C: Me too!

EXERCISE 7 YOUR BUCKET LIST

Ⓐ CONVERSATION **People sometimes make a list of things they want to achieve or experience in their lives. They call it a "bucket list." What's on your bucket list? Before you talk about it, make a list of four to six items.**

EXAMPLE: *visit Tahiti*
write a song and sing it on YouTube
buy a house
visit my hometown again

Ⓑ **Work with a partner. Talk about each other's lists. Choose one thing on your list. Why is it important to you? What will you need to do to achieve that goal?**

EXAMPLE: A: So, what's on *your* bucket list?
B: Well, I want to visit Tahiti, write a song and sing it on YouTube, buy a house, and visit my hometown again. Most of all I *really* want to visit Tahiti. They say it's incredibly beautiful.
A: OK. And what will you do to make your dream come true?
B: First I'll save some money for the trip. As soon as I have enough money, I'll look for good flights and hotels on the Internet. After I find a good flight, I'll . . .

EXERCISE 8 WHAT'S NEXT?

GAME **Work in a group and form a circle. One person says a sentence with a future time clause. The next person begins a new sentence using information from the main clause. Continue around the circle as long as you can. Use your imagination—your sentences don't have to be true!**

EXAMPLE:

FROM GRAMMAR TO WRITING

A BEFORE YOU WRITE **Think about a goal you have. Then complete the worksheet. Use future time clauses in some of your answers.**

Goal Planning Worksheet

What is your goal? ______________________________

Why do you want to achieve this goal? ______________________________

What are the first three steps of your action plan? Put them in order.

1. ______________________________

2. ______________________________

3. ______________________________

B WRITE **Use your worksheet to write a paragraph about your goal. Use future time clauses in your paragraph. Try to avoid the common mistakes in the chart.**

EXAMPLE: My goal is to buy a used car so I can take some trips. As soon as I have a car, I'm going to drive to Montreal to visit my cousins. While I'm Montreal, I'll take a cooking course . . .

Common Mistakes in Using Future Time Clauses

Use the **simple present** in the future time clause. Do not use *be going to* or *will* in the time clause.	I'll take a course when I **finish** school. NOT I'll take a course when I~~'ll finish~~ school.
Use a **comma after the time clause** when the time clause comes first. Do not use a comma after the main clause when the main clause comes first.	**When I finish school,** I'll take a course. NOT I'll take a course, when I finish school.

C CHECK YOUR WORK **Read your paragraph. Underline the future time clauses. Circle the verbs in the main clauses and in the time clauses. Use the Editing Checklist to check your work.**

Editing Checklist

Did you use . . . ?

- ☐ sentences with future time clauses
- ☐ the simple present in the time clauses
- ☐ the future in the main clauses
- ☐ commas after time clauses at the beginning of a sentence
- ☐ *when*, *after*, or *as soon as* for the first event
- ☐ *after* or *until* for the second event
- ☐ *while* for same-time events

D REVISE YOUR WORK **Read your paragraph again. Can you improve your writing? Make changes if necessary. Give your paragraph a title.**

UNIT 7 **REVIEW**

Test yourself on the grammar of the unit.

A **Circle the correct words to complete the sentences.**

1. What are you going to do after you will graduate / graduate?
2. We won't start a new chapter until we finished / finish this one.
3. When / Until Jorge gets a raise, he's going to buy a new car.
4. Is / Will Andrea find a job by the time she graduates?
5. Where will you live while you're learning / going to learn English?
6. We won't start the test until / when the teacher arrives. She has the tests.
7. Will you / Are you going to take another class after you finish this one?

B **Complete the sentences with the correct form of the verbs in parentheses.**

1. Yuri is going to take night classes while he ______________ (work) full-time.
2. Until he buys a new computer, he ______________ (not register) for online courses.
3. When he takes online courses, he ______________ (spend) more time at home.
4. He'll help his daughter with her homework while he ______________ (study) for his own courses.
5. He ______________ (not look) for a new job before he graduates.
6. As soon as he ______________ (graduate), he's going to find a job.
7. Before he starts his new job, he ______________ (take) a vacation.

C **Find and correct six mistakes. Remember to look at punctuation.**

A: Are you going to call Phil when we'll finish dinner?

B: No, I'm too tired. I'm just going to watch TV after I go to sleep.

A: Before I wash the dishes, I'm going answer some emails.

B: I'll help you, as soon as I'll drink my coffee.

A: No rush. I have a lot of emails. I won't be ready to clean up until you'll finish.

Now check your answers on page 476.

Present Perfect

UNIT 8

Present Perfect: *Since* and *For*

CAREERS

UNIT 9

Present Perfect: *Already*, *Yet*, and *Still*

PARTY PLANNING

UNIT 10

Present Perfect: Indefinite Past

ADVENTURE TRAVEL

UNIT 11

Present Perfect and Simple Past

FAILURE AND SUCCESS

UNIT 12

Present Perfect Progressive and Present Perfect

CLIMATE CHANGE

PART 3

OUTCOMES

- Describe events that began in the past and continue into the present
- Describe the duration of events, using the present perfect + *since/for*
- Identify key details in a short biography
- Identify the length of time of events in an interview
- Ask and answer questions about life events and experiences
- Write a paragraph about experiences and accomplishments

OUTCOMES

- Use *already*, *yet*, and *still* with the present perfect
- Discuss events that happened or did not happen at some time in the past
- Identify key details in an information article and a conversation
- Recognize and discuss tasks on a to-do list or plan
- Write a paragraph about a goal and the steps needed to reach it

OUTCOMES

- Describe events that happened at an indefinite time in the past
- Describe repeated actions and states in the past
- Identify main points of an article and a conversation about travel
- Discuss famous quotes, giving explanations and reasons for opinions
- Write a paragraph in response to a quote from literature

OUTCOMES

- Recognize when to use the present perfect and the simple past
- Identify key details in a short, factual text
- Understand the time frame of important details in an interview
- Discuss past events and experiences
- Research a famous person and present findings to the class
- Write a paragraph about a personal experience

OUTCOMES

- Describe actions that started in the past and are still in progress
- Describe actions that started at an indefinite time in the past and are finished
- Identify main points of a short text on a scientific topic
- Understand the time frame of main events in conversations
- Discuss climate change
- Write an email or letter about recent activities

UNIT
8 Present Perfect: *Since* and *For*
CAREERS

OUTCOMES
- Describe events that began in the past and continue into the present
- Describe the duration of events, using the present perfect + *since/for*
- Identify key details in a short biography
- Identify the length of time of events in an interview
- Ask and answer questions about life events and experiences
- Write a paragraph about experiences and accomplishments

STEP 1 GRAMMAR IN CONTEXT

BEFORE YOU READ

Look at Bob Burnquist's sports card. Discuss the questions.

1. What are his interests?
2. What are *your* interests?
3. What is Bob's motto?[1]
4. Do you have a motto? What is it?

SPORTS CARD
Bob Burnquist

Date of Birth	October 10, 1976
Place of Birth	Rio de Janeiro, Brazil
Residence	California, U.S.
Citizenship	Brazil and U.S.
Started Skateboarding	1987
Turned Professional	1991
Other Interests	Reading, travel, photography, snowboarding, mountain biking, surfing, skydiving
Motto	"Be good, be positive, respect individuality[2] and nature."

READ

08|01 **Read this article about a champion skateboarder.**

King of Skate

When he was only 11 years old, Bob Burnquist's life changed dramatically. A skate park opened just three blocks from his house in São Paulo, Brazil. Bob got his very first skateboard and started skating. He's been a skater since then.

1 *motto:* a short statement of life goals or beliefs
2 *individuality:* the way people are different from each other

At first, he did it just for fun, but soon he turned pro.[3] Before long, he made enough money to support himself while doing what he loved most. His first big international competition was in Canada in 1995. Bob won. Since then, he has won many more first-place prizes. And he is still winning. Since 2002, when he was voted "King of Skate" in a California contest, Bob has won twelve gold medals—three of them in 2013.

Bob has lived in California since 1995, but he frequently returns to Brazil. He's had dual citizenship (Brazil and the United States) for many years. Does he consider himself American? Bob says, "I'm American, South American. . . . A citizen of the world."

The skateboard isn't the only board Bob uses. He also enjoys snowboarding and surfing. Since he moved to California, he has been close to snow-topped mountains and the beach. His backyard and, of course, the streets provide opportunity for skating. As he once said, "If you snowboard, surf, and skate, you pretty much cover the whole earth."

3 *turned pro:* became a professional (did the sport for money)

AFTER YOU READ

A VOCABULARY **Choose the word or phrase that is closest in meaning to the word(s) in bold.**

1. Bob's life changed **dramatically**.
   a. slowly and a little　b. dangerously　c. quickly and a lot
2. He earned enough money to **support himself**.
   a. pay for lessons　b. pay for things he needs　c. buy a new skateboard
3. Does Bob **consider himself** American?
   a. want to be　b. like being　c. think he is
4. The streets provide **opportunity** for skating.
   a. some dangers　b. good chances　c. a lot of contests
5. Bob's **residence** is in California.
   a. home　b. office　c. family
6. Bob always says, "Be **positive**."
   a. 100 percent sure　b. hopeful　c. strong

B COMPREHENSION **Read the statements. Check (✓) *True* or *False*.**

	True	False
1. Bob Burnquist doesn't skate anymore.	☐	☐
2. He has won only one first-place prize since 1995.	☐	☐
3. Bob moved to California in 1995.	☐	☐
4. Bob is a citizen of many countries.	☐	☐
5. He lives close to the beach.	☐	☐

C DISCUSSION **Work with a partner. Compare your answers in B. Why did you check *True* or *False*?**

STEP 2 GRAMMAR PRESENTATION

PRESENT PERFECT WITH *SINCE* AND *FOR*

Statements

Subject	*Have (not)*	Past Participle		*Since / For*
I You* We They	**have (not)**	**been**	here	**since** 2002. **for** a long time.
He She It	**has (not)**	**lived**		

* *You* is both singular and plural.

Contractions

Affirmative	Negative
I have = **I've** you have = **you've** we have = **we've** they have = **they've** he has = **he's** she has = **she's** it has = **it's**	have not = **haven't** has not = **hasn't**

Yes / No Questions

Have	Subject	Past Participle		*Since / For*
Have	I you we they	**been**	here	**since** 2002? **for** a long time?
Has	he she it	**lived**		

Short Answers

Affirmative			Negative		
Yes,	you I / we you they	**have.**	**No,**	you I / we you they	**haven't.**
	he she it	**has.**		he she it	**hasn't.**

Wh- Questions

Wh- Word	*Have*	Subject	Past Participle	
How long	**have**	I you we they	**been**	here?
	has	he she it	**lived**	

Short Answers

Since 2002. **For** many years.

GRAMMAR NOTES

1 Present Perfect + *Since* or *For*

Use the present perfect with *since* or *for* to show that something **began in the past and continues into the present** (and may continue into the future).

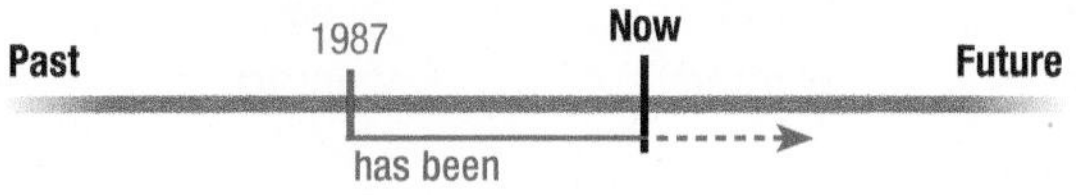

Bob **has been** a skater ***since*** 1987.
(He became a skater in 1987, and he is still a skater.)
He **has been** a skater ***for*** many years.
(He became a skater many years ago, and he is still a skater.)

2 *Since* and *For*

Since shows **when** something started. ***For*** shows **how long** something has lasted.

Use ***since*** + **point in time** (*since yesterday, since 5:00, since Monday, since 1995, since then*) to show when something started.	He **has won** many contests ***since 1995***. He **has become** famous ***since then***.
Since can also introduce a time clause.	He **has loved** sports ***since he was a child***.
Use ***for*** + **length of time** (*for 10 minutes, for two weeks, for years, for a long time*) to show how long something has lasted.	Bob **has had** a restaurant ***for years***. He **hasn't broken** a board ***for a long time***.
Expressions with ***since*** or ***for*** can go at the **end** or the **beginning** of the sentence.	He has become famous ***since then***. ***Since then***, he has become famous.
USAGE NOTE It is **more common** to put the expression with ***since*** or ***for*** at the **end** of the sentence.	He has lived in L.A. ***for many years***. *(more common)* ***For many years***, he has lived in L.A. *(less common)*
IN WRITING Use a **comma** when the expression with ***since*** or ***for*** comes at the **beginning** of the sentence.	***Since he turned pro,*** he hasn't taken a vacation. ***For many years,*** he's had dual citizenship.
Do not use a comma when the expression with *since* or *for* comes at the end of the sentence.	NOT He hasn't taken a vacation, since he turned pro. NOT He's had dual citizenship, for many years.

3 Past Participles

Form the present perfect with ***have* + past participle**.	He **has lived** there for years. They **have been** partners since 1998.		
	BASE FORM	**SIMPLE PAST**	**PAST PARTICIPLE**
To form the **past participle** of **regular verbs** add ***-d*** or ***-ed*** to the base form of the verb. It is the same as the regular simple past form of the verb.	love want	love**d** want**ed**	love**d** want**ed**
IN WRITING There are often **spelling changes** when you add ***-ed*** to the verb.	marry stop	marr**ied** stop**ped**	marr**ied** stop**ped**
Many common verbs are **irregular**. They do not form the past participle by adding *-d* or *-ed* to the base form of the verb. Here is a list of some of the **irregular verbs used in this unit**. It shows both the simple past and the past participle of each verb. Notice that most irregular verbs have a past participle form that is different from the simple past form.	be become go have meet take wear win write	was/were became went had met took wore won wrote	**been** **become** **gone** **had** **met** **taken** **worn** **won** **written**
USAGE NOTE Some verbs have **two past participle forms**—one **regular** and one **irregular**. In conversation, the irregular past participle form is more common. There is one exception: For *dream*, the regular form is more common.	kneel light prove dream	knelt/kneeled lit/lighted proved dreamed/dreamt	**knelt/kneeled** **lit/lighted** **proven/proved** **dreamed/dreamt**
USAGE NOTE A few verbs have **two irregular past participles**. The form *have gotten* is very common in American English.	beat get	beat got	**beaten/beat** **gotten/got**
BE CAREFUL! Do not form the **past participle of irregular verbs** by adding *-d* or *-ed* to the base form of the verb.	He has **won** many contests. NOT He has ~~winned~~ many contests.		

REFERENCE NOTE

For a more complete list of **irregular verbs**, see Appendix 1 on page 453.

STEP 3 FOCUSED PRACTICE

EXERCISE 1
DISCOVER THE GRAMMAR

GRAMMAR NOTES 1–3 **Read the information about a skater, Caterina. Then choose the sentence (*a* or *b*) that best describes the situation.**

1. Caterina has been a skater since 2008.
   (**a.**) She is still a skater.
   b. She is not a skater anymore.
2. She has lived in the same apartment for five years.
   a. She lived in a different apartment six years ago.
   b. She moved two years ago.
3. Caterina has been married for five years.
   a. She is not married now.
   b. She got married five years ago.
4. Catarina and her husband haven't been on a vacation since 2011.
   a. They are on a vacation now.
   b. They were on a vacation in 2011.
5. Caterina hasn't won a contest for two years.
   a. She won a contest two years ago.
   b. She didn't win a contest two years ago.
6. She has stayed positive about her career since she won her last contest.
   a. She expects to win more contests.
   b. She isn't hopeful anymore.

EXERCISE 2 *SINCE* OR *FOR*

GRAMMAR NOTE 2 **Complete the sentences about Brazilian sportswriter Mariana Andrade. Use *since* or *for*.**

1. Mariana Andrade has lived in São Paulo ___*since*___ 2000.
2. She has supported herself as a sportswriter ______________ four years.
3. ______________ June, she has written several articles about skateboarding.
4. This sport has been very popular in Brazil ______________ many years.
5. Mariana has met Burnquist twice ______________ she started her job.
6. She loves to skate, but she hasn't had much opportunity ______________ a long time.
7. She has been married to Alvaro, another skater, ______________ 2008.

EXERCISE 3 FORMS OF THE PRESENT PERFECT

GRAMMAR NOTE 3 **Complete this article about Lauren Jones. Use the correct form of the verbs in parentheses.**

Lauren Jones ___has loved___ (1. love) skating since she was a little girl. She began skating when she was 10, and she ________ (2. not stop) since then. She ________ (3. be) a professional skater now for several years. She and her husband ________ (4. live) in San Diego, California since the two got married. They ________ (5. have) the same one-bedroom apartment for three years. They ________ (6. not take) a vacation for many years, but they ________ (7. go) to several international skating contests since Lauren turned pro. Lauren ________ (8. skate) in three contests since last year, and she ________ (9. win) two second-place prizes since then. Lauren ________ (10. want) to be a pro since she was a child. "There aren't many professional female skateboarders," she says. "Ever since my dream came true, I ________ (11. consider) myself a lucky woman."

EXERCISE 4 FORMS OF THE PRESENT PERFECT WITH *SINCE* OR *FOR*

GRAMMAR NOTES 2–3 **Complete the sentences. Use the present perfect form of the verbs in parentheses and *since* or *for*.**

1. Skateboarding ___has been___ (a. be) popular ___for___ (b.) more than 50 years.
2. Skateboards ________ (a. be) around ________ (b.) a long time. In the 1930s, the first ones were simple wooden boxes on metal wheels. They ________ (c. change) dramatically ________ (d.) then!
3. The first skateboarding contest took place in California in 1963. ________ (a.) then, thousands of contests ________ (b. take) place internationally.
4. In 1976, the first outdoor skate park opened in the United States. ________ (a.) then, hundreds of parks ________ (b. open) in countries around the world such as Australia, China, England, France, Israel, Japan, and Kenya.
5. Skateboarding can be dangerous. ________ (a.) the 1960s, hundreds of thousands of people ________ (b. go) to hospital emergency rooms because of injuries.
6. When he was seven years old, Jon Comer lost his right foot as a result of a car accident. But that didn't stop him. ________ (a.) then, he ________ (b. become) one of the best-known professional skateboarders in the world, thanks to his great skill and very positive attitude.
7. Tony Hawk ________ (a. not compete) professionally ________ (b.) many years, but he is still the most famous and successful skateboarder of all time.

EXERCISE 5 QUESTIONS, STATEMENTS, AND SHORT ANSWERS

Ⓐ GRAMMAR NOTES 1–3 Amy Lu is applying for a job as a college sports instructor. Look at her résumé and the interviewer's notes. The year is 2016.

Amy Lu

525 Ahina St.
Honolulu, HI 96816

interviewed 09/19/16

Education:

2008 Certificate (American College of Sports Medicine)
2005 M.A. Physical Education (University of Texas)

moved to Honolulu in 2006

Employment:

2007-present part-time physical education teacher (high school)
2005-present sports trainer (private)

teaches tennis, swimming

Skills:

speaks English, Portuguese, and Chinese
practices martial arts

got black belt in tae kwon do 2 mos. ago

Other Interests:

travel, sports photography, skateboarding, surfing

Awards:

2008 Teacher of the Year Award
2005 First Prize in Sunburn Classic Skate Contest

Memberships:

2008-present member of National Education Association (NEA)

Ⓑ John Sakaino is interviewing Amy Lu for a job as a college sports instructor. Use the words in parentheses to complete the questions. Use the information in Amy's résumé to write her answers. Use contractions when possible.

1. (how long / live in Honolulu)

JOHN: *How long have you lived in Honolulu?*

AMY: *I've lived in Honolulu for 10 years.* **or** *I've lived in Honolulu since 2006.*

2. (how long / have your M.A. degree)

JOHN: ______

AMY: ______

3. (have any more training / since / you get your M.A.)

JOHN: ______________________________

AMY: ______________________________

4. (how long / be a physical education teacher)

JOHN: ______________________________

AMY: ______________________________

5. (how long / work as a sports trainer)

JOHN: ______________________________

AMY: ______________________________

6. (how long / have a black belt in tae kwon do)

JOHN: ______________________________

AMY: ______________________________

7. (win any awards since then)

JOHN: I see you won a medal in skateboarding. ______________________________

AMY: ______________________________ I won the Teacher of the Year Award in 2008.

8. (how long / be a member of NEA)

JOHN: ______________________________

AMY: ______________________________

EXERCISE 6 EDITING

GRAMMAR NOTES 1–3 **Read these posts to a skateboard message board. There are ten mistakes in the use of the present perfect with *since* and *for*. The first mistake is already corrected. Find and correct nine more.**

THE SKATEBOARDING BOARD Tell us your skating stories here!

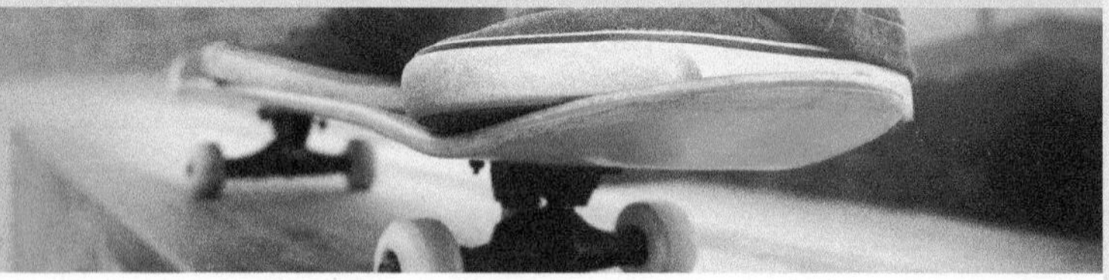

Jennifer, U.S.
~~I have~~ I've had my skateboard for two years. For me, it's much more than just a sport. It's a form of transportation. It's much faster than walking!

Paulo, Brazil
I've been a skater since five years. Since December, I won two contests. I'd love to turn pro one day and support myself skating.

Sang-Ook, South Korea
Help! I've broken three boards for January!!! Is this normal? How long you have had *your* board?

Marta, Mexico	Broken boards?! That's nothing! Consider yourself lucky! I've break my wrist twice since I started skating!
Megan, Australia	Last year, my board hit a rock while I was skating in the street. I fell and hit my head and had to go to the emergency room. I always worn a helmet since then!
Ming, U.S.	I live in California since 2006. My first love is surfing, but when there aren't any waves, I jump on my skateboard and take to the streets! My motto is "Make the best of what you have!"
Todd, Canada	Wow! Yesterday, my friend gave me a copy of the video "OP King of Skate." I've watch it three times since then. The Burnquist part is awesome!
Sylvie, France	At last! A skate park opened near my home last week. Since then, I gone every day. It's a lot more fun than skating in the streets!

STEP 4 COMMUNICATION PRACTICE

EXERCISE 7 LISTENING

08|02 **A** **Listen to Eliana Serrano's job interview. Then listen again and complete the interviewer's notes. Use *since* and *for*.**

— WSPR Radio —

Eliana Serrano   Interviewed Sept. 9

Eliana has been an athlete *for fifteen years* ________________________.
1.

She's been an announcer ________________________.
2.

She's lived in L.A. ________________________.
3.

She hasn't worked full-time as an announcer ________________________.
4.

She's worked part-time at WABC ________________________.
5.

She's written sports articles ________________________.
6.

She's considered herself an announcer ________________________.
7.

08|02 **B** Listen to the interview again and read the interviewer's notes. Do you think Eliana should get the job? Why or why not? Discuss your opinion with a partner.

EXAMPLE: A: I think Eliana should get the job. She has had a lot of experience. She . . .
B: Yes, but she hasn't . . .

EXERCISE 8 WHO GETS THE JOB?

A ROLE PLAY Work with a partner. You are going to role-play two interviews for a job as a college music teacher. Look at the résumés. Write five or more interview questions. Begin your questions with *How long*, *How many*, and *Have you . . . since?*

EXAMPLE: *How long have you been a music teacher?*

CHIN HO CHO

EDUCATION:
2005 M.A. in Music Education (Boston University)

TEACHING EXPERIENCE:
2005–present The Juilliard School

COURSES TAUGHT:
Voice and Piano
History of Music
Symphonies of Beethoven
Twentieth-century Jazz

PUBLICATIONS:
"Introducing Computers into Music Class" (*The Journal of Music*, 2007)

AWARDS:
Teacher of the Year, 2007
Winner of University of Maryland Piano Competition, 2014

CLARA RESTON

EDUCATION:
1991 M.A. in Music Education (Boston University)

TEACHING EXPERIENCE:
2011–present Barnard College
2006–2010 Boston University
1997–2005 Yale University
1994–1996 Sarah Lawrence College
1991–1993 Boston University

COURSES TAUGHT:
Music Theory I
Music and Culture

PUBLICATIONS:
"Rachmaninoff Revisited" (*MJ*, 1996)
"Favorite Instruments of High School Students" (*Music Education*, 1996)
"World Music in a Small World" (*Music and Culture*, 1998)

B Work with your partner. Role-play two interviews (one for Chin Ho Cho and one for Clara Reston). Take turns being the interviewer.

EXAMPLE: A: How long have you been a music teacher, Chin Ho?
B: I've been a music teacher since 2005.

C Work in a group. Decide who to hire for the job and why. Remember to use *since* and *for*.

EXAMPLE: A: Chin Ho Cho has had the same job since he got his M.A. degree.
B: Clara Reston has a lot more experience. She's been a teacher since 1991.
C: But Chin has taught . . .

EXERCISE 9 WHAT ABOUT YOU?

A CONVERSATION **Before you talk with your partner about your life, complete these notes.**

1. I live in ______________________________ .
(a country, city)
2. I study ______________________________ .
(a language, another subject)
3. I am a(n) ______________________________ .
(an occupation)
4. I play ______________________________ .
(a sport, a game, a musical instrument)
5. I want to ______________________________ .
(a goal)
6. *Other:* ______________________________

B Work with a partner. Show your partner your notes. Ask and answer questions with *How long* to learn more about your partner. Do you and your partner have anything in common?

EXAMPLE: A: How long have you lived in Canada?
B: For about five years. What about you?
A: Oh, since . . .

FROM GRAMMAR TO WRITING

A BEFORE YOU WRITE **You are going to write about a person's experience and accomplishments. You can write about yourself, a famous person, a person you know, or one of the people in Exercise 8. You can also make up information. Choose a person and complete the outline.**

Name: ______________________________

Occupation: ______________________ **From:** ________ (year) **To:** ________ (year)

Accomplishments: ______________________________

____

____

B WRITE **Use your outline to write a paragraph about that person's accomplishments. Remember to use the present perfect with *since* and *for*. Try to avoid the common mistakes in the chart.**

EXAMPLE: Amy Lu has been a high school physical education teacher and a private sports trainer for many years. She has received two awards since 2005, one for teaching and the other for skateboarding. She has been a member of the National Education Association since 2008. Amy has many interests. She speaks three languages. She has also been . . .

Common Mistakes in Using the Present Perfect with *Since* and *For*

Use *for* with a **length of time**. Do not use *since*.	She's been a teacher ***for* five years**. NOT She's been a teacher ~~since~~ five years.
Use a **comma** after a time clause that begins with *since* when the **time clause comes first**. Do not use a comma when the time clause comes last.	***Since* I moved here,** I've had two jobs. NOT I've had two jobs, since I moved here.
Be careful to make **spelling changes** in some regular past participles. Do not just add *-ed*.	They've **studied** English since May. NOT They've ~~studyed~~ English since May.

C CHECK YOUR WORK **Read your paragraph. Underline the present perfect verbs. Circle *since* and *for* and the time expressions. Use the Editing Checklist to check your work.**

Editing Checklist

Did you use . . . ?

- ☐ *since* with a point in time
- ☐ *for* with a length of time
- ☐ *have* + the correct past participle
- ☐ the correct spelling for the past participles

D REVISE YOUR WORK **Read your paragraph again. Can you improve your writing? Make changes if necessary. Give your paragraph a title.**

UNIT 8 **REVIEW**

Test yourself on the grammar of the unit.

A Complete the sentences with *since* or *for*.

1. Sara has lived in San Francisco ______________ 10 years.
2. She has wanted to be a tennis player ______________ she was a little girl.
3. She's been a professional player ______________ several years.
4. Sara has had the same trainer ______________ a long time.
5. ______________ 2010, she has won several competitions.
6. ______________ the past few weeks, she has had a wrist injury.
7. ______________ then, she hasn't been able to practice.

B Complete the sentences with the present perfect form of the verbs in parentheses. Use contractions when possible.

1. I ______________________ (be) a skateboarder for many years.
2. Since 2010, I ______________________ (not have) any skating accidents.
3. My brother ______________________ (love) the sport since he was a little boy.
4. Together we ______________________ (compete) in many competitions.
5. He ______________________ (win) several competitions since last year.
6. We ______________________ (not see) each other for a few months.

C Find and correct seven mistakes.

1. Marta and Tomás lived here since they got married in 2013.
2. Tomás has been a professional tennis player since he has come to this country.
3. He has won several competitions for then.
4. Since I have known Tomás, he had three different coaches.
5. I haven't see Marta for several weeks.
6. She have been in Brazil since April 1.
7. I've wanted to visit Brazil since years, but I haven't had any vacation time since I got this new job.

Now check your answers on page 476.

UNIT 9

Present Perfect: *Already, Yet,* and *Still*

PARTY PLANNING

OUTCOMES

- Use *already, yet,* and *still* with the present perfect
- Discuss events that happened or did not happen at some time in the past
- Identify key details in an information article and a conversation
- Recognize and discuss tasks on a to-do list or plan
- Write a paragraph about a goal and the steps needed to reach it

STEP 1 GRAMMAR IN CONTEXT

BEFORE YOU READ

Look at the photo. Discuss the questions.

1. How do you feel about parties?
2. Which do you prefer: giving a party or going to one? Why?

READ

09|01 Read this article about how to plan a party.

It's Party Time!

It's almost the end of the year, and you've already been to several parties, but you haven't given a party of your own yet. You're a little nervous, but you decide it's time to take the plunge.[1]

First things first: Have you chosen the date yet? What about the time?

OK. You've already chosen the date and the time and emailed the invitations. But you still haven't decided on the menu, and now your party is just one week away! Don't panic!

1 *take the plunge:* do an activity that seems difficult or frightening

We spoke to Patty Cake, a professional party planner. She says, "It *is* very important to be organized, but remember: You don't need a whole new set of skills. Think about your everyday life. You've already done many of the things you need to do for a party. You know how to shop for food, put it on plates, and introduce friends to one another. Now, all you need to do is just bring your many skills together."

Still need help? Party planners, like Patty Cake, can offer specific advice. She says, "We've already helped hundreds of people plan successful parties—big and small. If you haven't used a party-planning service yet, you should give it a try." And you don't have to spend a lot of money. Free advice is available on the Internet. There, you will also find handy[2] lists where you can check off things you've already done (and see the things you haven't done yet!). So, take a deep breath, relax, and enjoy the party!

2 *handy:* useful; easy to use

AFTER YOU READ

A VOCABULARY **Complete the sentences with the words from the box.**

available	organized	professional	specific	successful

1. OK. The drinks are on the table over there. Extra chairs are in the bedroom. The cake is in the refrigerator. I'll take it out at 8:00 p.m. That's it! I think I'm quite ________________.
2. I can meet you for lunch any day this week to discuss plans for your party. You can also call me anytime—day or night. As you can see, I'm pretty ________________.
3. The party is for my friend Marta. She's a writer. Her latest book is on the bestseller list! She's really ________________.
4. Please bring two large bags of Crispy Chips. The ones in the blue bag—they're low in fat, but not low in salt. You'll find them at Shopwise in aisle 6. I know I'm being very ________________, but I want to be sure you get the right ones!
5. Jake offered to paint the apartment before the party, but I prefer to hire ________________ painters. They have training, job experience—and insurance if something goes wrong!

B COMPREHENSION **Reread the first three paragraphs in the article. Check (✓) the correct answers.**

The party giver . . .

- ☐ **1.** went to several parties
- ☐ **2.** gave a party of her own
- ☐ **3.** chose a date for the party
- ☐ **4.** chose the time
- ☐ **5.** sent invitations
- ☐ **6.** decided on a menu

C DISCUSSION **Work with a partner. Compare your answers in B. Why did you or didn't you check each item?**

STEP 2 GRAMMAR PRESENTATION

PRESENT PERFECT: *ALREADY*, *YET*, AND *STILL*

Affirmative Statements: *Already*

Subject	*Have*	*Already*	Past Participle		*Already*
They	**have**	*already*	**emailed**	the invitations.	
She	**has**		**chosen**	the menu.	

They	**have**		**emailed**	the invitations	*already*.
She	**has**		**chosen**	the menu	

Negative Statements: *Yet*

Subject	*Have not*	Past Participle		*Yet*
They	**haven't**	**emailed**	them	*yet*.
She	**hasn't**	**chosen**	it	

Negative Statements: *Still*

Subject	*Still*	*Have not*	Past Participle	
They	*still*	**haven't**	**emailed**	them.
She		**hasn't**	**chosen**	it.

Yes/No Questions: *Yet*

Have	Subject	Past Participle		*Yet*
Have	they	**emailed**	them	*yet*?
Has	she	**chosen**	it	

Short Answers

Affirmative		Negative	
Yes,	they **have**.	**No,**	they **haven't**.
	she **has**.		she **hasn't**.
			not *yet*.

GRAMMAR NOTES

1 Present Perfect + *Already*, *Yet*, or *Still*

Use the present perfect with *already*, *yet*, or *still* to show that something **happened or did not happen at an indefinite** (not exact) **time in the past.**

- *already* — I**'ve** ***already*** **emailed** the invitations.
- *yet* — We **haven't ordered** the cake ***yet***.
- *still* — He ***still*** **hasn't replied.**

BE CAREFUL! Do not use ***already***, ***yet***, or ***still*** with past time expressions.

NOT I've *already* mailed the invitations ~~last week~~.

USAGE NOTE In American English, we sometimes use the **simple past** with *already* and *yet*.

Jenna **has *already* left**. or Jenna ***already* left**.
Ebo **hasn't left *yet***. or Ebo **didn't leave *yet***.

2 Statements

In **affirmative statements**, use *already*. In **negative statements**, use *yet* or *still*.

Use *already* in **affirmative statements** to show that something **has happened before now**.	Jenna **has *already* met** Carlos.
USAGE NOTE We often use the present perfect with *already* for something that happened sooner than expected.	You**'ve *already* set** the table. Great!
Use *yet* in **negative statements** to show that something **has not happened before now** (in the near past).	A: Jenna **has*n't* called *yet***. B: Oh, I'm sure we'll hear from her later.
USAGE NOTE We often use the present perfect with *not yet* for something we expected to happen earlier, but did not happen. It is possible that it will happen soon.	Where's Tom? I expected him at 8:00, but he **hasn't arrived *yet***. I hope he gets here soon.
You can also use *still* in **negative statements**. *Still* has a similar meaning to *not yet*.	Jenna ***still* hasn't called**.
USAGE NOTE We often use the present perfect with *still* to show that we are surprised or unhappy with the situation.	I don't know if Jenna is coming or not. I've texted her several times, but she ***still* hasn't answered**. She promised to help me.

3 Questions

In questions, we usually use *yet*.

Use the present perfect with *yet* in **questions** to ask if something has happened before now.	A: **Have** you **bought** the soda ***yet***?
Notice the different possible ways of giving **negative answers**.	B: **No, I haven't.** or **No, *not yet*.** or ***Not yet*.**
USAGE NOTE We sometimes use *already* in questions to express **surprise** that something has happened sooner than expected.	**Has** Carlos **arrived *already***? What's he doing here? The party doesn't start until 8:00!

4 Word Order

Already usually goes **before the past participle**. It can also go at the **end of the clause**.	**I've *already* made** the cake. **I've made** the cake ***already***.
Yet usually goes at the **end of the clause**.	They **haven't arrived *yet***. She **hasn't invited** Mehmet ***yet***.
Still goes **before *have not***.	They ***still* haven't arrived**. She ***still* hasn't invited** Mehmet.

REFERENCE NOTES

For a list of **irregular past participles**, see Appendix 1 on page 453.
For more information on the **indefinite past**, see Unit 10 on page 131.

STEP 3 FOCUSED PRACTICE

EXERCISE 1 DISCOVER THE GRAMMAR

GRAMMAR NOTES 1–3 **Read the first statement. Then decide if the second statement is *True (T)* or *False (F)*.**

1. I've already given many parties.
   __F__ This will be my first party.
2. I haven't made the cake yet.
   ____ I plan to make a cake.
3. Has Bev arrived yet?
   ____ I'm surprised that Bev is here.
4. Tom and Lisa still haven't arrived.
   ____ I expect them to arrive.
5. Has Jenna left already?
   ____ I'm surprised that Jenna left.
6. Have you had a cup of tea yet?
   ____ I don't know if you had a cup of tea.
7. Carlos has already met my sister.
   ____ I need to introduce Carlos to her.
8. I still haven't called Mehmet.
   ____ I don't plan to call him.
9. Has Tom bought the chips yet?
   ____ I think Tom is going to bring the chips.
10. I still haven't talked to the party planner.
    ____ I should call her.
11. Have you taken any photos yet?
    ____ I saw you take some photos.
12. We've already finished all the cake.
    ____ There is more cake.

EXERCISE 2 QUESTIONS, STATEMENTS, SHORT ANSWERS

A GRAMMAR NOTES 1–3 **Complete these conversations that take place at Marta's party. Use the present perfect form of the verbs in parentheses with *already* or *yet* and short answers. Use contractions when possible. See Appendix 1 on page 453 for help with irregular verbs.**

1. A: This is a great party. Marta made the cake. She's a professional baker. ____Have____ you ____tried____ (try) it ____yet____?
   B: ____No____, I ____haven't____.
   But I'm going to have a piece now.

2. A: Jenna, I'd like you to meet my friend Carlos.

B: We ______________ ______________ ______________ (meet). Marta introduced us.

3. A: Would you like another cup of coffee?

B: No, thanks. I ______________ ______________ ______________ (have) three cups!

4. A: ______________ Jenna ______________ (leave) ______________? It's still early!

B: ______________, she ______________. She's in the kitchen.

5. A: ______________ you ______________ (see) Tarantino's new movie ______________?

B: ______________, I ______________. It's great. What about you?

A: I ______________ ______________ (see) it ______________, but I want to.

6. A: This was a great party. I'm giving my own party next week. I ______________ ______________ ______________ (plan) the whole thing, but I'm still nervous about it.

B: Don't worry. If you organize it well, the rest will take care of itself!

09|02 **B** LISTEN AND CHECK **Listen to the conversations and check your answers in A.**

EXERCISE 3 WORD ORDER

GRAMMAR NOTE 4 **Unscramble the words to complete what some of the guests at Marta's party said.**

1. (tried / have / yet / the cake / you)

   Have you tried the cake yet?

2. (Jenna / yet / haven't / seen / I)

   ____.

3. (already / met / I've / Carlos)

   ____.

4. (yet / seen / Bruno / you / have)

   ____?

5. (still / tried / I / the cake / haven't)

   ____.

6. (some of the guests / left / already / have)

   ____.

7. (Bruno / arrived / hasn't / still)

   ____!

EXERCISE 4 AFFIRMATIVE AND NEGATIVE STATEMENTS

GRAMMAR NOTES 1–4 Read Dante's party-planning checklist. Write statements about the things that he *has already done* and the things that he *hasn't done yet* (or the things that he *still hasn't done!*). See Appendix 1 on page 453 for help with irregular verbs.

1. *He's already picked a date.*
2. *He hasn't chosen a time yet.* **or** *He still hasn't chosen a time.*
3. ____________________
4. ____________________
5. ____________________
6. ____________________
7. ____________________
8. ____________________
9. ____________________
10. ____________________

EXERCISE 5 EDITING

GRAMMAR NOTES 1–4 Read this online bulletin board. There are nine mistakes in the use of the present perfect with *already*, *yet*, and *still*. The first mistake is already corrected. Find and correct eight more.

Doug asked: Help! My party is next week, and I ~~already~~ *still* haven't figured out the food! I'm not at all organized. I've yet wasted three days worrying, and I still don't have any ideas. What should I do?

The Party Planner's Advice: Don't panic! Your guests haven't started arriving already, so there's still time. Ask everyone to bring something! (You've already invite people, right?) Or order pizza. I haven't met anyone already who doesn't like pizza.

Rosa asked: I'd like to find a "theme" for my next birthday party. I've already have a pasta party (10 kinds of pasta!), and I've already gave a movie party (everyone dressed up as a movie character). Both were very successful, but I haven't still decided what to do this time. Any ideas?

The Party Planner's Advice: Sure. Has you tried this one yet? Ask each guest to bring a baby photo of himself or herself. Collect the photos. People try to match the photos with the guests! Your guests will love it!

STEP 4 COMMUNICATION PRACTICE

EXERCISE 6 LISTENING

09|03 **A** A couple is planning a party. Look at their "To Do" list. Then listen to their conversation. Listen again and check (✓) the things they've already done.

09|03 **B** Listen to the conversation again. Then work with a partner. Discuss your answers in A. Why did or didn't you check each item?

EXAMPLE: A: Did you check item 2?
B: Yes. They've already found a place.
A: Right. They're going to have the party at Jason's. What about item 3? Have they invited people yet?

C Work with your partner. What are some additional things the couple may need to do? Brainstorm ideas. Ask questions with *yet*. Compare your questions with another pair.

EXAMPLE: A: Have they bought a gift yet?
B: If they bought a gift, have they wrapped it yet?

EXERCISE 7 PARTY CHORES

A INFORMATION GAP **Work with a partner. Student A will follow the instructions below. Student B will follow the instructions on page 486.**

STUDENT A

- **Look at the picture of the Stangers' dining room and at Gisela's "To Do" list. Check (✓) the chores that Gisela has already done. Then answer your partner's questions about Gisela's chores.**

  EXAMPLE: B: Has Gisela vacuumed the carpet yet?
  A: No, she hasn't. or No, not yet.

- **Look at Karl's "To Do" list. Ask your partner questions to find out which chores Karl has already done. Check (✓) those chores.**

  EXAMPLE: A: Has Karl bought a memory card yet?
  B: Yes, he has. or Yes, he's already gotten one.

To Do: Karl

- ☑ buy memory card for camera
- ☐ bake the cake
- ☐ put the turkey in the oven
- ☐ mop the floor
- ☐ wash the dishes
- ☐ cut up the vegetables

To Do: Gisela

- ☐ vacuum the carpet
- ☑ buy flowers
- ☐ wash the windows
- ☐ set the table
- ☐ hang the balloons
- ☐ wrap the gift

B **Now compare lists with your partner. Are they the same?**

EXERCISE 8 WHAT ABOUT YOU?

A CONVERSATION **Before you talk with a partner about your plans, write a list of things that you planned or wanted to do by this time (for example, organize a big party for my parents, find a new job, paint the apartment, buy a new computer). Include things that you *have already done* and things that you *haven't done yet*.**

B **Work with a partner. Exchange lists and ask and answer questions about the items on the lists.**

EXAMPLE: A: Have you organized the party for your parents yet?
B: No, not yet. I'm still trying to find a place to have it. or Yes, I have. What about you? Have you . . . ?

FROM GRAMMAR TO WRITING

A BEFORE YOU WRITE **Think about a goal you are working on at the moment. Write a list of things people do to reach this goal. Then check (✓) the things you have already done to reach *your* goal.**

My Goal: ______________________________

☐ **1.** ______________________________

☐ **2.** ______________________________

☐ **3.** ______________________________

☐ **4.** ______________________________

☐ **5.** ______________________________

B WRITE **Use your list to write a paragraph. Describe your goal. Then write about the things you *have already done* and things you *haven't done yet* or that you *still haven't done* to reach your goal. Try to avoid the common mistakes in the chart.**

EXAMPLE: I would like to find a new apartment. I've already done a few things to reach my goal. For example, I've already chosen a neighborhood where I would like to live. However, I haven't been to see any apartments yet. And I still haven't spoken to . . .

Common Mistakes in Using the Present Perfect with *Already*, *Yet*, and *Still*

Put ***already*** between ***have*** and the past participle. Do not put ***already*** after the past participle.	**I've *already* chosen** a neighborhood. NOT ~~I've chosen already~~ a neighborhood.
Put ***yet*** at the end of the clause. Do not put ***yet*** after the past participle.	I **haven't seen** apartments ***yet***. NOT I ~~haven't seen yet~~ apartments.
Put ***still*** before ***haven't***. Do not put ***still*** between ***haven't*** and the past participle or at the end of the clause.	I ***still* haven't found** an apartment. NOT I ~~haven't still found~~ an apartment. NOT I haven't found an apartment ~~still~~.

C CHECK YOUR WORK **Read your paragraph. Underline the present perfect verbs and circle *already*, *yet*, and *still*. Use the Editing Checklist to check your work.**

Editing Checklist

Did you use . . . ?

☐ the present perfect with *already* for things that have happened before now

☐ the present perfect with *yet* or *still* for things that haven't happened before now

☐ the correct word order

D REVISE YOUR WORK **Read your paragraph again. Can you improve your writing? Make changes if necessary. Give your paragraph a title.**

UNIT 9 **REVIEW**

Test yourself on the grammar of the unit.

A **Circle the correct words to complete the sentences.**

1. I've started planning your graduation party last night / already.
2. We still / yet haven't chosen a restaurant for the party. I'm getting nervous.
3. I met Nita yesterday, but I haven't met her boyfriend already / yet.
4. Did / Has Marla left already? The party just started!
5. Have you told / tell your friends about the party yet?
6. No, not already / yet.

B **Complete the conversations with the present perfect form of the verbs in parentheses and *already*, *still*, or *yet*.**

1. ANN: Ed ____________ ____________ ____________. Amazing!
   a. (graduate / already)

   BEN: I know, but don't relax yet. We ____________ ____________ ____________ the party.
   b. (have / still)

2. ANN: ____________ they ____________ the food ____________? Should I begin to worry?
   a. (deliver / yet)

   BEN: It just arrived. But Ed ____________ ____________ ____________ the tables.
   b. (set / still)

   ANN: Well, he ____________ ____________ ____________. I'll help him finish.
   c. (start / already)

3. BEN: Some of Ed's friends ____________ ____________ ____________.
   a. (arrive / still)

   ANN: I know . . . I don't think his new girlfriend ____________ ____________ ____________.
   b. (arrive / yet)

   ED: Mom and Dad, ____________ you ____________ Christy ____________?
   c. (meet / yet)

C **Find and correct six mistakes.**

A: I can't believe it's the 10th already. And we still didn't finished planning.

B: We haven't checked the guest list for a while. Who hasn't replies yet?

A: Sally hasn't called about the invitation already. I wonder if she's coming.

B: Maybe she just forgot. Have you called yet her?

A: I've already call her a couple of times. She hasn't called back still.

Now check your answers on page 477.

UNIT
10

Present Perfect: Indefinite Past
ADVENTURE TRAVEL

OUTCOMES
- Describe events that happened at an indefinite time in the past
- Describe repeated actions and states in the past
- Identify main points of an article and a conversation about travel
- Discuss famous quotes, giving explanations and reasons for opinions
- Write a paragraph in response to a quote from literature

STEP 1 GRAMMAR IN CONTEXT

BEFORE YOU READ

Look at the photos and at the title of the article. Discuss the questions.

1. What do you think the article is about?
2. Would you like to do the things in the photos? Why or why not?

READ

10|01 **Read this article about unusual vacations.**

Been There? Done That?

Maybe it's time for something new . . .

Today's world is getting smaller. People are traveling the globe[1] in record numbers.[2] Our readers have been to Rome. They've visited Greece. They've seen the ancient pyramids of Egypt. They've gone skiing in the Swiss Alps. Now, they're looking for new places to see and new things to do. They want adventure. *Travel Today* has just come out with its annual survey. As part of the survey, the magazine asks its readers the following question: "What would you like to do that you've never done before?"

Here are some of their answers:

1 *the globe:* the world
2 *in record numbers:* much more than in the past

I've made several trips to Egypt, but I've never ridden a camel. I've always wanted to do that.

Riding a camel, hot-air ballooning, ice climbing . . . These are just a few activities that travelers can choose from today. All you need is time, money (a lot of it!), and a sense of adventure.[3] But you don't have to go to a faraway place in an unusual type of transportation to have a great vacation! Have you ever spent the day walking in the woods, heard the sound of the wind, or watched the sun set over the ocean? These can be wonderful adventures, too! And a lot more affordable!

3 *sense of adventure:* the ability to enjoy new things

AFTER YOU READ

A VOCABULARY **Match the words with their definitions.**

____ **1. adventure**	**a.** very old
____ **2. survey**	**b.** an exciting, unusual experience
____ **3. affordable**	**c.** happening every year
____ **4. transportation**	**d.** a questionnaire
____ **5. ancient**	**e.** a way of traveling someplace
____ **6. annual**	**f.** not expensive

B COMPREHENSION Which activities have the readers of *Travel Today* tried? Check (✓) them.

☐ **1.** skiing in the Alps
☐ **2.** riding a camel
☐ **3.** hot-air ballooning
☐ **4.** ice-skating
☐ **5.** mountain climbing
☐ **6.** ice climbing

C DISCUSSION Work with a partner. Compare your answers in B. Why did you or didn't you check each activity?

STEP 2 GRAMMAR PRESENTATION

PRESENT PERFECT: INDEFINITE PAST

Statements

Subject	*Have (not)*	Past Participle	
They	**have (not)**	**visited**	Egypt.
She	**has (not)**	**been**	there.

Statements with Adverbs

Subject	*Have (not)*	Adverb	Past Participle		Adverb
They	**have**	*never* / *just* / *recently*	**visited**	Egypt.	
She	**has**		**been**	there.	
They	**have (not)**		**visited**	Egypt	*twice.* / *lately.* / *recently.*
She	**has (not)**		**been**	there	

Yes/No Questions

Have	Subject	*(Ever)*	Past Participle	
Have	they	*(ever)*	**visited**	Egypt?
Has	she		**been**	there?

Short Answers

Affirmative		Negative	
Yes,	they **have.**	**No,**	they **haven't.**
	she **has.**		she **hasn't.**
			never.

Wh- Questions

Wh- Word	*Have*	Subject	Past Participle	
How often	**have**	they	**visited**	Egypt?
	has	she	**been**	there?

GRAMMAR NOTES

1 Present Perfect

Use the present perfect to show that something **happened at an indefinite** (not exact) **time in the past**.

Use the present perfect when you **don't know when** something happened or when the specific **time is not important**.

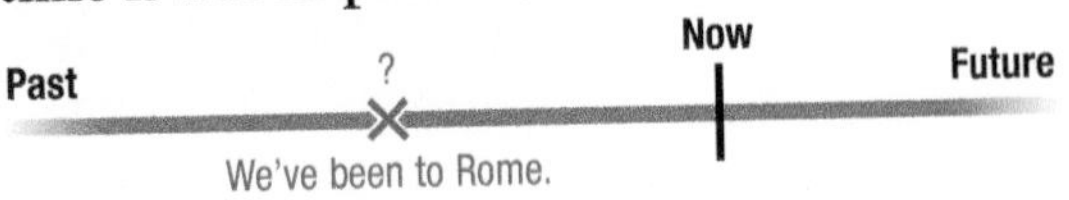

They**'ve traveled** to Egypt.
(You don't know the exact time.)
We**'ve been** to Rome.
(The exact time isn't important.)

Use the present perfect (not the simple past) to show a **connection to the present**: the result of the action or state is important in the present.

The hotel **has closed.**
(So we can't stay there now.)

USAGE NOTE For many speakers ***have been to*** and ***have gone to*** have different meanings.

He**'s been to** France.
(At some point in the past, he visited France, but he's not necessarily there now.)
He**'s gone to** France.
(He's in France now.)

2 Present Perfect + Adverbs of Time or Time Expressions

You can also use the present perfect with **adverbs of time** or **time expressions** to show that something happened at an **indefinite time in the past**.

For **repeated actions** at some indefinite time in the past, use adverbs of time or time expressions such as:

- ***twice***
- ***often***
- ***many times***

They**'ve seen** the Pyramids ***twice***.
We**'ve *often* stayed** at that hotel.
We**'ve stayed** there ***many times***.

For **repeated actions** or **states** that continue up to the present and may continue into the future, use:

- ***so far***

So far, I**'ve taken** more than 1000 photos. I'm sure I'll take many more before this trip is over!
So far, the weather **has been** great.

USAGE NOTE We often use ***so far*** with numbers, adverbs like *twice*, and *only*.

So far, she's bought ***four*** souvenirs.
So far, they've traveled to Egypt ***twice***.
So far, he's ***only*** been to Cairo.

For states or actions that **continue in the present**, use:

- ***always***
- ***never***

We**'ve *always* wanted** to go to Egypt.
I**'ve *never* ridden** a camel.

CONTINUED ▶

To ask **questions** and give **negative answers**, use:	
• *ever* (= at any time before now)	A: **Have** you ***ever*** **been** to Rome?
• *never*	B: **No, I've *never* been** there. or **No, *never*.**
To stress that something happened in the very **recent past**, use:	
• *just* (= a very short time before now)	**I've *just* gotten** back from China.
• *lately/recently* (= in the near past)	They **haven't been** there ***lately***. He**'s flown** a lot ***recently***.
USAGE NOTE In American English, we often use *just* and *recently* with the **simple past**. You can't, however, use *lately* with the simple past.	**I've *just* returned** or **I *just* returned.** NOT I returned ~~lately~~.
BE CAREFUL! Do not use the present perfect with adverbs or expressions that refer to a **specific time in the past**. Use the simple past.	I **got** back ***yesterday***. NOT ~~I've gotten~~ back *yesterday*.

3 Word Order

With the present perfect, most **adverbs of time** or **time expressions** can go at the **end of the clause** or **before the past participle**.

Some adverbs of time and time expressions go at the **end of the clause**:	
• *twice*	She**'s been** there ***twice***.
• *many times*	**I've been** there ***many times***.
• *lately*	I **haven't traveled *lately*** because it's too expensive.
Other adverbs go **before the past participle**:	
• *always*	**I've *always* wanted** to stay there.
• *often*	We**'ve *often* talked** about it.
• *ever*	**Have** you ***ever*** **seen** the pyramids?
• *never*	We**'ve *never* been** to Egypt.
• *just*	His plane **has *just* landed.**
Recently can go **at the end of the clause** or **before the past participle**.	They**'ve traveled** a lot ***recently***. They**'ve *recently* traveled** a lot.
So far usually goes at the **beginning** or **end of the clause**.	***So far***, I've read 100 pages of my guide book. I've read 100 pages of my guide book ***so far***.

REFERENCE NOTES

For a list of **irregular past participles**, see Appendix 1 on page 453.
For all **present perfect forms**, see Unit 8 on page 106.
For **present perfect with *already*, *yet*, and *still***, see Unit 9 on page 120.

STEP 3 FOCUSED PRACTICE

EXERCISE 1 DISCOVER THE GRAMMAR

GRAMMAR NOTES 1–3 **Read the first statement. Then decide if the second statement is *True (T)* or *False (F)*. If there isn't enough information in the first statement to know the answer, put a question mark *(?)* on the line.**

1. Adventure vacations have become very popular.

   __T__ They are popular now.

2. I've been to Italy twice.

   ____ I was there two years ago.

3. I have never been to the Himalayas.

   ____ I went to the Himalayas a long time ago.

4. I've just returned from China.

   ____ I was in China a short time ago.

5. Greg asks you, "Have you ever been to Costa Rica?"

   ____ Greg wants to know when you were in Costa Rica.

6. Marta asks you, "Have you read any good travel books lately?"

   ____ Marta wants to know about a travel book you read last year.

7. We have visited Egypt several times.

   ____ This is not our first visit to Egypt.

8. He's recently been to Greece.

   ____ He's been to Greece recently.

9. I've spent $100 so far.

   ____ I've spent $100 up to now.

10. I've been on an African safari.[1]

    ____ I'm on a safari now.

---

1 *safari:* a trip through the country areas of Africa in order to watch wild animals

EXERCISE 2 STATEMENTS AND QUESTIONS

A GRAMMAR NOTES 1–2 *Travel Today* (TT) interviewed travel writer Rosa García (RG). **Complete this interview. Use the present perfect form of the verbs in parentheses. Use contractions when possible.**

TT: As a travel writer, you *'ve visited* (1. visit) many places. Any favorites?

RG: Thailand. It's a beautiful, amazing country. I ________ (2. be) there five times.

TT: What ________ (3. be) your most unusual travel experience?

RG: My *most* unusual? I ________ (4. have) so many! I ________ (5. swim) near sharks (in a cage, of course!), I ________ (6. eat) dinner next to a very active volcano, I ________ (7. sleep) in an ice hotel in Finland . . .

TT: The world ________ (8. become) a lot smaller. There are fewer and fewer "undiscovered" places. ________ you ever ________ (9. find) a really great place and decided not to tell your readers about it?

RG: No, never. I ________ (10. think) about doing that a few times, but so far, I ________ never actually ________ (11. do) it. I ________ always ________ (12. write) about it.

TT: Where ________ you ________ (13. be) recently?

RG: I ________ just ________ (14. return) from a hot-air ballooning trip in Australia. It was really fantastic. In fact, ballooning is my new favorite form of transportation!

TT: Where are you going next?

RG: On an African safari! I ________ never ________ (15. be) on one, and I'm really excited. I ________ always ________ (16. want) to do that.

TT: Good luck! And I look forward to your African safari article.

10|02 **B** LISTEN AND CHECK **Listen to the interview and check your answers in A.**

EXERCISE 3 AFFIRMATIVE AND NEGATIVE STATEMENTS

GRAMMAR NOTES 1–3 Look at this survey. Then write sentences about things Andy *has done* and things he *hasn't done* (or *has never done*). Use contractions when possible.

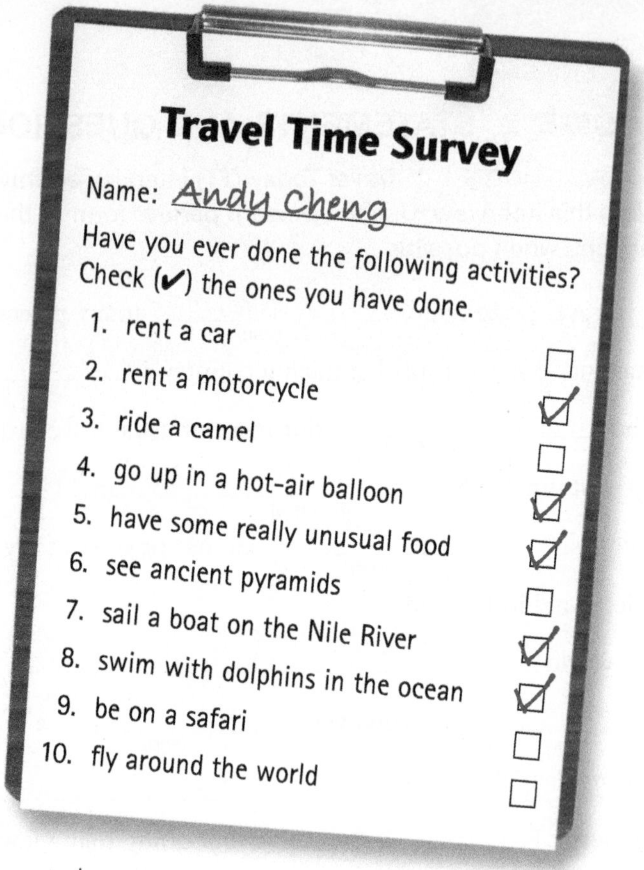

1. *He hasn't rented a car.* **or** *He's never rented a car.*
2. *He's rented a motorcycle.*
3. __________
4. __________
5. __________
6. __________
7. __________
8. __________
9. __________
10. __________

EXERCISE 4 WORD ORDER

A GRAMMAR NOTE 3 Complete this conversation. Put the words in parentheses in the correct order. Use the present perfect form of the verbs. Include short answers. Use contractions when possible.

EVAN: Hot-air ballooning! What's it like? *I've never done this* before!
1. (I / do this / never)

ANDY: You'll love it. __________,
2. (I / a few times / go up)

but __________.
3. (not do it / lately / I)

EVAN: __________?
4. (you / a lot / travel)

ANDY: Yes, __________. I'm a travel writer, so it's part of my job.
5.

EVAN: That's great! ______________________ on a safari?
6. (you / be / ever)

ANDY: No, ______________, but ______________________.
7. 8. (want / to go / always / I)

EVAN: Me too. ______________________.
9. (I / several times / to Africa / be)

In fact, ______________________ back from a trip there.
10. (I / get / just)

But ______________________ on a safari.
11. (so far / I / not be)

ANDY: Look. ______________________ getting the balloon ready. It's time to go up!
12. (they / finish / just)

10|03 **B** LISTEN AND CHECK Listen to the conversation and check your answers in A.

EXERCISE 5 STATEMENTS

GRAMMAR NOTES 1–3 Look at some of Rosa's things. Write sentences using the present perfect form of the verbs from the box. Use adverbs of time or time expressions when possible.

~~be~~	ride	see	stay	travel	write

1. *She's been to Egypt twice.*

2. ______________________

3. ______________________

4. ______________________

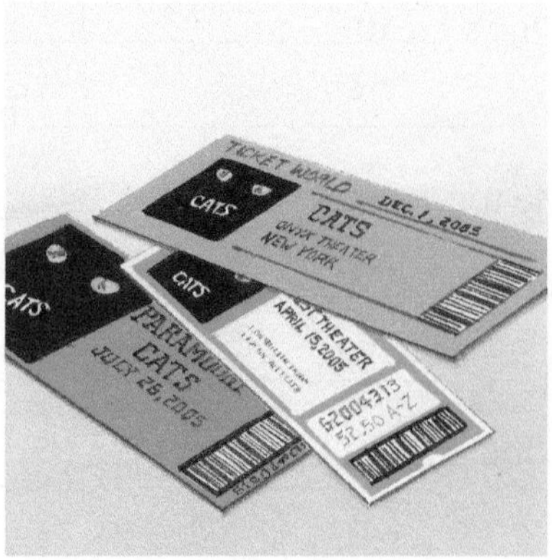

5. ______________________________ 6. ______________________________

EXERCISE 6 EDITING

GRAMMAR NOTES 1–3 Read these comments found on a hot-air ballooning website. There are twelve mistakes in the use of the present perfect and adverbs. The first mistake is already corrected. Find and correct eleven more.

We ~~has~~ *have* **received many comments from our clients. We'd like to share some with you.**

Britta Kessler
GERMANY
I have always be afraid of heights. But after I saw the beautiful photos on your website, I knew I had to go hot-air ballooning! This have been one of the best experiences of my life so far. Thank you!

James Hudson
CANADA
We've returned just from a fantastic vacation. I've told all my friends about your company.

Antonio Vega
MEXICO
I've always wanted to go up in a hot-air balloon. I was not disappointed!

Bill Hampton
USA
I just seen some new photos posted on the website! Awesome!

Amalia Lopes
BRAZIL
I've never went hot-air ballooning, but after visiting your wonderful website, I've decided to sign up!

Pat Calahan
IRELAND
We gave our parents a balloon trip as an anniversary gift. They've just wrote to say it was fantastic. They've ever been very adventurous, but now they want to go whitewater rafting!

Lydia Hassan
NEW ZEALAND
You have ever seen the face of a kid on a hot-air balloon ride? The cost of the ride: a lot. That look on her face: priceless!

May Roa
PHILIPPINES
I broken my leg last month, so I haven't lately been able to do sports—boring! Your mountain balloon trip has just gave me a lift—in more than one way!

STEP 4 COMMUNICATION PRACTICE

EXERCISE 7 LISTENING

▶10|04 **A** Read the statements. Then listen to the conversation and look at the brochures. Listen again and check (✓) *True* or *False*.

	True	False
1. The woman has gone to a travel agent.	☑	☐
2. She has just been on her annual vacation.	☐	☐
3. She has never done adventure traveling.	☐	☐
4. She wants to do something new.	☐	☐
5. She has been hang gliding a few times.	☐	☐
6. She has been skydiving several times.	☐	☐
7. She has never been shark diving.	☐	☐
8. She's never been snowmobiling in Canada.	☐	☐

▶10|04 **B** Listen to the conversation again. Then work with a partner. Look at the travel brochures. Together, decide on a good vacation choice for the woman. Give your reasons.

EXAMPLE: A: I think she would like whitewater rafting.
B: Oh, I don't know about that. She's done whitewater rafting. She says she wants to try something new. What about shark diving?
A: Shark diving? Well, she . . .

EXERCISE 8 QUOTABLE QUOTES

DISCUSSION **Work with a partner. Read the quotes about travel. Choose three quotes and discuss them. What do they mean? Do you agree with them? Why or why not?**

1. Once a year, go someplace you've never been before.
—Dalai Lama (1935– , Tibetan Buddhist religious leader)

EXAMPLE: A: I think the quote means that it's important to go someplace new every year.
B: I agree with you. I also agree with the idea of the quote.
A: Me too. I think you learn a lot from traveling. I know I've always learned a lot from my trips.
B: I'm going to Rome next summer. I've never been there, and I'm really looking forward to it.

2. Like all great travelers, I have seen more than I remember, and remember more than I have seen.
—Benjamin Disraeli (1804–1881, British politician and writer)

3. Every dreamer knows that it is entirely possible to be homesick[1] for a place you've never been to, perhaps more homesick than for familiar ground.
—Judith Thurman (1946– , U.S. writer)

4. The traveler sees what he sees. The tourist sees what he has come to see.
—G.K. Chesterton (1874–1936, British writer and poet)

5. Tourists don't know where they've been, travelers don't know where they're going.
—Paul Theroux (1941– , U.S. travel writer and novelist)

6. I haven't been everywhere, but it's on my list.
—Susan Sontag (1933–2004, U.S. writer and filmmaker)

1 *homesick:* feeling sad because you are away from your home

EXERCISE 9 FIND SOMEONE WHO . . .

A GAME **Walk around your classroom. Try to find someone for each of the activities below. When you find someone, write the person's name next to the activity. You have 10 minutes. The student with the most names is the winner.**

EXAMPLE: A: Ana, have you ever been on a boat?
B: No, I haven't.
A: Dimitris, have *you* ever been on a boat?
C: Yes, I have. I used to go boating a lot when I lived in Greece.
A: Olga, have you ever taken a long car trip?
D: Yes, I have. Two years ago . . .

Activities	Names
be on a boat	__________
take a long car trip	__________
climb a mountain	__________
eat something unusual	__________
ride a horse	__________
go camping	__________
swim in a river	__________
see a beautiful sunset	__________
hear a mariachi band	__________
have dinner on the beach	__________

B **Report back to the class.**

EXAMPLE: I have six names on my list: Dimitris, Olga, Murat, Vania, Nai-Kwan, and Kunio. Dimitris has been on a boat. Olga has taken a long trip. Murat . . .

FROM GRAMMAR TO WRITING

A BEFORE YOU WRITE **Read this quote by U.S. photographer Diane Arbus. Discuss it with a partner. Answer the questions.**

My favorite thing is to go where I've never been.
—*Diane Arbus (1923–1971, U.S. photographer)*

1. What does Arbus mean?
2. Do you feel the same way?
3. What is your favorite thing about travel?
4. Where have you been so far?
5. Would you like to go there again?
6. Where have you never been that you would like to go?

B WRITE **Use your answers to write a paragraph about the quote from Diane Arbus. Give reasons why you agree or disagree with Arbus. Use the present perfect and give examples. Try to avoid the common mistakes in the chart.**

EXAMPLE: Diane Arbus said, "My favorite thing is to go where I've never been." This means that she . . . I don't feel the same way. I enjoy returning to places I have already been. For example, I've been to China several times, but I would like to go back there because . . .

Common Mistakes in Using the Present Perfect for the Indefinite Past

Use the present perfect with or without adverbs or time expressions to talk about the indefinite past. Do not use **adverbs or expressions** that refer to a **specific time in the past**.	**I've seen** a beautiful sunset. **I've seen** a beautiful sunset ***many times***. NOT **I've seen** a beautiful sunset ~~yesterday~~.
Put adverbs of time such as ***twice*** and ***lately*** or time expressions such as ***many times*** at the **end of the clause**. Do not put them **before or after the past participle**.	I've been to Greece ***twice***. NOT I've ~~been twice~~ to Greece. NOT I've ~~twice been~~ to Greece.

C CHECK YOUR WORK **Read your paragraph. Underline all the verbs in the present perfect. Circle the adverbs of time and time expressions. Use the Editing Checklist to check your work.**

Editing Checklist

Did you use . . . ?

☐ the present perfect without adverbs of time or time expressions
☐ the present perfect with adverbs of time or time expressions such as *twice, often, many times, always, never, just, lately, recently, so far*
☐ the correct word order

D REVISE YOUR WORK **Read your paragraph again. Can you improve your writing? Make changes if necessary. Give your paragraph a title.**

UNIT 10 **REVIEW**

Test yourself on the grammar of the unit.

A **Circle the correct words to complete the sentences.**

1. Have you twice / ever been to Egypt?
2. I've just / lately returned from Cairo.
3. I've was / been there twice, and I'm returning next summer.
4. Has / Have Jon ever ridden a camel?
5. I haven't read any good travel books lately / never.
6. One of my classmates is / has recommended a good book.

B **Complete the sentences with the present perfect form of the correct verbs from the box. Use contractions when possible.**

be	give	read	see	show	take	want

1. ____________ you ever ____________ the pyramids?
2. I ____________ never ____________ to Egypt.
3. Elena ____________ just ____________ an interesting book about ancient Egypt.
4. She ____________ ____________ it to me to read.
5. I ____________ always ____________ to ride a camel.
6. My brother ____________ ____________ several trips there.
7. He ____________ recently ____________ me his photos.

C **Find and correct seven mistakes.**

1. I've lately traveled a lot.
2. We've returned just from an African safari.
3. I've never have so much fun before.
4. Have you been ever on a safari?
5. No, but I've recently went hot-air ballooning.
6. My wife and I has decided to go next summer.
7. I've saw a lot of great photos on a hot-air ballooning website.

Now check your answers on page 477.

UNIT 11

Present Perfect and Simple Past

FAILURE AND SUCCESS

OUTCOMES

- Recognize when to use the present perfect and the simple past
- Identify key details in a short, factual text
- Understand the time frame of important details in an interview
- Discuss past events and experiences
- Research a famous person and present findings to the class
- Write a paragraph about a personal experience

STEP 1 GRAMMAR IN CONTEXT

BEFORE YOU READ

Look at the photo of Thomas Edison. Discuss the questions.

1. What is Thomas Edison famous for?
2. Why do you think people call him a "first-time failure"?

READ

11|01 **Read this article about failure and success.**

Famous First-Time Failures

Have you ever tried and failed, and then quit something really very important to you? Thomas Alva Edison failed thousands of times before he created the first successful electric light bulb. But the famous inventor had a great attitude. He never lost hope and never gave up. "I have not failed, not once. I've discovered ten thousand ways that don't work," he said after one of many tries.

Thomas Alva Edison

Like Edison, author Melissa de la Cruz didn't have it easy at first. She wrote her first book at age 22 and sent it to many publishers.[1] They all rejected it. Nobody wanted her next few books either. Then, when she decided to take a writing course, every school rejected her. The young writer probably wanted to give up many times, but she didn't quit. Since her early failures, de la Cruz has written more than twenty-five

1 *publishers:* people or companies that arrange the writing, printing, and sale of books

books—many of them best sellers. She has won several awards and has sold millions of copies of her books around the world.

Have you ever quit too soon? Has your own failure really been a success that is waiting for a few more tries? Maybe you haven't failed enough times yet? Try again, and when you feel discouraged, remember Edison and de la Cruz and follow the advice in the famous saying: "If at first you don't succeed, try, try, try again."

Melissa de la Cruz

AFTER YOU READ

A VOCABULARY **Choose the word or phrase that best completes each sentence.**

1. Edison **created** many things. This means that he ____ many new things.
   a. bought b. made c. wanted
2. The opposite of **failure** is ____.
   a. health b. happiness c. success
3. If you are **discouraged**, you don't feel ____.
   a. hopeful b. nervous c. tired
4. If people **reject** your ideas, they ____ them.
   a. say *yes* to b. think about c. say *no* to
5. Your **attitude** is how you ____ about something.
   a. act b. feel or think c. learn
6. You win an **award** for being ____ at something you do.
   a. pretty good b. good c. the best

B COMPREHENSION **Read the statements. Check (✓) *True* or *False*.**

	True	False
1. Thomas Edison was immediately successful.	☐	☐
2. Edison never quit.	☐	☐
3. Publishers immediately accepted Melissa de la Cruz's first book.	☐	☐
4. Publishers rejected de la Cruz's next books.	☐	☐
5. De la Cruz is still writing books.	☐	☐
6. De la Cruz is very successful.	☐	☐

C DISCUSSION **Work with a partner. Compare your answers in B. Why did you check *True* or *False*?**

STEP 2 GRAMMAR PRESENTATION

PRESENT PERFECT AND SIMPLE PAST

Present Perfect	Simple Past
She **has been** here since 2014.	She **was** in the Philippines in 2013.
They**'ve lived** here for 20 years.	They **lived** there for 10 years.
She**'s written** ten pages today.	She **wrote** twenty pages yesterday.
He **hasn't flown** this month.	He **didn't fly** last month.
Has she **called** him today?	**Did** she **call** him yesterday?

GRAMMAR NOTES

1 Present Perfect or Simple Past + *For*

The present perfect with *for* has a **very different meaning** from the simple past with *for*.

Use the **present perfect** to show that something began in the past and **continues into the present** (and may continue into the future).

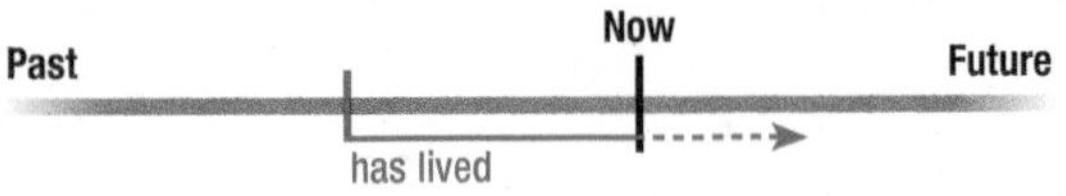

She **has lived** in the United States for more than thirty years.
(She moved to the United States more than thirty years ago, and she is still living there.)

Use the **simple past** to show that something happened in the past and has **no connection to the present**.

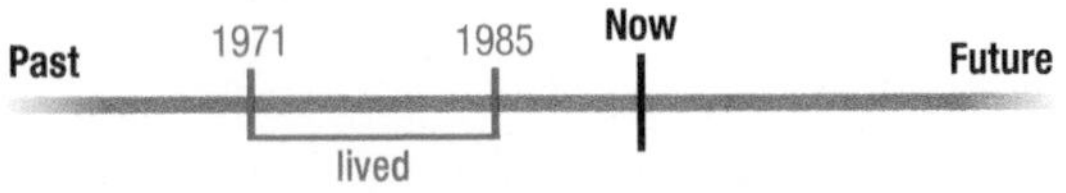

She **lived** in the Philippines for fourteen years.
(She lived there until 1985, but she no longer lives there.)

2 Indefinite Time or Specific Time in the Past

Use the **present perfect** to show that something happened at an **indefinite time** in the past. The exact time is not known or not important.

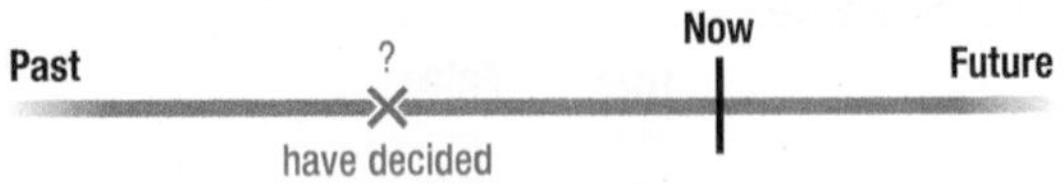

They **have decided** to write another book.
(We don't know exactly when they made the decision, or the time of the decision is not important.)

Use the **simple past** to show that something happened at a **specific time** in the past. The exact time is known and often included.

She **wrote** her first book ***in 2001***.
(We know the exact time and it is important information.)

BE CAREFUL! Do not use the present perfect with a specific time in the past. The only exception is with *since*.

I **lived** in Manila ***in 2007***.
NOT ~~I've lived~~ in Manila ***in 2007***.
I've lived in Manila ***since 2007***.

3 Unfinished Time or Finished Time

Use the **present perfect** to show that something happened in a time period that is **unfinished**, such as *today, this morning, this month, this year.*	Her publisher **has called** three times ***today***. *(Today isn't finished, and it's possible that the publisher will call again.)*
Use the **simple past** to show that something happened in a time period that is **finished**, such as *yesterday, yesterday morning, last month, last year.*	Her publisher **called** three times ***yesterday***. *(Yesterday is finished.)*
BE CAREFUL! Some time expressions such as ***this morning***, ***this month***, or ***this year*** can refer to an **unfinished** or a **finished** time period. Use the present perfect if the time period is unfinished. Use the simple past if the time period is finished.	It's 10:00 a.m. She**'s had** three cups of coffee ***this morning***. *(The morning isn't finished.)* It's 1:00 p.m. She **had** three cups of coffee ***this morning***. *(The morning is finished.)*

REFERENCE NOTES

For the **simple past**, see Unit 2 on page 20.
For the **present perfect** with *since* and *for*, see Unit 8 on page 106.
For the **present perfect** for **indefinite past**, see Unit 10 on page 131.
For a list of **irregular verbs**, see Appendix 1 on page 453.

STEP 3 FOCUSED PRACTICE

EXERCISE 1 DISCOVER THE GRAMMAR

GRAMMAR NOTES 1–3 **Read the information about Melissa de la Cruz. Then choose the sentence (*a* or *b*) that best describes the situation.**

1. Melissa de la Cruz was born in the Philippines in 1971. She lived there until she moved to the United States.
   - (**a.**) She lived in the Philippines for fourteen years.
   - **b.** She's lived in the Philippines for fourteen years.
2. She moved to the United States in 1985. She still lives there.
   - **a.** She lived in the United States for more than thirty years.
   - **b.** She's lived in the United States for more than thirty years.
3. She was a computer programmer for nine years.
   - **a.** She has had a job as a computer programmer for nine years.
   - **b.** She had a job as a computer programmer for nine years.
4. She has always loved to read.
   - **a.** Her love of books started early.
   - **b.** She didn't love books until she became an adult.

5. At first, many publishers rejected her books.
   a. She was not successful.
   b. She has not been successful.

6. In 2013, she returned to the Philippines for a book-signing tour.
   a. She has been there for a few weeks.
   b. She was there for a few weeks.

7. In 2002, she married architect Michael Johnston. The couple is still married.
   a. The couple has been married for many years.
   b. The couple was married for many years.

8. They write books together.
   a. They have written together for a while.
   b. They wrote together for a while.

9. Their books sell all over the world.
   a. Their books have been a great success.
   b. Their books were a great success.

10. It's April and they are on their third book-signing tour.
    a. They went on several trips this year.
    b. They've been on several trips this year.

Stephen King

EXERCISE 2 PRESENT PERFECT OR SIMPLE PAST

GRAMMAR NOTES 1–3 **Complete this article about best-selling author Stephen King (1947–). Circle the correct verb forms.**

Stephen King **(has written)** / wrote (1.) more than 60 novels and almost 200 short stories. As a child in Portland, Maine, he has enjoyed / enjoyed (2.) reading horror comics.[1] He has begun / began (3.) writing in school, where he has sold / sold (4.) his stories to his friends. But his early success as a writer did not continue without problems. In 1973, he has written / wrote (5.) his first novel, *Carrie*, about a teenage girl with frightening magical powers. It has received / received (6.) thirty rejections. Discouraged, King has thrown / threw (7.) the book away. Luckily for him and his many future fans, his wife has removed / removed (8.) it from the trash and encouraged him to submit it again. This time the publishers have accepted / accepted (9.) it.

1 *horror comics:* magazines (often for children) that use pictures to tell very frightening stories

Since 1974, King has sold / sold (10.) more than 350 million books around the world. In addition to his books, he has written / wrote (11.) scripts for movies and television. He has received / received (12.) many awards including the World Fantasy Award for Life Achievement, which he has won / won (13.) in 2004. In spite of his huge success, King lives a simple life. He has continued / continued (14.) to live in Maine and he has remained / remained (15.) married to the same woman who has rescued / rescued (16.) *Carrie* from the trash can many years ago. In a 2014 interview with *Rolling Stone Magazine*, the interviewer has asked / asked (17.) King about his fear of failure. "I'm afraid of failing at whatever story I'm writing," King has admitted / admitted (18.). His fear, however, never stops him. King continues to be one of the best-selling authors in the world.

EXERCISE 3 PRESENT PERFECT OR SIMPLE PAST STATEMENTS

GRAMMAR NOTES 1–3 **Complete this entry in a writer's online journal. Use the present perfect or simple past form of the verbs in parentheses.**

Thursday, 4:00 p.m.

It ___has been___ (1. be) a very difficult day, and it's not over yet! I ________ (2. begin) working at 8:00 a.m. this morning. I ________ (3. want) to finish the next chapter of my book, but I ________ (4. write) only two pages all day! It's so frustrating. It's already Thursday, and I ________ (5. not have) a good idea all week. (Last week, I ________ (6. write) two whole chapters!) Yesterday, I ________ (7. feel) so discouraged that I almost ________ (8. quit). But then I ________ (9. remember) Thomas Edison and the trouble he ________ (10. experience) when he was trying to create the light bulb. He ________ (11. have) such a great attitude about failure and success. It really ________ (12. help) me to go on. I guess I can look at today in a positive way and say "This morning, I ________ (13. discover) another way not to finish this chapter!"

EXERCISE 4 PRESENT PERFECT OR SIMPLE PAST QUESTIONS

A GRAMMAR NOTES 1–3 *Success Magazine* (SM) is interviewing a famous author, Emil Karlsson (EK). Complete the interview questions. Use the words in parentheses. Choose between the present perfect and simple past.

SM: *How long have you been an author?*
1. (how long / you / be an author)

EK: Oh, for about fifteen years.

SM: And ______________________________
2. (when / you / write your first book)

EK: I wrote my first book when I was twenty-one.

SM: ______________________________
3. (be / it / immediately successful)

EK: Yes. I was very lucky. And very surprised!

SM: ______________________________
4. (how many copies / it / sell during its first year)

EK: More than a million.

SM: More than a million copies? That's a lot of copies! Now, tell me about your most recent book.

____
5. (when / it / come out)

EK: It came out about a year ago.

SM: And ______________________________ since then?
6. (it / win / any awards)

EK: Yes. It won *Mystery Mag's* Best Book of the Year Award.

SM: Congratulations! ______________________________?
7. (how many copies / it / sell)

EK: I'm not sure. You'll have to ask my publisher!

11|02 **B** LISTEN AND CHECK Listen to the interview and check your answers in A.

EXERCISE 5 EDITING

GRAMMAR NOTES 1–3 **Read these online comments about a book called *Failure and Success*. There are twelve mistakes in the use of the present perfect and simple past. The first mistake is already corrected. Find and correct eleven more.**

Comments from Readers

November 4

I've just finished reading *Failure and Success* by Nila Sciretta. Actually, ~~I read~~ I've read several of her books this year. The book is great! It's no surprise that it sold so many copies. **—Marta Lopez**

I was a big fan of this author for many years, so I was very happy to find her latest book online. I've downloaded it last week and I finished it in two days. It's a great book—perhaps the best book I read so far this year. I highly recommend it. **—Burak Mardin**

Have these other people read the same book as me? I haven't liked it at all. I thought it was boring. I've finished it last night, but I'm sorry I bought it. Save your money! **—Felipe Casa**

For the last few months, I tried suggestions from *Failure and Success*. This book has changed my attitude about failure. Everyone has failed at some time, but the author has not failed in communicating her message: Failure can be a great teacher! **—Soon-Bok Park**

I only read two chapters so far, but I think it's a very interesting and helpful book. I've already learned a lot from it. I especially like all the examples about famous people, like Edison, who have failed at first before they became successful. **—Jason Morgen**

My husband and I are both college professors. Before we finally have found teaching jobs at the same school, we had to live in different cities. It was a very difficult time for us. A friend recommended one of Sciretta's earlier books and it really helped. We're also authors, but we didn't find a publisher yet. But thanks to Sciretta's advice, we won't give up! **—Ann Braid**

STEP 4 COMMUNICATION PRACTICE

EXERCISE 6 LISTENING

11|03 **A** A student is interviewing two college professors for the school newspaper. Read the list. Then listen to the interview. Listen again and check (✓) the items that are true now.

The professors ____.

- ☑ **1.** are married
- ☐ **2.** live in different cities
- ☐ **3.** live in Boston
- ☐ **4.** live in Los Angeles
- ☐ **5.** teach at the same university
- ☐ **6.** have a house
- ☐ **7.** teach creative writing 101
- ☐ **8.** write books together
- ☐ **9.** have best-selling books
- ☐ **10.** love teaching
- ☐ **11.** are happy in Los Angeles
- ☐ **12.** get positive reviews from their students

11|03 **B** Work with a partner. Listen again. In your opinion, what successes have the couple had? What failures have they had? Give reasons for your answers. Remember to use the present perfect and simple past.

EXAMPLE: A: Well, they seem to have a successful marriage.
B: Yes, they've been married for ten years.
A: And times haven't always been easy for them, but they've stayed together.

EXERCISE 7 A FAMOUS WRITER

ROLE PLAY Work with a partner. Take turns being a magazine interviewer (A) and a famous writer (B). The interviewer asks questions using the words in the box with the present perfect or simple past. The writer answers the interviewer's questions, using his or her imagination.

EXAMPLE: A: How long have you been a writer?
B: I've been a writer since I was twenty-one.

how long / be a writer?
when / write your first book?
you / successful right away?
how many books / write?
why / become a writer?
when / your new book / come out?
how many copies / it / sell?
how many copies / your first book / sell?
your books / win / awards?
how many awards / your books / win?
Other: ____________?

EXERCISE 8 LAST YEAR AND THIS YEAR

COMPARISON Work with a partner. Sumni Wook is a successful musician. Look at her records from last year and this year. It is now the end of August. Compare what she did last year and what she has done this year. You can use the verbs from the box.

EXAMPLE: A: Last year, she performed in New York twice.
B: So far this year, she's only performed there once.

attend	give	go	have	perform	practice	study	win

LAST YEAR

January	February	March	April	May	June
• concert in N.Y. • L.A. – violin workshop	• L.A. – violin workshop • 1 seminar	• concert in N.Y.	• attend lecture	• 10 vacation days	• 2 concerts – Ottawa • 1 concert – Toronto
July	**August**	**September**	**October**	**November**	**December**
• receive Young Musician award	• music conference – Seoul	• Mom's visit • attend lecture	• concert in Toronto	• Modern Day interview	• 10 vacation days

THIS YEAR

January	February	March	April	May	June
• concert in San Francisco	• concert in N.Y. • attend lecture	• Nan's wedding	• concert in Toronto	• concert in Paris	• 5 vacation days • 1 seminar
July	**August**	**September**	**October**	**November**	**December**
• visit Tania	• music conference • attend lecture				

EXERCISE 9 TRY, TRY, TRY

DISCUSSION Work with a partner. Think about the famous saying "If at first you don't succeed, try, try, try again." Do you agree with the saying? Give an example about a time when this worked, or didn't work, for you or someone you know who is still alive. Think about the questions below.

EXAMPLE: A: I think the saying is true. I remember when I wanted to learn to drive. I failed my road test three times! But I didn't give up. I took some more driving lessons and I finally passed. I've had my license now for three years and I've never even gotten a parking ticket!
B: That's great. I think it's good to try and not give up, but . . .

1. What did the person want to achieve?
2. What did the person do to try to reach his or her goal?
3. Did he or she succeed?
4. How has it changed the person's life?
5. How does the person feel now?

EXERCISE 10 FAMOUS FIRST-TIME FAILURES

A GROUP PROJECT **Work in a group. Look at the photos of six famous first-time "failures." Choose one of them and research that person online. Discuss the person with your group.**

EXAMPLE: A: So, what did we find out about James Dyson?
B: He's a British inventor.
C: What's he famous for?
B: He invented a vacuum cleaner that works without a bag.
C: Oh! That's right! I've seen TV ads for it!
B: And he wasn't successful right away. He . . .

James Dyson (inventor)

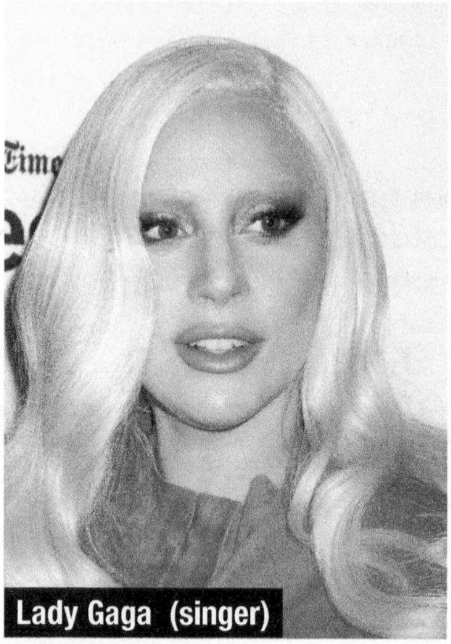
Lady Gaga (singer)

Michael Jordan (retired athlete)

Oliver Stone (filmmaker)

J.K. Rowling (author)

Vera Wang (fashion designer)

B **Report back to the class.**

EXAMPLE: James Dyson is a British inventor. He created the first vacuum cleaner that worked without a bag. Before he succeeded, he failed more than 5,000 times and he went through all his savings. Today, his vacuum cleaner has become very popular and he has made billions of dollars with his invention.

FROM GRAMMAR TO WRITING

A BEFORE YOU WRITE **Choose one of the titles below for a paragraph about failure and success. You can also choose your own title. Give an example to support your title.**

Failure Is a Good Teacher	Everyone Fails Some of the Time
From Failure to Success	There Is Nothing Good About Failure
You Can't Always Succeed	*Other:* ______________________

An example for ____
(the title you chose)

____

____

B WRITE **Use your example to write a paragraph about failure and success. Remember to use the present perfect and simple past. Write your title above the paragraph. Try to avoid the common mistakes in the chart.**

EXAMPLE: Failure Is a Good Teacher

I believe that failure is a good teacher. For example, when I was younger, I tried to . . . Even though I failed several times, I still learned a lot. I . . . As a result of my experience, I have become . . .

Common Mistakes in Using the Present Perfect and Simple Past

Use the **past participle** form of the verb **after *have***. Do not use the simple past form.	She **has written** many books. NOT She has ~~wrote~~ many books.
Use the **simple past** with a **specific time in the past**. Do not use the present perfect.	She **won** an award ***last year***. NOT She ~~has won~~ an award ***last year***.

C CHECK YOUR WORK **Read your paragraph. Underline the verbs in the present perfect and circle the verbs in the simple past. Use the Editing Checklist to check your work.**

Editing Checklist

Did you use . . . ?

- ☐ the present perfect for things that began in the past and continue into the present
- ☐ the simple past for things that happened in the past and have no connection to the present
- ☐ the present perfect for things that happened at an indefinite time in the past
- ☐ the simple past for things that happened at a specific time in the past
- ☐ the present perfect for things that have happened in a time period that is not finished
- ☐ the simple past for things that happened in a time period that is finished

D REVISE YOUR WORK **Read your paragraph again. Can you improve your writing? Make changes if necessary.**

UNIT 11 **REVIEW**

Test yourself on the grammar of the unit.

A **Imagine you are interviewing Ken Sousa, an engineer. Write questions with the words in parentheses. Use the present perfect or the simple past.**

2010	2011	2012	2013	2014	2015	2016	July, this year
Ken moves to Vancouver		gets engineering degree	starts first professional job	marries Tina	loses job	moves to Singapore to work	Tina joins him in Singapore

1. When did you move to Vancouver
(when / move to Vancouver)
2. How long have you been an engineer
(how long / be an engineer)
3. Did you work in Vancouver for a long time?
(work / in Vancouver for a long time)
4. When did you get married?
(when / get married)
5. How many years have you lived in Singapore?
(how many years / live in Singapore)
6. Has your wife lived in Singapore a long?
(your wife / live in Singapore long)

B **Complete the paragraph from Tina's journal. Use the present perfect or the simple past form of the verbs in parentheses.**

I has been (1. be) in Singapore for a month. It's great to be with Ken, but there's so much to do! We saw (2. see) five apartments last week, and so far this evening we have crossed (3. cross) three places off our list. I still haven't seen (4. not see) very much of the city, but this morning we took (5. take) a boat tour. It was (6. be) great! Ken has learned (7. learn) some Chinese already, so he ordered (8. order) lunch for us. I didn't learn (9. not learn) much Chinese in Vancouver, but I'll learn fast here.

C **Find and correct five mistakes.**

Tina and Ken lived apart for a while, but then Tina found a job in Singapore. She has moved there last month. Here are some of their thoughts:

KEN: I'm so glad Tina is finally here. Last year has been the hardest time of my life.

TINA: Before I got here, I didn't understood Ken's experiences. But I was in culture shock since I arrive. Now I know what a difficult time Ken had at first. But he never gave up.

Now check your answers on page 477.

UNIT 12

Present Perfect Progressive and Present Perfect

CLIMATE CHANGE

OUTCOMES

- Describe actions that started in the past and are still in progress
- Describe actions that started at an indefinite time in the past and are finished
- Identify main points of a short text on a scientific topic
- Understand the time frame of main events in conversations
- Discuss climate change
- Write an email or letter about recent activities

STEP 1 GRAMMAR IN CONTEXT

BEFORE YOU READ

Look at the photo and at the title of the article. Discuss the questions.

1. What is happening to the Earth?
2. Why does the Earth have a thermometer in it?
3. What is a hot topic?

READ

12|01 **Read this article about climate change.**

Global Warming:[1] A Hot Topic

The Earth's climate has changed many times. Warm oceans covered the Earth for millions of years. Then those oceans turned to ice for millions more. If the climate has been changing for five billion years, why is global warming such a hot topic today?

Almost everyone agrees that the Earth has been getting hotter. But not everyone agrees about the cause. Most climate experts think that human activities have added to global warming. The coal and oil we burn for energy have been sending more and more gases into the air around the Earth. The gases keep the

1 *global warming:* the continuing increase in the Earth's temperatures (including air and oceans) since the 1950s

heat in the atmosphere[2] and also cause air pollution.[3] These experts believe humans can slow global warming.

Others say global warming is mostly the result of natural causes, such as changes in the sun. They don't believe that human activities can make things better or worse.

Human or natural, the effects of global warming have been powerful. Here are just two examples:

- In the Arctic,[4] ice has been melting quickly. As a result, polar bears and other animals have become endangered species.[5] Arctic towns and villages are also in danger as sea levels rise.
- In parts of Africa, rainfall has decreased. Water and food have become very hard to find. Both people and animals have been suffering badly.

Recently, people have been taking steps to slow these dangerous trends. They have been developing ways to use clean solar energy. In addition, they have been designing homes and cars that use less energy.

Does it really matter what causes global warming? Environmentalists[6] believe that it does, and they say that if we have been part of the cause, then we can also be part of the solution.

---

2 *atmosphere:* the air that surrounds the Earth
3 *air pollution:* something dirty and unhealthy in the air
4 *the Arctic:* the most northern part of the Earth
5 *endangered species:* a type of animal or plant that may not continue to exist
6 *environmentalists:* people who want to protect the environment (land, water, and air)

AFTER YOU READ

A VOCABULARY **Match the words with their definitions.**

_____	**1. expert**	**a.** the power that makes machines work
_____	**2. climate**	**b.** to create a drawing that shows how to build something
_____	**3. develop**	**c.** someone with special knowledge of a subject
_____	**4. energy**	**d.** the typical weather in an area
_____	**5. design**	**e.** the way a situation is generally changing
_____	**6. trend**	**f.** to work on a new idea or product to make it successful

B COMPREHENSION **Read the statements. Check (✓) *True* or *False*.**

	True	False
1. Climate change is something new.	☐	☐
2. Almost everyone believes that the Earth used to be cooler.	☐	☐
3. Coal and oil are still sending gases into the air around the Earth.	☐	☐
4. Ice in the Arctic has stopped melting.	☐	☐
5. In parts of Africa, people and animals are still suffering.	☐	☐
6. People are no longer developing ways to use solar energy.	☐	☐

C DISCUSSION **Work with a partner. Compare your answers in B. Why did you check *True* or *False*?**

STEP 2 GRAMMAR PRESENTATION

PRESENT PERFECT PROGRESSIVE AND PRESENT PERFECT

Present Perfect Progressive

Statements

Subject	*Have (not)*	*Been*	Base Form of Verb + *-ing*	*(Since/For)*
I You* We They	**have (not)**	**been**	**working**	(**since** 2009). (**for** years).
He She It	**has (not)**			

* *You* is both singular and plural.

***Yes/No* Questions**

Have	Subject	*Been*	Base Form of Verb + *-ing*	*(Since/For)*
Have	you	**been**	**working**	(**since** 2009)? (**for** years)?
Has	she			

Short Answers

Affirmative		
Yes,	I/we	**have.**
	she	**has.**

Negative		
No,	I/we	**haven't.**
	she	**hasn't.**

***Wh-* Questions**

Wh- Word	*Have*	Subject	*Been*	Base Form of Verb + *-ing*
How long	**have**	you	**been**	**working?**
	has	she		

Present Perfect Progressive and Present Perfect

Present Perfect Progressive
They **have been living** here for many years.
I**'ve been reading** this book since Monday.
Dr. Owen **has been writing** articles since 2000.
She**'s been working** in Kenya for a year.

Present Perfect
They **have lived** here for many years.
I**'ve read** two books about solar energy.
Dr. Owen **has written** many articles.
She**'s worked** in many countries.

GRAMMAR NOTES

1 Present Perfect Progressive or Present Perfect

The present perfect progressive and the present perfect usually have **different meanings**.

Use the **present perfect progressive** to show that something is **unfinished**. It started in the past and is still continuing. The focus is on the **continuation** of the action.

I've been reading a book about solar energy.
(I'm still reading it.)
She**'s been writing** an article.
(She's still writing it.)

Use the **present perfect** to show that something is **finished**. It happened at an indefinite time in the past. The focus is on the **result** of the action.

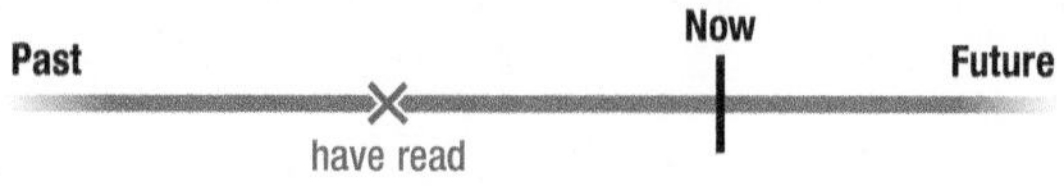

I've read a book about solar energy.
(I finished the book.)
She**'s written** an article.
(She finished the article.)

USAGE NOTE We also use the **present perfect progressive** for finished actions that **ended in the very recent past**. You can often still see the results of the action.

Look! The streets are wet. It**'s been raining**.
(It stopped raining very recently.)
NOT It~~'s rained~~.

BE CAREFUL! We usually do not use **non-action verbs**, such as *be*, *have*, and *know* in the progressive.

She**'s had** the same job since 2000.
NOT She~~'s been having~~ the same job since 2000.

2 With Time Expressions, Quantifiers, and Numbers

Use the **present perfect progressive** with *for* + **time expression** to show *how long* something has been happening.

I've been reading books about wind energy ***for two months***.

Use the **present perfect** with a **quantifier or number** to show:

- *how much* someone has done — **I've read *a lot*** about it.
- *how many things* someone has done — She**'s written *three*** articles.
- *how many times* someone has done something — **I've read** that book ***twice***.

BE CAREFUL! Do not use the present perfect with a **specific time in the past**. The only exception is with *since*.

She**'s read** three articles.
NOT She~~'s read~~ three articles ***last week***.
She**'s read** three articles ***since last week***.

3 With Verbs of Duration + *For* or *Since*

With verbs that show **duration** such as ***live***, ***study***, ***teach***, and ***work***, you can use the **present perfect progressive** or the **present perfect** with ***for*** or ***since***. The meaning is the same: something is **unfinished**.

• **present perfect progressive**	He**'s been studying** global warming ***for*** ten years.
	or
• **present perfect**	He**'s studied** global warming ***for*** ten years. *(In both examples, he is still studying it.)*
USAGE NOTE We often use the **present perfect progressive** to show that something is **temporary**.	They**'ve been living** here ***since*** 1995, but they are moving next month.
USAGE NOTE We often use the **present perfect** to show that something is **permanent**.	They**'ve lived** here ***since*** they were children, and they're not planning on moving.

REFERENCE NOTES

For a list of **non-action verbs**, see Appendix 2 on page 454.
For the **present perfect with *since* and *for***, see Unit 8 on page 106.
For the **present perfect for the indefinite past**, see Unit 10 on page 131.
For the **present perfect and simple past**, see Unit 11 on page 146.

STEP 3 FOCUSED PRACTICE

EXERCISE 1 DISCOVER THE GRAMMAR

GRAMMAR NOTES 1–3 **Read each statement. Decide if something is finished or unfinished. Check (✓) *Finished* or *Unfinished*.**

		Finished	Unfinished
1.	I've been reading a book about global warming.	☐	☑
2.	I've read a book about global warming.	☐	☐
3.	She's written two magazine articles about air pollution.	☐	☐
4.	She's been waiting for some supplies.	☐	☐
5.	They've lived in Ontario since 2002.	☐	☐
6.	They've been living in Ontario since 2002.	☐	☐
7.	We've been developing plans with the leaders of many countries.	☐	☐
8.	We've developed these plans with many leaders.	☐	☐
9.	Look out the window—it's been raining.	☐	☐
10.	Look. Someone has watered the plants.	☐	☐

EXERCISE 2 PRESENT PERFECT PROGRESSIVE OR PRESENT PERFECT

GRAMMAR NOTES 1–3 **Complete the statements about an expert on climate change, Professor Jane Owen, and her work. Circle the correct words. Sometimes both answers are correct.**

1. *Green Earth* magazine has been publishing / (has published) Professor Owen's third annual report on environmental trends. It's an excellent report.
2. Professor Owen is working on two articles for the next issue of *Green Earth* magazine. She has been writing / has written these articles since Monday.
3. She has been writing / has written about global warming many times.
4. Professor Owen has been speaking / has spoken at our school several times about climate change.
5. She has been speaking / has spoken since 8:00 p.m., and she still has a lot more to tell us.
6. Professor Owen has a lot of work to do. Lately, she has been studying / has studied the use of solar energy for homes. She's learning about pollution from buildings.
7. She was late for a meeting with the members of her group. When she arrived they said, "At last, you're here. We've been waiting / We've waited for you."
8. Professor Owen has been living / has lived in Kenya for the last two years, but she will return to the United States in January.
9. She has been working / has worked with environmentalists in Kenya and Tanzania.
10. Kenyans have been planting / have planted 30 million trees since the 1970s.

EXERCISE 3 PRESENT PERFECT PROGRESSIVE

GRAMMAR NOTES 1–2 Look at the two pictures of Professor Owen. Complete the sentences describing what has been happening. Use the present perfect progressive form of the verbs in parentheses. Choose between affirmative and negative.

1. She 's been working (work) in her office.
2. She ______________ (write) a book.
3. She ______________ (watch) TV.
4. She ______________ (use) her computer.
5. She ______________ (drink) coffee.
6. She ______________ (drink) tea.
7. She ______________ (eat) her sandwich.
8. She ______________ (wear) her new black sweater.
9. She ______________ (work) hard.
10. It ______________ (rain) all day.

EXERCISE 4 STATEMENTS

GRAMMAR NOTES 1–3 Complete Professor Owen's blog about the European Solar Decathlon, a competition for the best solar houses (homes that get all their energy from the sun). Use the present perfect progressive or the present perfect form of the verbs in parentheses. Sometimes both forms are possible.

One of the solar houses in this year's competition

Green Mail

JUNE 28, 2014 VERSAILLES, FRANCE – A beautiful solar village *has appeared* (1. appear) on the grounds of the Versailles Palace. Twenty teams from universities in Europe, Asia, and North and South America ____________ (2. bring) these houses here for an international competition of solar houses. Universities ____________ (3. participate) in this competition since 2007. For all the contests, talented students ____________ (4. design) the energy-efficient houses, and they ____________ (5. build) them as well. Over the years, the homes ____________ (6. get) more energy efficient *and* more beautiful. This year, twenty houses ____________ (7. enter) the competition. I ____________ (8. visit) the houses since I got here. I still have several more to see, and I am looking forward to it. I ________ also ____________ (9. talk) to many of the student designers. So far, what I hear most often is, "I could *totally* live in this house!" I agree.

Check back in about two weeks for the winners.

JULY 14 – Well, the contest is finally over and Team RhOME (RhOME = Rome home) from Italy ____________ (10. win) this year's first prize. The teams from France and the Netherlands also ____________ (11. receive) prizes for their creative work. Tomorrow, it's back to Kenya for me. This ____________ (12. be) a really great event.

EXERCISE 5
QUESTIONS AND ANSWERS

GRAMMAR NOTE 2 **Professor Owen is interviewing one of the student designers at Solar Decathlon Europe. Use the words in parentheses to write Professor Owen's questions. Use her notes to complete the student's answers. Choose between the present perfect progressive and the present perfect. Use contractions when possible.**

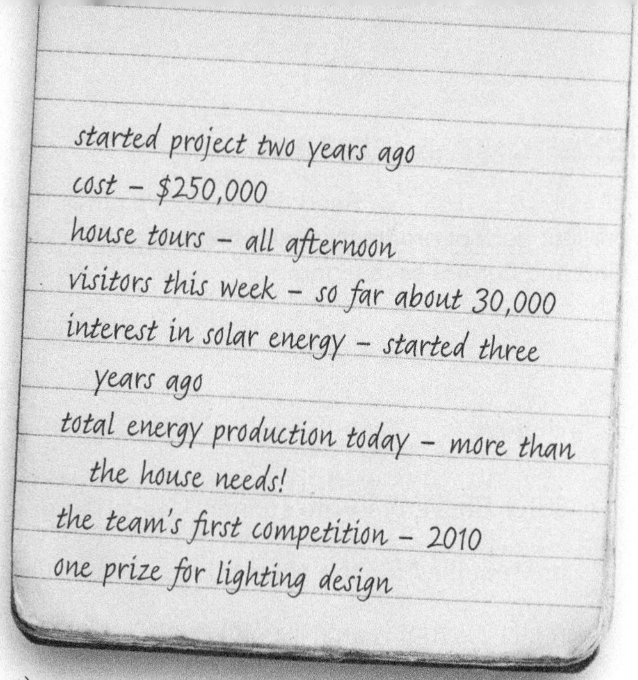

1. (how long / your team / work / on this project)

OWEN: *How long has your team been working on this project?*

STUDENT: *We've been working on this project for two years.*

2. (how much money / the team / spend / on the house)

OWEN: ______________________________

STUDENT: ______________________________

3. (how long / you / lead tours / today)

OWEN: ______________________________

STUDENT: ______________________________

4. (how many people / visit / this week)

OWEN: ______________________________

STUDENT: ______________________________

5. (how long / you / be / interested in solar energy)

OWEN: ______________________________

STUDENT: ______________________________

6. (how much energy / the house / produce today)

OWEN: ______________________________

STUDENT: ______________________________

7. (how long / your team / compete)

OWEN: ______________________________

STUDENT: ______________________________

8. (how many prizes / your team / win)

OWEN: ______________________________

STUDENT: ______________________________

EXERCISE 6 EDITING

GRAMMAR NOTES 1–3 Read this student's email. There are eight mistakes in the use of the present perfect progressive and the present perfect. The first mistake is already corrected. Find and correct seven more.

Hi guys,

Sorry I haven't ~~wrote~~ *written* sooner. I haven't been having any free time since we arrived in Versailles for the solar house competition. (Our house got here before us!) I'm really excited and also really tired. Since we arrived, we've been lived on pizza and coffee. I haven't sleeping more than a few hours since . . . well, I can't remember when. Our team has been working day and night for the last two weeks, and today the house looks wonderful. I'm so proud—we've designed a home that's beautiful AND reduces pollution. We're finally ready for the judges, so I've spent most of the day looking at other teams' houses. I've been visiting ten houses today. They are so interesting and creative! I hope they help start a new trend in housing that is good for the environment. For the last hour, I've just been hanging out in a café with some people from the other teams. I've already been drinking three cups of coffee—it's delicious, but really strong! We been practicing our French. I still don't understand too much, but our teammate Jacques Renard is from Quebec, Canada, and he's been helped me out a lot. Wish us luck and check your text messages for photos of the house.

Katie

STEP 4 COMMUNICATION PRACTICE

EXERCISE 7 LISTENING

12|02 **A** You're going to listen to six short conversations. Before you listen, look at the photos. Then listen. Do the photos match the conversations? Check (✓) *Matches* or *Doesn't Match*.

1. ☐ Matches ☑ Doesn't Match

2. ☐ Matches ☐ Doesn't Match

3. ☐ Matches ☐ Doesn't Match

4. ☐ Matches ☐ Doesn't Match

5. ☐ Matches ☐ Doesn't Match

6. ☐ Matches ☐ Doesn't Match

12|02 **B** **Listen to each conversation again. Work with a partner. Compare your answers in A. Give reasons for your choices.**

EXAMPLE: A: For Conversation 1, the answer is *Doesn't Match*.
B: Right. The photo doesn't match the conversation. The man said "They've planted some trees." But in the photo, they haven't planted any trees yet.
A: OK. What about the photo in Conversation 2?

EXERCISE 8 CLIMATE CHANGE

A GROUP PROJECT **Work in a group. Do an online search for "climate change." How have things been changing? What have some of the effects been? Consider some of the topics below.**

EXAMPLE: A: The average air temperature around the world has increased by more than 1.53 degrees Fahrenheit (0.85 degrees Celsius) in the last 100 years.
B: There have been more . . .

- air temperature
- ocean temperature
- water level (how high the ocean is)
- amount and frequency of rain
- rain storms
- ice caps (large areas of thick ice that cover the North and South Poles)

B **Compare your results with those of your classmates. Did you find the same information online?**

EXAMPLE: A: I read that the temperature *hasn't* been changing.
B: One report says that it hasn't changed since 1958.
C: But there has definitely been evidence of . . .

EXERCISE 9 A PICTURE IS WORTH A THOUSAND WORDS

A PICTURE DISCUSSION **Work with a partner. Look at the photo and discuss the questions.**

EXAMPLE: A: The photo shows a polar bear. It's . . .
B: I think it means . . .

1. What does the photo show?
2. What does it mean?
3. Is it a strong message? Why or why not?
4. Do you agree with the message?

B **Compare your ideas with those of another pair of students.**

EXAMPLE: A: We think it means . . .
B: We think it's a strong message because . . .

EXERCISE 10 WHAT ABOUT YOU?

DISCUSSION **Work in a group. What changes have you made or experienced recently? Discuss some of the questions below. Use the present perfect progressive and the present perfect to talk about them.**

EXAMPLE: A: Recently, I've gotten more interested in the environment. I've been recycling paper and other things. I've also been walking or riding my bike more.
B: I've just started a job, so I've been wearing business clothes instead of jeans.
C: You look good, Ben! For myself, I've been . . .

Have you changed . . . ?

- your opinions about society or the environment
- the way you look or dress
- the people you hang out with
- your hobbies or interests
- your goals
- *Other:* ____________________

FROM GRAMMAR TO WRITING

A BEFORE YOU WRITE **Think about your recent activities—things you have been doing and things you have done lately. Complete the lists.**

Unfinished Activities	Finished Activities

B WRITE **Use the information from your lists to write an email to a friend or family member about your recent activities. Try to avoid the common mistakes in the chart.**

EXAMPLE: Hi everyone,

A new semester has started, and I've been pretty busy lately. I've been working really hard on a science project. We're learning how to check the water quality in the lake. I've gotten more interested in the environment because of this project, so I've been . . .

Common Mistakes in Using the Present Perfect Progressive and Present Perfect

Use the **present perfect progressive** for things that are **unfinished**. Do not use the present perfect.	**I've been reading** Owen's book. I'm almost finished. NOT ~~I've read~~ Owen's book. I'm almost finished.
Use the **present perfect** for things that are **finished**. Do not use the present perfect progressive (except for something that ended in the very recent past and whose results you can still see).	**I've read** Owen's book. It was great. NOT ~~I've been reading~~ Owen's book. It was great.

C CHECK YOUR WORK **Read your email. Underline the verbs in the present perfect progressive and circle the verbs in the present perfect. Use the Editing Checklist to check your work.**

Editing Checklist

Did you use . . . ?

- ☐ the present perfect progressive for things that are unfinished
- ☐ the present perfect for things that are finished
- ☐ the present perfect progressive to show how long something has been happening
- ☐ the present perfect to show how much, how many, and how many times something has happened
- ☐ the present perfect progressive or the present perfect with verbs of duration

D REVISE YOUR WORK **Read your email again. Can you improve your writing? Make changes if necessary.**

UNIT 12 **REVIEW**

Test yourself on the grammar of the unit.

A **Circle the correct words to complete the sentences.**

1. Professor Ortiz has been writing / has written ten articles on global warming.
2. Today, he has been writing / has written since 6:00 a.m.
3. I've been reading / I've read one of his books. I'll give it to you when I'm finished.
4. My sister has been reading / has read it twice already.
5. I wanted to finish it today, but I've been having / I've had a headache all day.
6. I've been taking / I've taken aspirin all day.

B **Complete the conversations with the present perfect progressive or present perfect form of the verbs in parentheses. Use contractions when possible.**

1. A: How long ______ you ______ (a. live) in Dallas?
   B: I ______ (b. be) here for more than ten years. What about you?
   A: I moved here last month. I ______ (c. enjoy) it a lot.
2. A: ______ you ______ (a. read) any books by Peter Robb?
   B: Yes. In fact, I'm reading one now.
   A: Really? How many books ______ he ______ (b. write)?
3. A: Why are your books all over the place? I ______ (a. try) to clean up!
   B: I ______ (b. study) for my exam.
4. A: How long ______ Vilma ______ (a. be) a student here?
   B: This is her third semester.
   A: ______ she ______ (b. choose) her major?

C **Find and correct five mistakes.**

1. Janet hasn't been writing a word since she sat down at her computer.
2. Since I've known Dan, he's been having five different jobs.
3. I've drunk coffee all morning. I think I've been having at least ten cups!
4. We've been lived here for several years, but we're moving next month.

Now check your answers on page 477.

Modals and Similar Expressions

UNIT **13** **Ability and Possibility: *Can, Could, Be able to***
MULTILINGUALISM

UNIT **14** **Permission: *Can, Could, May, Do you mind if***
ROOMMATES

UNIT **15** **Requests: *Can, Could, Will, Would, Would you mind***
MESSAGES

UNIT **16** **Advice: *Should, Ought to, Had better***
INTERNET RULES

PART 4

OUTCOMES
- Express ability and possibility in the past, present, and future
- Identify main points in a social sciences text
- Identify important details in a job interview
- Compare and contrast different possibilities for improving language skills
- Discuss an academic topic
- Write a paragraph about past, present, and future abilities

OUTCOMES
- Ask for, give, or deny permission
- Identify main points in a short reading
- Recognize when a speaker gives permission or refuses permission
- Come to a resolution with others by asking for and giving permission to do something
- Write a short note, explaining a situation and asking for permission to do something

OUTCOMES
- Make and respond to requests
- Identify important details related to requests in emails and text messages
- Identify details related to a schedule in a conversation
- Discuss a daily schedule that involves making requests of others
- Write and respond to a request in a text or email message

OUTCOMES
- Give and ask for advice
- Identify main points in a short text about rules and advice
- Recognize statements of advice in a radio show
- Discuss possible solutions to everyday situations, giving reasons and explanations
- Write an email or letter of complaint, giving advice on making improvements

UNIT

13 Ability and Possibility: *Can, Could, Be able to*

MULTILINGUALISM

OUTCOMES
- Express ability and possibility in the past, present, and future
- Identify main points in a social sciences text
- Identify important details in a job interview
- Compare and contrast different possibilities for improving language skills
- Discuss an academic topic
- Write a paragraph about past, present, and future abilities

STEP 1 GRAMMAR IN CONTEXT

BEFORE YOU READ

Look at the photo. Discuss the questions.

1. What do you think a *polyglot* is?
2. Do you recognize any of these languages?
3. Which languages can *you* speak?

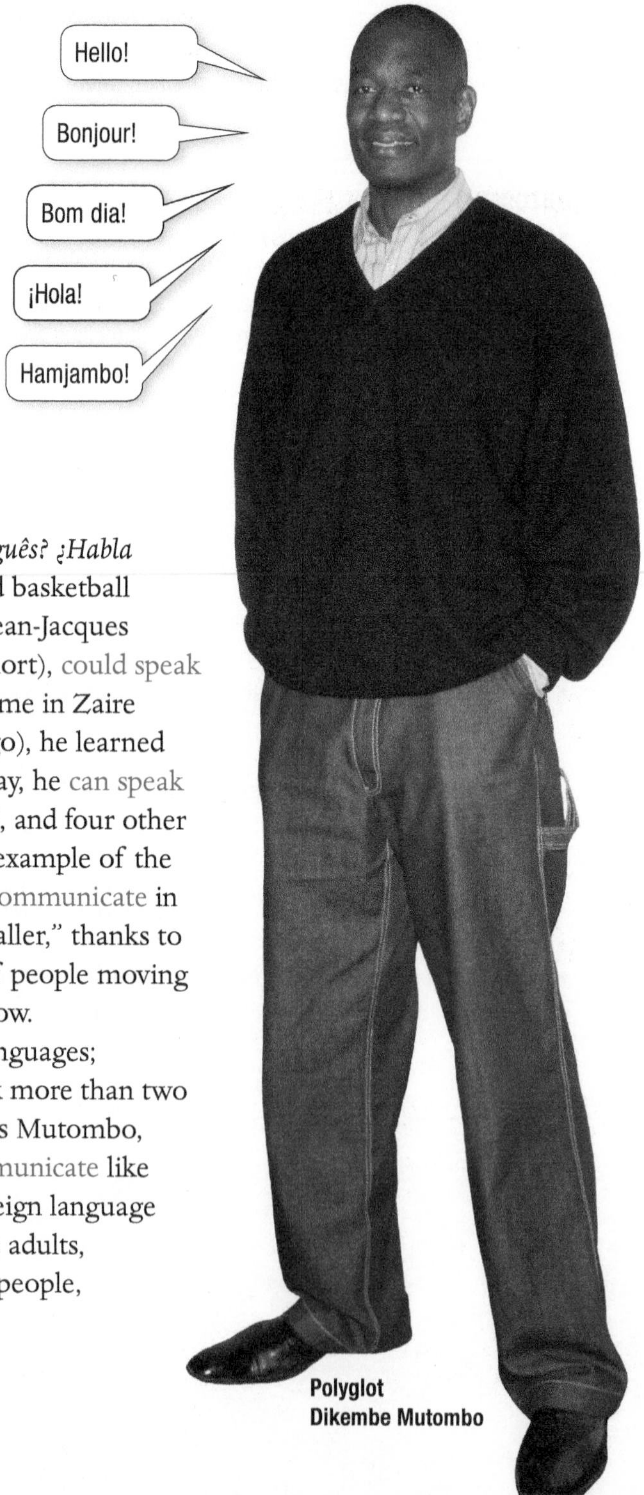

Polyglot
Dikembe Mutombo

READ

13|01 Read this article about multilingualism.

Multilingualism

Do you speak English? Parlez-vous français? Fala português? ¿Habla Usted español? Unaongea Kiswahili? As a child, retired basketball player, Dikembe Mutombo Mpolondo Mukamba Jean-Jacques Wamutombo (known as Dikembe Mutombo for short), could speak several languages. Growing up in a multilingual home in Zaire (today called the Democratic Republic of the Congo), he learned some languages at home and others at school. Today, he can speak nine: English, French, Portuguese, Spanish, Swahili, and four other African languages. Dikembe Mutombo is just one example of the more than 50% of the world population who can communicate in two or more languages. And as the world "gets smaller," thanks to the Internet, increased travel, and large numbers of people moving to other countries, this number will continue to grow.

Bilingualism describes people who speak two languages; *multilingualism* usually describes the ability to speak more than two languages. Being multilingual, or a polyglot, such as Mutombo, does not always mean that a person is able to communicate like a native speaker in each language. In fact, most foreign language speakers, especially people who learn a language as adults, cannot speak like native speakers. The majority of people, even if they become fluent,[1] are not able to totally

1 *fluent:* able to speak or write a language very well

lose their foreign accents, and they will usually make some mistakes when they use the language. But they will be able to communicate well enough to understand and allow people to understand them.

Multilingualism has many advantages in today's world. Speaking other languages can help you get a job in many fields such as tourism, health services, banking, teaching, and sales. And recent research shows that learning a new language can make you smarter and help slow down the signs of aging. But, most of all, learning and knowing other languages can be fun and exciting. You can use your languages when you travel, and you can learn more about other people and cultures. Dikembe Mutombo loves to travel. In an interview with the magazine *Condé Nast Traveler*, he said, "People think of travel for work or play, but it can also be a lesson that will change your life." However, even if you don't travel, you still can enjoy songs, books, and movies in other languages—without ever leaving home.

AFTER YOU READ

A VOCABULARY **Choose the word or phrase that best completes each sentence.**

1. A **retired** language teacher ____.
   a. teaches many classes b. used to teach c. works very hard
2. An **adult** is a person who ____.
   a. is not a child b. is good at languages c. speaks well
3. People do **research** when they want to ____ about a subject.
   a. learn new facts b. forget c. complain
4. One **advantage** of speaking several languages is ____.
   a. a good dictionary b. hard work c. more job opportunities
5. "What **field** are you in?" is a question about your ____.
   a. native language b. occupation c. country
6. If the **majority** of people speak more than one language, this means that ____ are multilingual.
   a. less than 50% b. 50% c. more than 50%

B COMPREHENSION **Circle the correct information to complete each statement.**

1. As a child, Dikembe Mutombo had the ability to speak two / more than two languages.
2. Today, one of the many languages he speaks is French / Chinese.
3. A multilingual person usually speaks / doesn't speak like a native speaker.
4. Most multilingual people lose / don't lose their foreign accent.
5. Knowing other languages helps you in the field of sports / tourism.
6. Learning another language is often enjoyable / difficult.

C DISCUSSION **Work with a partner. Compare your answers in B. Why did you choose each answer?**

STEP 2 GRAMMAR PRESENTATION

ABILITY AND POSSIBILITY: *CAN* AND *COULD*

Statements

Subject	*Can/Could (not)*	Base Form of Verb	
I You He She We You They	**can (not)**	**speak** French	now.
	could (not)		last year.

Contractions

cannot or can not	=	**can't**
could not	=	**couldn't**

Yes/No Questions

Can/Could	Subject	Base Form of Verb
Can	I you he she we you they	**speak** French?
Could		

Short Answers

Affirmative		
Yes,	you I he she you we they	**can.**
		could.

Negative		
No,	you I he she you we they	**can't.**
		couldn't.

***Wh-* Questions**

Wh- Word	*Can/Could*	Subject	Base Form of Verb
How well	**can**	she	**speak** French?
	could	you	

ABILITY AND POSSIBILITY: *BE ABLE TO*

Statements

Subject	*Be*	*(Not) Able to*	Base Form of Verb
I	**am**	**(not) able to**	**practice.**
You	**are**		
He She	**is**		
We You They	**are**		

Yes/No Questions

Be	Subject	*Able to*	Base Form of Verb
Is	she	**able to**	**practice?**
Are	you		

Short Answers

Affirmative		
Yes,	she	**is.**
	I	**am.**

Negative		
No,	she	**isn't.**
	I'm	**not.**

Wh- Questions

Wh- Word	*Be*	Subject	*Able to*	Base Form of Verb
When How often	**is**	she	**able to**	**practice?**
	are	you		

GRAMMAR NOTES

1 *Can, Could, Be able to*: Forms

Can and its past form ***could*** are modals. ***Be able to*** is an expression similar to a modal. Modals are auxiliaries: we use modals with other verbs.

Like all modals, ***can*** and ***could***:

- are followed by the base form of a verb: **modal + base form of verb**

  Marti **can speak** Arabic.
  Marti **could speak** Arabic when he was a child.

- have only **one form** (Do not use *-s* for the third-person singular, and do not add *-s* to the base form of the verb.)

  I **can** speak French, and she **can** speak Arabic.
  NOT She ~~cans~~ speak Arabic.
  NOT She can ~~speaks~~ Arabic.

- form the **negative with *not*** (Do not use *do, does,* or *did.*)

  She **can't** understand me.
  NOT She ~~doesn't can~~ understand me.

- go **before the subject** in **questions** (Do not use *do, does,* or *did.*)

  Can Antonio speak Italian?
  NOT ~~Does~~ can Antonio speak Italian?

Be able to is similar to a modal, but it has different forms (*am, is, are; was, were; will be*).

Was she **able to speak** French as a child?
Will I **be able to learn** French by next year?

IN WRITING ***Can*** and ***could*** are more common in conversation than in writing. ***Be able to*** is more common in formal writing.

A lot of people **can speak** several languages. *(conversation)*
Many people **are able to speak** several languages. *(formal writing)*

2 *Can, Could, Be able to*: Meanings

A modal adds meaning (such as the meaning of ability or possibility) to the verb that follows it. For example, ***can, could***, or ***be able to*** shows that somebody has the **ability** and/or the **possibility** to do something.

• **ability** (natural or learned)	She **can speak**, but she **can't hear**. We **could read**, but we **couldn't write**. Soon, you**'ll be able to write** to me in English.
• **possibility**	You **can take** English as a second language this year. I **couldn't take** it last year. My school didn't offer it. You**'ll be able to take** that course next semester.
Can, could, and ***be able to*** often have both meanings of **ability and possibility**. This is especially true when we use them with a human or animal subject.	I **can help** you study for your French test. *(I have the ability and the possibility to help you.)*
We sometimes use ***can*** with a non-human or non-animal subject, but in this case the meaning is just **possibility**.	Speaking a foreign language **can be** fun. *(It has the possibility of being fun.)*

3 Present Ability or Possibility

Use ***can*** or ***am/is/are able to*** for present ability or possibility.

• ***can***	She **can speak** English, but she **can't speak** French.
• ***am/is/are able to***	She **is able to speak** English, but she **isn't able to speak** French.
USAGE NOTE ***Can*** is very common. It is much more common than *be able to* in everyday **conversation** about present ability.	**Can** you **speak** French? *(more common)* **Are** you **able to speak** French? *(less common)*
USAGE NOTE We often use ***be able to*** when the ability to do something comes after a lot of **hard work**.	French was difficult for me, but now I**'m able to have** a conversation because I spent a year studying in France.

4 Future Ability or Possibility

Use ***can*** or ***will be able to*** for future ability or possibility.

• ***can***	I hope I **can understand** people when I'm in France next month.
• ***will be able to***	I hope I**'ll be able to understand** people when I'm in France next month.
BE CAREFUL! Use ***will be able to*** (not *can*) for things you **learn**.	When I finish this course, I**'ll be able to** speak French well. NOT When I finish this course, I ~~can~~ speak French well.

5 Past Ability or Possibility

Use ***could*** or ***was/were able to*** for past ability or possibility.

• ***could*** • ***was/were able to***	**Could** he **speak** Spanish when he was a child? **Was** he **able to speak** Spanish when he was a child?
BE CAREFUL! Do not use *could* in affirmative statements for a **single event in the past.** Use ***was/were able to.***	After a lot of hard work, they **were able to pass** the French test. NOT . . . they ~~could~~ pass the French test.
However, it is possible to use the negative ***couldn't*** for single past events.	They studied hard, but they **couldn't pass** the test.

REFERENCE NOTES

For ***can*** and ***could*** for **permission**, see Unit 14 on page 191; for **requests**, see Unit 15 on page 204.
For ***can't*** and ***could*** for **present conclusions**, see Unit 32 on page 440.
For ***could*** for **future possibility**, see Unit 31 on page 429.
For a list of **modals and their functions**, see Appendix 19 on page 460.

STEP 3 FOCUSED PRACTICE

EXERCISE 1 DISCOVER THE GRAMMAR

A GRAMMAR NOTES 1–5 **Read this article about two famous polyglots. Underline all the verbs that express ability or possibility.**

Julio Iglesias

Singing in Another Language

What do Spanish-born Julio Iglesias and Canadian-born Celine Dion have in common? They are both world-famous superstars who can sing in many languages. As a young man, Iglesias played football professionally until a serious car accident changed everything. He couldn't walk for two years, and he wasn't able to play football anymore. But he soon discovered that he could sing. Now more than seventy years old, he can still entertain audiences of all ages. He has recorded songs in fourteen languages including French, Portuguese, German, and Japanese. Did he miss football? Maybe, but he's happy with his career. He realized long ago, he said in a recent interview, "I can sing until the end. I won't be able to play football until the end."

Celine Dion

Celine Dion dreamed at an early age of becoming a professional singer, and by the time she was 14, she was able to turn that dream into reality. She entered many singing competitions and was able to take home prizes including the World Music Award for the best-selling female singer of all time. At first, she only sung in her native French, but she took lessons and soon she was able to sing and record in English. Today, she mostly records in French and English, but, like Julio Iglesias, she can also sing in many languages including Spanish, German, Italian, Japanese and Mandarin Chinese. Because of family health problems, she stopped performing for a while. After taking a break from her career, she resumed her schedule. Her fans hope that she will be able to continue entertaining them for many more years.

B Look at the words you underlined in A. Write three sentences about Julio Iglesias and three sentences about Celine Dion. Write one sentence about the present, one sentence about the past, and one sentence about the future.

Julio Iglesias

present: *He can sing in many languages.*

past: ______________________________

future: ______________________________

Celine Dion

present: ______________________________

past: ______________________________

future: ______________________________

EXERCISE 2 STATEMENTS AND QUESTIONS

A GRAMMAR NOTES 2–5 **Some language students are talking in the school cafeteria. Circle the correct words to complete their conversations.**

Conversation 1

A: I heard your sister wants to take Chinese lessons before her trip. (Could she find) / Is she able to find (1.) a class?

B: Yes. In fact, she started classes last month. She can understand a little now, but even with lessons and a lot of practice, she still can say / can't say (2.) very much.

Conversation 2

A: How is Chang doing with his English?

B: Good. He's made a lot of progress. Last semester, he can't order / couldn't order (3.) a meal in a restaurant or talk on the phone. His friends helped him do everything. Now he can speak / could speak (4.) English in a lot of situations. It won't be long before he was able to get / he'll be able to get (5.) a part-time job here.

Conversation 3

A: What about Emma? Was she able to pass / Could she pass (6.) her final exam?

B: Yes, but she had trouble with her presentation because she got so nervous. She really can communicate / can't communicate (7.) well in small groups, but she still doesn't feel comfortable in big ones. She plans to take a course in public speaking.

A: That's good. I'm sure that with her dedication she was able to improve / she'll be able to improve (8.) very quickly.

Conversation 4

A: Can you speak / Could you speak (9.) Russian as a child, Alex?

B: Yes. We spoke it at home, so I'm able to speak / I could speak (10.) it fluently when I was very young.

A: Do your children speak Russian, too?

B: No. Unfortunately, they don't. We always only spoke French at home, so, sadly, they never was able to become / were able to become (11.) really fluent. But they're going to take Russian lessons next year, so I hope that someday they can speak / they'll be able to speak (12.) and understand it. Languages are so important!

13|02 **B** LISTEN AND CHECK **Listen to the conversations and check your answers in A.**

EXERCISE 3 *CAN* AND *COULD*: AFFIRMATIVE AND NEGATIVE STATEMENTS

GRAMMAR NOTES 1–3 **Look at the English Language Ability Checklist. Complete the teacher's comments about Andreas. Use *can*, *can't*, *could*, and *couldn't* and the correct verb from the checklist.**

English Language Ability Checklist

Student: *Andreas Koblin*

	LAST YEAR	NOW
read a newspaper	☑	☑
read a book	☒	☑
write an essay	☑	☑
write an academic paper	☑	☑
understand a movie	☒	☒
understand the words to songs	☒	☑
understand the news on TV	☒	☑
discuss the news with classmates	☒	☑
give a presentation	☒	☒

1. Last year, Andreas *could read* a newspaper in English, but he *couldn't understand* the news on TV.
2. Now, he ____________ the news on TV.
3. Last year, he ____________ the news with his classmates, but now he ____________ the news with other students.
4. Andreas ____________ a book in English now. Last year, he ____________ a book in English.
5. Andreas ____________ an essay now. And he ____________ an academic paper, too.
6. Last year, he ____________ a movie in English. He still ____________ a movie in English today.
7. Now, he ____________ the words to songs in English very well, but last year he ____________ them.
8. Andreas has improved a lot, but he still ____________ a presentation in English. I am sure he will be able to do this with a little more practice.

EXERCISE 4 *CAN*, *COULD*, OR *BE ABLE TO*

GRAMMAR NOTES 1–5 **Complete this FAQ (Frequently Asked Questions) about language learning. Use *can*, *could*, or *be able to* and the correct form of the verb in parentheses. There is often more than one correct answer.**

Can **everyone** ***become*** (1. become) **multilingual?**

Yes. Almost everyone has the ability to learn more than one language, but some people ____________ (2. learn) languages more easily than others.

What are some characteristics of good language learners?

Good learners ______________ (3. tolerate) mistakes. This means they accept mistakes as a natural part of the language-learning process. They don't feel frustrated or get embarrassed. They understand that people learn through mistakes. Good learners also enjoy learning languages. They know that it is hard work, but they also know that after they learn a new language, they ______________ (4. enjoy) many advantages.

What is the best way to learn a language?

There is no one "best way." Polyglot, author, language teacher, and world traveler Susanna Zaraysky says that people ______________ (5. learn) any language anywhere. As an example, she describes how people in post-war Bosnia ______________ (6. practice) their English by listening to weak radio or TV signals. She also strongly believes that listening to music ______________ (7. help) with the learning process. In fact, research shows that singing in a foreign language ______________ (8. assist) people in their fluency and pronunciation.

Does knowing one foreign language help you learn another?

Definitely. People who speak a second language ______________ (9. pick up) a third or fourth language more easily.

I'm studying French this semester. ______________ I ______________ (10. learn) Italian more easily next semester?

Yes. Especially because French and Italian have a lot in common—similar vocabulary for example. But even if the third language is unrelated to the second, as with Spanish and Chinese, it helps to have the experience of "learning to learn" another language.

What about age? Can people learn at any age?

Yes, again. Most people find it much easier to learn when they are younger, but people ______________ (11. acquire) a new language at any age. I had a student who, after a lot of hard work, ______________ (12. learn) Portuguese when she was 82. She ______________ (13. not lose) her accent, but today she ______________ (14. communicate) with Portuguese language speakers when she travels.

EXERCISE 5 EDITING

GRAMMAR NOTES 1–5 **Read these postings from an online language-learning message board. There are ten mistakes in the use of *can*, *could*, and *be able to*. The first mistake is already corrected. Find and correct nine more.**

I just read an article about polyglot Dikembe Mutombo. It's an amazing story. When he first went to the United States, he was able to speak French and several other languages, but he couldn't ~~spoke~~ speak a word of English. He studied six hours a day and soon he is able to join in discussions in his classes at Georgetown University. He was also able become a professional basketball player—something he never really planned to do. Today, he can speak nine languages, and he is able to help a lot of people with the money he made as a star basketball player! —Martha O'Neill, Canada

I grew up in Finland, where children learn at least two foreign languages. By the time I was 18, I was able speaking Finnish, Swedish, English, and German. I'm studying Russian now. Last week, I could get an A on my final exam. And in a few years, I can speak my fourth foreign language. I think everyone should learn foreign languages! —Matias Laine, Finland

In India, we grow up speaking many languages. I was born in Bangalore. As a child, I spoke Gujarati at home with my parents. In school, I also learned Kannada (the state language) and India's two official languages (Hindi and English). As a result, today I able to communicate in four languages. —Tanvi Patel, India

My mother could understands both English and Spanish, but she only spoke Spanish with me. I never really knew if she couldn't speak English or if she just didn't want to. It had an advantage for me, though. I learned English at school at an early age, but I was also able to keep my family's native language. Now, I'm fluent in both languages. —Lia Gomez, USA

Here in Europe, we generally learn more than one language because there are so many different countries close together. As a result, we can often communicate with other Europeans when we travel. When I went to Germany last year, I were able to speak to the people there and I learned a lot about their country. That wasn't true on my trip to Hungary, though. Hungarian is very different from French. I can't understand a word when I was there! —Philippe Michaud, France

STEP 4 COMMUNICATION PRACTICE

EXERCISE 6 LISTENING

13|03 **A** Karl is interviewing for the job of office assistant at Lang's Language Lab, a school that teaches foreign languages. Look at the list of job skills and other job requirements. Then listen to the interview. Listen again and check (✓) all the things Karl says he can do now.

Lang's Language Lab

FULL-TIME OFFICE ASSISTANT wanted for busy language school. Must be friendly and speak fluent English. Other languages a definite plus! Computer skills important. Contact us at 555-TALK.

- ☑ **1.** answer the phones
- ☐ **2.** greet visitors to the school
- ☐ **3.** speak fluent English
- ☐ **4.** speak other languages
- ☐ **5.** do word processing
- ☐ **6.** do Excel spreadsheets
- ☐ **7.** type 50 words per minute
- ☐ **8.** design a monthly newsletter
- ☐ **9.** order office supplies
- ☐ **10.** work weekends

13|03 **B** Work with a partner. Listen to the interview again. Do you think Karl is a good person for this job? Why or why not? Discuss your answers.

EXAMPLE: A: Well, he seems pretty friendly. That's important for the job.
B: I agree. I think he'll be able to get along well with the students. But will he be able to . . . ?

EXERCISE 7 WHAT ABOUT YOU?

A CONVERSATION Before you talk about your abilities in English, complete the English Language Ability Checklist. Use your own information. Check (✓) things you *could do last year* and/or *can do now*. Put an ✗ next to things you *couldn't do last year* and/or *can't do now*.

English Language Ability Checklist

Student: ______________________

	LAST YEAR	NOW
read a newspaper	☐	☐
read a book	☐	☐
write an essay	☐	☐
write an academic paper	☐	☐
understand a movie	☐	☐
understand the words to songs	☐	☐
understand the news on TV	☐	☐
discuss the news with classmates	☐	☐
give a presentation	☐	☐

B Work with a partner. Ask and answer questions about your abilities in English. Give examples. Use *can, can't, could, couldn't* or the correct form of *be able to*.

EXAMPLE: A: Can you read a newspaper in English?
B: Sometimes. It all depends on the topic. Sometimes I can understand it, but sometimes I can't. For example, I can understand articles about soccer because I know the vocabulary, but I'm not really able to understand scientific articles very well. What about you?
A: It's the same with me. What about movies? Can you . . . ?

EXERCISE 8 LANGUAGE LEARNING TIPS

PROBLEM SOLVING **Work in a group. Look at the list of language learning skills in the box. What can you do to improve your skills? Think of as many suggestions as possible. Make a list of tips. Compare your list of tips with another group's.**

SKILLS
- listening comprehension
- grammar
- pronunciation
- reading
- vocabulary
- writing

EXAMPLE: A: For listening comprehension, you can listen to a lot of TV.
B: You can also listen to songs. The more you listen, the more you'll be able to understand!
C: You can also . . .

EXERCISE 9 A WORLD OF ADVANTAGES

A BRAINSTORMING **Work in a group. Brainstorm advantages of being multilingual. Think about the topics in the list below.**

EXAMPLE: A: You can get a better job.
B: You can talk to customers in their own language.
C: You can . . .

TOPICS
- employment
- travel
- social life
- free-time activities
- politics
- health
- *Other:* ____________

B Compare your answers with those of the rest of the class.

EXAMPLE: A: We said languages can help you get a better job.
B: We said that, too. If you're multilingual, you can get specific types of jobs, too.
C: Right. You can become a translator, for example.

FROM GRAMMAR TO WRITING

A BEFORE YOU WRITE Think about your English. How has it changed? How hasn't it changed? What are your hopes for the future? Complete the outline about your English language abilities.

Past Abilities	Present Abilities	Future Abilities
______________	______________	______________
______________	______________	______________
______________	______________	______________

B WRITE Use your outline to write a paragraph about your English abilities. Compare your language ability now to your abilities at some time in the past. What do you think you'll be able to do in the future that you can't do now? Include examples. Try to avoid the common mistakes in the chart.

EXAMPLE: When I first came to this country five years ago, I couldn't speak a word of English. I wasn't able to . . . and I couldn't . . . Now, I can do many things that I couldn't do then. For example, I can . . . I hope in the future, I will be able to . . .

Common Mistakes in Using *Can*, *Could*, and *Be able to* for Ability or Possibility

Use the **base form** of the verb after ***can*** or ***could***. Do not add *-s* to the base form after *he*, *she*, or *it*.	She **can speak** Arabic. NOT She can ~~speaks~~ Arabic.
Use ***will be able to*** for things you **learn**. Do not use *can*.	Next year, **I'll be able to speak** Russian. NOT Next year, I ~~can speak~~ Russian.
Use ***was/were able to*** for a **single event in the past**. Do not use *could*.	Last year, I **was able to get** an A in Spanish. NOT Last year, I ~~could get~~ an A in Spanish.

C CHECK YOUR WORK Read your paragraph. Circle all the verbs with *can* or *could*. Underline all the verbs that use a form of *be able to*. Use the Editing Checklist to check your work.

Editing Checklist

Did you use . . . ?

- ☐ the base form of the verb after *can* or *could*
- ☐ *can*, *can't*, or *am able to* for present ability
- ☐ *can* or *will be able to* for future ability
- ☐ *could* or *was able to* for past ability
- ☐ *was able to* for a single past event

D REVISE YOUR WORK Read your paragraph again. Can you improve your writing? Make changes if necessary. Give your paragraph a title.

UNIT 13 **REVIEW**

Test yourself on the grammar of the unit.

A Circle the correct words to complete the sentences.

1. How many languages can she speak / speaks?
2. After a lot of studying, Stefan could / was able to get an A on his Russian test.
3. Keep practicing and soon you can / will be able to understand the TV news.
4. Sorry, but I can't / couldn't help you with your Spanish homework right now.
5. I can't / couldn't understand the movie. They spoke too fast.

B Complete the paragraph with *can*, *could*, or *be able to* and the verbs in parentheses. Choose between affirmative and negative. There is often more than one correct answer.

As a child, Lia Romano ___Was able to speak___ (1. speak) two languages fluently—English and Italian. Then, in high school, she studied French, and after a few years, she ___Was able to win___ (2. win) an award for "Best Foreign Language Learner." Last year, she took Chinese classes, and now she ___can speak___ (3. speak) a little. But she ___can't write___ (4. write). It's still too difficult for her. She's really working very hard, though, and she believes that with some more practice, she ___can improve___ (5. improve) soon. Lia hopes she ___can travel___ (6. travel) to China some day, but right now she ___can't afford___ (7. afford) the air fare. She just got a part-time job, so she hopes that after she saves some money, she ___can make___ (8. make) the trip. Last summer, she went to Cuba. Because she speaks Italian, she ___Was able to communicate___ (9. communicate) well enough to get along. It was a great experience, and Lia hopes she ___can visit___ (10. visit) other countries soon.

C Find and correct five mistakes.

A: I can't ~~to see~~ see the board. The guy in front of me is very tall.

B: Let's change seats. ~~You be~~ You'll be able to see from this seat.

A: Thanks. I don't want to miss anything. I ~~no can~~ can't believe what a great teacher Ms. Acosta is.

B: I know. My sister had her last semester. She ~~could~~ was able to get an A on her final exam!

A: ~~Were~~ Was your sister able to speak any Spanish before taking that class?

B: No. She couldn't speak a word!

A: That's amazing!

Now check your answers on page 478.

UNIT

14

Permission: *Can, Could, May, Do you mind if*

ROOMMATES

OUTCOMES

- Ask for, give, or deny permission
- Identify main points in a short reading
- Recognize when a speaker gives permission or refuses permission
- Come to a resolution with others by asking for and giving permission to do something
- Write a short note, explaining a situation and asking for permission to do something

STEP 1 GRAMMAR IN CONTEXT

BEFORE YOU READ

Look at the cartoon and at the title of the article. Discuss the questions.

1. Where are these people?
2. What is their relationship?
3. How are they getting along? Why?

READ

14|01 **Read this article about getting along with a roommate.**

Always Ask First

Heather immediately liked Tara, her neat, non-smoking college roommate. Their first week together was great. But the second week, the cookies from Heather's mother disappeared. Tara didn't ask Heather, "Could I have one?" She just assumed it was all right. Tara's friends always helped themselves to[1] food without asking for permission. The third week, Heather was halfway out the door when she asked Tara, "Can I wear your new jacket today?" She was already wearing it. Tara was angry, but she stayed calm and answered, "Sorry, but I was planning on wearing it today." The fourth week, Tara looked annoyed whenever Heather's friends stopped by to visit. Heather never asked Tara, "Hey, do you mind if they hang out here for a while?" At

1 *helped themselves to:* took without asking for permission

home, Heather's friends were always welcome. By October, Heather and Tara weren't talking. Luckily, their dorm counselor was able to help them fix their relationship with three simple rules.

1. Always ask for permission before you touch your roommate's stuff. Say: "My computer isn't working. Could I use yours for a few hours?"
2. Establish times when it's OK to have visitors. If it's not "visiting hours," ask for your roommate's permission: "Can Luis and Ming-Hwa work here tonight? We're doing a presentation in class tomorrow."
3. Try to solve problems. Say: "Your music is too loud for me, but you can borrow my headphones."

Follow these guidelines, and who knows? You may gain a happier roommate *and* a good friend.

AFTER YOU READ

A VOCABULARY **Complete the sentences with the words from the box.**

annoyed	assumed	established	gained	guidelines	presentation

1. Ahmed is ________________ at his roommate for using his computer without asking first.

2. We didn't get any ________________ for our science report. Could you please give us some instructions?

3. I just ________________ it was OK to eat the cookies because you left them on the table.

4. We ________________ those rules when we became roommates. That means we both agreed to follow them.

5. For his class ________________, Raoul showed a video about getting along with roommates.

6. I ________________ a better understanding of relationships from my roommate.

B COMPREHENSION **Read the statements. Check (✓) *True* or *False*.**

	True	False
1. Tara didn't ask for permission before taking Heather's cookies.	☐	☐
2. Tara's friends never asked for permission before taking food.	☐	☐
3. Heather asked for permission to wear Tara's jacket.	☐	☐
4. Tara gave Heather permission to wear her jacket.	☐	☐
5. Heather asked for permission before her friends visited.	☐	☐

C DISCUSSION **Work with a partner. Compare your answers in B. Why did you check *True* or *False*?**

STEP 2 GRAMMAR PRESENTATION

PERMISSION: *CAN, COULD, MAY, DO YOU MIND IF*

Yes/No Questions: *Can/Could/May*

*Can/Could/May**	Subject	Base Form of Verb	
Can **Could** **May**	I he she we they	**stay**	here?

Short Answers

Affirmative	Negative
Certainly. Of course. Sure. No problem.	Sorry, but . . .

* *Can, could,* and *may* are modals. Modals have only one form. They do not have *-s* in the third-person singular.

Wh- Questions: *Can/Could/May*

Wh- Word	*Can/Could/May*	Subject	Base Form of Verb
When	**can** **could** **may**	I he she we they	**call?**

Statements: *Can/May*

Subject	*Can/May (not)*	Base Form of Verb	
You He She	**can** (**not**) **may** (**not**)	**stay**	here.

Contractions*

cannot or can not	=	**can't**

* There is no contraction for ***may not***.

Questions: *Do you mind if*

Do you mind if	Subject	Verb	
Do you mind if	I we they	**stay**	here?
	he she it	**stays**	

Short Answers

Affirmative	Negative
Not at all. **No,** I **don't**. Go right ahead.	Sorry, but . . .

GRAMMAR NOTES

1 *Can, Could, May*

Use the modals ***can***, ***could***, and ***may*** to ask for **permission**.

• *can* • *could* • *may*	**Can** I **borrow** your book? LESS FORMAL **Could** he **come** tomorrow? ↕ **May** we **leave**, Professor Lee? MORE FORMAL *(student speaking to teacher)*
USAGE NOTE ***May*** is not very common. It is much **more formal** and polite than *can* and *could*. We sometimes use it when we are speaking to a person in authority (for example, a teacher, police officer, doctor, librarian, counselor, etc.).	
USAGE NOTE We often use ***please*** when we ask for permission. Notice the word order.	**Could** I **ask** a question, ***please***? or **Could** I ***please*** **ask** a question?
Could refers to the **present** or the **future**. It does not refer to the past (even though *could* is the past form of *can*).	**Could** I **call** you ***tomorrow***?
IN WRITING **Asking for permission** is much more common in **conversation** than in writing, but you can ask for permission in **informal notes**, **emails**, and **text messages**.	**Can** I **make** an appointment to discuss my presentation with you? *(conversation)* Hi Professor Chin. **Could** I **make** an appointment to discuss my presentation with you? *(note/email)*

2 Answers

There are **several ways to answer** when someone asks for permission.

When we **give permission**, we usually use **informal expressions** instead of modals in answers.	A: **Could** I close the window? B: ***Sure.*** or ***Of course.*** or ***Go ahead.***
When we use a **modal** in an **affirmative answer**, we almost always use ***can***. We do not use *could*, and we rarely use *may* in short answers.	A: **Could** I borrow this pencil? B: ***Yes***, of course you **can**. NOT Yes, of course you ~~could~~. A: **May** I please see your notes? B: ***Sure*** you **can**. or ***Yes***, you **may**. *(rare)*
USAGE NOTE When we **refuse permission**, we usually **apologize** and give an **explanation**.	A: **Can** I please use your computer? B: ***I'm sorry***, ***but*** I need it today.
USAGE NOTE *No, you can't* and *No, you may not* are **not common** answers, and they don't sound polite. People sometimes use these short negative answers when they are angry. And adults sometimes use them when talking to children.	A: **Can** I wear your new sweater? B: ***No, you can't!*** I haven't even worn it yet! A: Mommy, **can** I have ice cream for breakfast? B: ***No, you can't.***

3 Do you mind if

Use the expression ***do you mind if*** to ask for permission when an **action may annoy** or inconvenience someone.

Use the **simple present** of the verb after ***do you mind if***.	A: **Do you mind if** he ***cleans up*** later? B: No, I don't. He can do it tomorrow.
BE CAREFUL! Do not use ***please*** with *do you mind if*.	**Do you mind if** I **ask** a question? NOT Do you mind if I ask a question ~~please~~?
BE CAREFUL! When we **give permission**, we use ***Not at all*** or ***No, I don't***, but we're really saying: *It's OK.*	A: **Do you mind if** Ian comes over tonight? B: ***Not at all.*** or ***No, I don't.*** *(It's OK for Ian to come over tonight.)*
When we **refuse permission**, we can use ***Yes, I do***, but we're really saying: *It's not OK.*	B: ***Yes, I do.*** *(It's not OK for Ian to come over tonight.)*
USAGE NOTE It's **not common** to refuse permission with ***Yes, I do***. As with questions with *can, could,* and *may*, when we refuse permission to a question with ***do you mind if***, we usually **apologize** and give an **explanation**.	A: **Do you mind if** Ian comes over tonight? B: ***Sorry***, ***but*** I have to study tonight.
IN WRITING As with *can, could,* and *may*, ***do you mind if*** is much more common in **conversation** than in writing, but you can use it in **informal notes, emails**, and **text messages**.	Hi. **Do you mind if** I **invite** Paulo to have dinner with us tomorrow night? *(email)*

REFERENCE NOTES

For general information on **modals**, see Unit 13, Grammar Notes 1–2, on page 177.

For ***can*** and ***could*** for **ability and possibility**, see Unit 13 on page 176; for **requests**, see Unit 15 on page 204.

For ***could*** and ***may*** for **future possibility**, see Unit 31 on page 429; for **present conclusions**, see Unit 32 on page 440.

For a list of **modals and their functions**, see Appendix 19 on page 460.

STEP 3 FOCUSED PRACTICE

EXERCISE 1 DISCOVER THE GRAMMAR

GRAMMAR NOTES 1–3 Read the quiz. Underline all the modals and expressions for permission. Then if you'd like to, you can take the quiz. The answers are below.

Are You a Good Roommate?

Take this short quiz and find out.

1. You want to use your roommate's computer.
You say:
○ **a.** I may use your computer tonight.
○ **b.** Can I use your computer tonight?
○ **c.** I'm using your computer tonight.

2. You don't have any food in the house.
You say:
○ **a.** Can you make dinner for me?
○ **b.** I don't mind eating some of your food.
○ **c.** Do you mind if I have some of your food?

3. You may not have time to wash the dishes tonight.
You say:
○ **a.** Could you wash the dishes?
○ **b.** I can't wash the dishes.
○ **c.** Can I wash the dishes tomorrow?

4. Your roommate asks you: "Could my best friend stay overnight?"
You answer:
○ **a.** Can she stay in a hotel instead?
○ **b.** Sure she can!
○ **c.** I'm sure she could, but I don't want her to!

5. You can find nothing to wear to the party next Friday.
You say:
○ **a.** Could I borrow your new sweater?
○ **b.** I may borrow your new sweater.
○ **c.** You could lend me your new sweater.

6. You want to hang your favorite poster in your dorm room.
You say:
○ **a.** Could I hang my poster here?
○ **b.** Maybe you could hang my poster here.
○ **c.** I assume I can hang my poster here.

ANSWERS: 1. b, 2. c, 3. c, 4. b, 5. a, 6. a

EXERCISE 2 QUESTIONS AND ANSWERS

GRAMMAR NOTES 1–3 **Look at the signs. Complete each question and answer. Use the words in parentheses and the correct pronouns. Write appropriate short answers. There can be more than one correct short answer.**

1. PIERRE: <u>Do you mind if</u> I <u>eat</u> my lunch here while I get on the Internet? I'll be neat.
a. (do you mind if / eat)

ASSISTANT: <u>Sorry</u>. Please look at the sign.
b.

2. SÉBASTIEN: Those guys next door are making a lot of noise!

__________ they __________ that?
a. (can / do)

NATHANIEL: __________. They aren't going to gain any friends that way, but according to the guidelines, it's OK to play music now. It's 8:00 a.m.
b.

SÉBASTIEN: Well, __________ I __________ your earplugs? I have to prepare for my English presentation.
c. (can / borrow)

3. CARMEN: __________ we __________ our bikes on this path?
a. (may / ride)

GUARD: __________.
b.

4. DONOVAN: __________ I __________ my dog next semester? My roommate doesn't mind.
a. (could / bring)

COUNSELOR: __________. But some of the other dorms allow pets.
b.

5. GABRIELLE: __________ I __________ my cell phone in here?
a. (may / use)

LIBRARIAN: __________. People get really annoyed by cell phone conversations.
b.

EXERCISE 3 QUESTIONS AND ANSWERS

GRAMMAR NOTES 1–3 **Heather and her roommate Tara are planning a party in Kent Hall. Use the words in parentheses to ask for permission. Answer the questions.**

1. Tara's friend Troy is in town. She wants him to come to the party.

   TARA: *Do you mind if Troy comes to the party?*
   (do you mind if)

   HEATHER: *Not at all.* I'd love to meet him.

2. Heather wants to borrow her roommate's black sweater.

   HEATHER: I have nothing to wear. ______________________
   (can)

   TARA: ______________________ I'm planning to wear it myself!

3. Tara's sister is coming from out of town. Tara wants her to stay in their room.

   TARA: ______________________
   (do you mind if)

   HEATHER: ______________________ She can sleep on the couch.

4. Heather and Tara would like to have the party in the dormitory lounge. Heather asks her dormitory counselor for permission.

   HEATHER: ______________________
   (may)

   COUNSELOR: ______________________ It's available next Friday. We just have to establish some guidelines.

5. Heather and Tara would like to hang decorations from the ceiling of the lounge.

   HEATHER: ______________________
   (could)

   COUNSELOR: ______________________ Fire regulations won't allow it.

6. Heather and Tara want the party to go until midnight.

   HEATHER: ______________________
   (could)

   COUNSELOR: ______________________ Quiet hours start at 11:00 on Friday.

7. Tara wants to play some of her friend Erica's CDs at the party.

   TARA: ______________________
   (could)

   ERICA: ______________________ Which ones should I bring?

8. It's Friday night. A student wants to study in the lounge.

   STUDENT: ______________________
   (can)

   HEATHER: ______________________ We're having a party. Want to join us?

EXERCISE 4 EDITING

GRAMMAR NOTES 1–3 Read Sharif's English test. There are seven mistakes in the use of *can*, *could*, *may*, and *do you mind if*. The first mistake is already corrected. Find and correct six more.

Class: *English 102*

Name: *Sharif Halabi*

Directions: These conversations take place on a train. Find and correct the mistakes.

1. A: May we board the train now?

   B: Sorry, you ~~couldn't~~ *can't* board until 12:30.

2. A: Can he comes on the train with me?

   B: Sorry. Only passengers can board.

3. A: Do you mind if I'm sitting here?

   B: No, I don't. My friend is sitting here.

4. A: Could I looked at your newspaper?

   B: Yes, of course you could.

5. A: Do you mind if my son play his computer game?

   B: No, not at all. It won't disturb me.

   A: Thanks.

   B: No problem.

STEP 4 COMMUNICATION PRACTICE

EXERCISE 5 LISTENING

14|02 **A** Listen to seven short conversations. For each one, check (✓) *Permission Given* or *Permission Refused*.

	Permission Given	Permission Refused
Conversation 1	☑	☐
Conversation 2	☐	☐
Conversation 3	☐	☐
Conversation 4	☐	☐
Conversation 5	☐	☐
Conversation 6	☐	☐
Conversation 7	☐	☐

14|02 **B** Work with a partner. Read the list of people. Listen again to the conversations. Decide who is speaking. What do you think their relationship is? Match each conversation with the correct people.

EXAMPLE: A: So, Conversation 1 is between a driver and a police officer.
B: Yes. The driver is very polite. She uses "may." It's clear she's speaking to an authority figure like a police officer. So what about Conversation 2?

Conversation	People
d 1.	a. roommate and roommate
____ 2.	b. child and parent
____ 3.	c. travel agent and customer
____ 4.	~~d.~~ driver and police officer
____ 5.	e. boyfriend and girlfriend's mother
____ 6.	f. employee and employer
____ 7.	g. student and teacher

EXERCISE 6 DO YOU MIND IF . . . ?

BRAINSTORMING Work in a group. Read each situation and decide what to say. Think of as many things to say as possible.

1. You have a small apartment. Two of your friends are coming to visit your town for a week, and they want to stay with you. What can you say to your roommate?

   EXAMPLE: A: Do you mind if Anton and Eva stay here for a week?
   B: Could Anton practice his guitar in the evening?
   C: Can Eva keep her bike in the hall?

2. You're visiting some good friends. The weather is very cold, but they don't seem to mind. Their windows are open and the heat is off. You're freezing.

3. You're at a concert with some friends. You like the performer very much. You have your smartphone with you and you'd like to take some photos or maybe a short video. Sometimes this performer talks to fans and signs programs after the concert.
4. You have formed a study group with some classmates. You want to use a classroom on Thursday evenings to study. Some of your classmates come directly from work. They would like to eat their dinner in the classroom. What can you say to your teacher?

EXERCISE 7 COULD I . . . ?

ROLE PLAY **Work with a partner. Read the situations. Take turns being Student A and Student B.**

	Student A	Student B
1.	You were absent from class yesterday. Student B, your classmate, always takes good notes.	Student A is in your class. You're always willing to help your classmates.

EXAMPLE: A: Can I copy your notes from class yesterday?
B: Sure. Here they are.
A: Could I call you tonight if I have questions?
B: Of course. I'll give you my number.

	Student A	Student B
2.	You're at work. You have a terrible headache. Student B is your boss.	Student A is your employee. You have a lot of work for Student A to do today.
3.	You're a teenager. You and your friend want to travel to another city to see a concert. Student B is your father/mother. You want to borrow his or her car. Your friend has a license and wants to drive.	Student A is your son/daughter. You like this friend, and you have no objection to lending him or her the car. However, you want the friend to be careful.
4.	Student B has invited you to a small party. At the last minute, your two cousins show up. They have nothing to do the night of the party.	Your party is a small party for a few of your close friends. It's also at a restaurant, and you have already arranged for a certain number of people to attend.

FROM GRAMMAR TO WRITING

A BEFORE YOU WRITE **Think of two situations for which you need to write a short note asking for permission. Complete the outline.**

EXAMPLE: My computer isn't working. I want to borrow my roommate's laptop.

	Situation	Reason you will ask for permission
1.	______________________	______________________
2.	______________________	______________________

B WRITE **Use the information from your outline to write two notes asking for permission. Then exchange notes with two classmates. Write answers to your classmates' notes. Try to avoid the common mistakes in the chart.**

EXAMPLE:

Ana, my computer isn't working. I have to write a report for my class tomorrow. Could I please borrow your laptop? —Melissa	Sorry, Melissa. I can't lend you my laptop. I'm going home for the weekend, and I'm taking my laptop with me. —Ana

Common Mistakes in Using *Can, Could, May,* and *Do you mind if* for Permission

Use the **base form** of the verb after ***can***, ***could***, or ***may***. Do not add *-s* to the base form after *he*, *she*, or *it*.	**Can** my roommate **come** with us? NOT Can my roommate ~~comes~~ with us?
To be **more polite**, use ***please*** with ***can***, ***could***, or ***may***. Do not use ***please*** with *do you mind if*.	**Could** I ***please*** borrow your notes? NOT Do you mind if I borrow your notes~~, please~~?
Use **informal expressions** in **answers**. Do not use *can*, *could*, or *may*.	A: **Can** my roommate come with us? B: ***Of course.*** NOT ~~Yes, he can.~~

C CHECK YOUR WORK **Read your four notes. Circle all the modals or expressions that ask for permission. Underline all the informal expressions in your answers. Use the Editing Checklist to check your work.**

Editing Checklist

Did you use . . . ?

- ☐ the base form of the verb after *can, could,* or *may*
- ☐ *do you mind if* when an action may annoy or inconvenience someone
- ☐ *please* with *can, could,* or *may* (but not with *do you mind if*) to be more polite
- ☐ informal expressions in your answers
- ☐ an apology and an explanation if you refused permission

D REVISE YOUR WORK **Read your notes again. Can you improve your writing? Make changes if necessary.**

UNIT 14 **REVIEW**

Test yourself on the grammar of the unit.

A **Circle the correct words to complete the questions.**

1. Can my roommate come / comes to class with me?
2. Could / Do you mind if I call you at home?
3. Could I borrow / borrowed a pen?
4. Do you mind if / when I ask a question?
5. May I shut please / please shut the door?

B **Read the situations in parentheses. Complete the questions to ask for permission.**

1. Could ____?
(You want to borrow a pen.)
2. Can ____?
(Your sister wants to leave.)
3. Do you mind if ____?
(You want to open a window.)
4. Could ____?
(You and a friend want to come early.)
5. May ____?
(You want to ask a question.)

C **Find and correct ten mistakes.**

1. A: Do you mind if I changed the date of our next meeting?
   B: Yes, I do. When would you like to meet?
2. A: Could I calling you tonight?
   B: Sorry, but you couldn't. I won't be home.
3. A: Mom, I may have some more ice cream?
   B: No, you mayn't. You've already had a lot. You'll get sick.
4. A: Do you mind if my son turn on the TV?
   B: Not at all. I can't study with the TV on.
5. A: Can my sister borrows your bike?
   B: Could I letting you know tomorrow?
   A: Sure. No problem.

Now check your answers on page 478.

UNIT 15

Requests: *Can, Could, Will, Would, Would you mind*

MESSAGES

OUTCOMES
- Make and respond to requests
- Identify important details related to requests in emails and text messages
- Identify details related to a schedule in a conversation
- Discuss a daily schedule that involves making requests of others
- Write and respond to a request in a text or email message

STEP 1 GRAMMAR IN CONTEXT

BEFORE YOU READ

Look at the title of the text messages and the emails. Discuss the questions.

1. What do you think the title means?
2. Why do people use abbreviations in text messages?
3. Do you prefer text messages or emails? Why?

READ

15|01 Read these text messages between Marta and her mother. Then read the emails to Marta from her boss and from Marta to her assistant.

Messages 4 u!

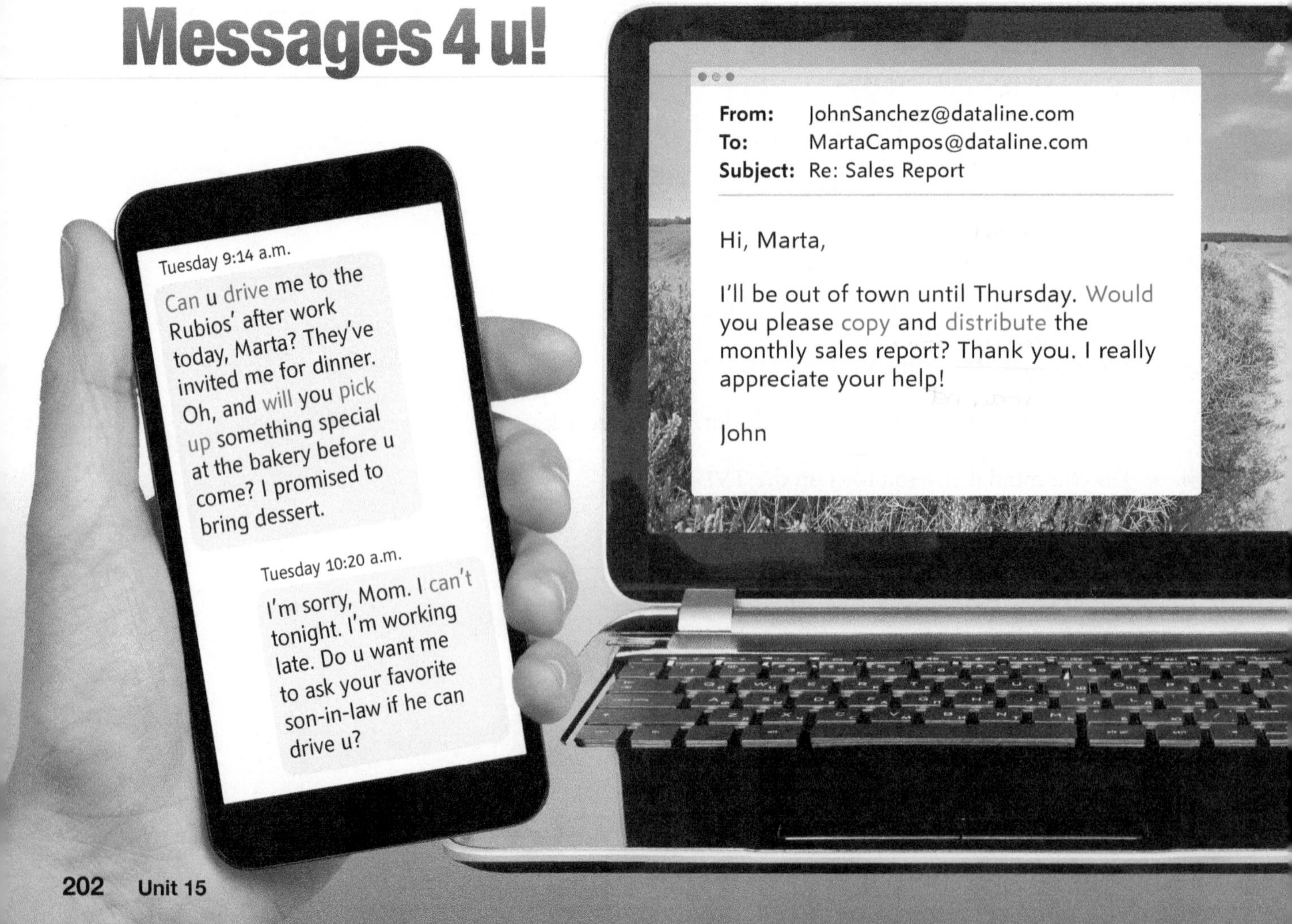

AFTER YOU READ

A VOCABULARY **Choose the word or phrase that best completes each sentence.**

1. A **request** is a polite way of _____ something.
a. asking for **b.** doing **c.** answering

2. When you **deliver** a report, you _____ it to someone.
a. promise **b.** describe **c.** bring

3. When you **respond** to a message you give a(n) _____.
a. answer **b.** report **c.** opinion

4. When a question is **urgent**, you need to react to it _____.
a. carefully **b.** immediately **c.** slowly

5. When you **distribute** reports, you _____ one to each person in a group.
a. give **b.** read **c.** talk about

6. When you **appreciate** what someone does for you, you feel _____.
a. worried **b.** sorry **c.** thankful

B COMPREHENSION **Read the statements. Check (✓) *True* or *False*.**

	True	False
1. Marta's mother made three requests to her daughter.	☐	☐
2. Marta's mother needs a ride.	☐	☐
3. Marta is going to drive her.	☐	☐
4. John is going to copy and distribute the sales report.	☐	☐
5. Marta wants Ann to give her the copies of the sales report.	☐	☐
6. Marta wants to know how her boss responds to a request.	☐	☐

C DISCUSSION **Work with a partner. Compare your answers in B. Why did you check *True* or *False*?**

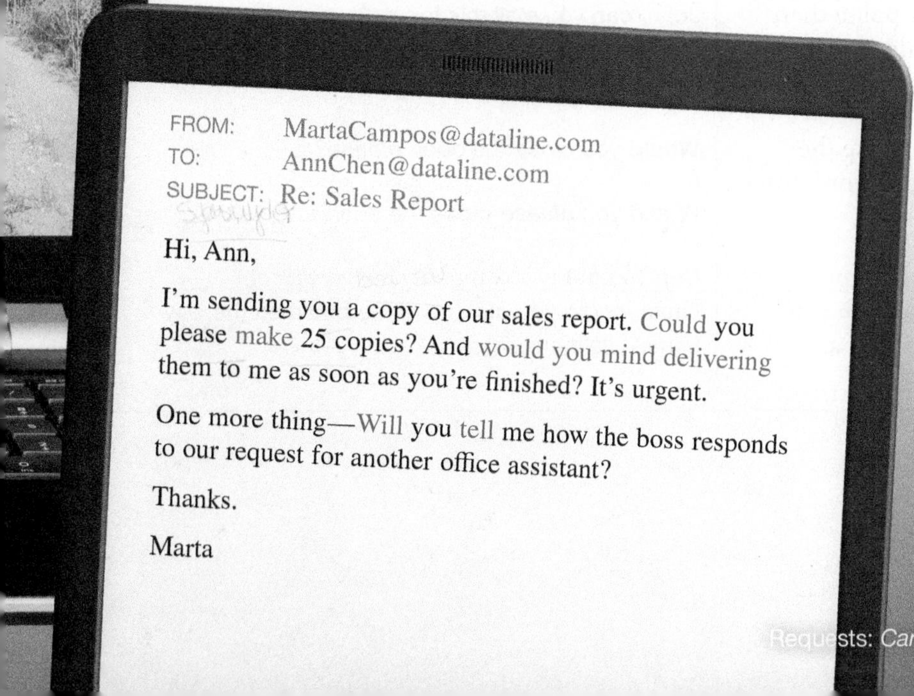

FROM: MartaCampos@dataline.com
TO: AnnChen@dataline.com
SUBJECT: Re: Sales Report

Hi, Ann,

I'm sending you a copy of our sales report. Could you please make 25 copies? And would you mind delivering them to me as soon as you're finished? It's urgent.

One more thing—Will you tell me how the boss responds to our request for another office assistant?

Thanks.

Marta

STEP 2 GRAMMAR PRESENTATION

REQUESTS: *CAN, COULD, WILL, WOULD, WOULD YOU MIND*

Questions: *Can/Could/Will/Would*

*Can/Could/Will/Would**	*You*	Base Form of Verb	
Can **Could** **Will** **Would**	you	**distribute**	this report for me?
		drive	me to the doctor?
		pick up	some groceries?

Short Answers

Affirmative	Negative	
Sure. Certainly. No problem. Of course. I'd be glad to.	I'm sorry, (but)	**I can't.**
	I'm afraid	

* *Can, could, will,* and *would* are modals. Modals do not have *-s* in the third-person singular.

Questions: *Would you mind*

Would you mind	Gerund	
Would you mind	**distributing**	this report for me?
	driving	me to the doctor?
	picking up	some groceries?

Short Answers

Affirmative	Negative	
Not at all. I'd be glad to. No problem. Of course not.	I'm sorry, (but)	**I can't.**
	I'm afraid	

GRAMMAR NOTES

1 *Can, Could, Will, Would*

Use the modals ***can***, ***could***, ***will***, and ***would*** to make a **request**.

- ***can***
- ***could***
- ***will***
- ***would***

Can you **email** me?
Could you **copy** Danica?
Will you **call** me tomorrow?
Would you **remind** me to call Mason?

USAGE NOTE ***Could*** and ***would*** are more polite than *can* and *will*. We use *could* and *would* to soften requests.

John, **can** you mail this for me?
Ms. Lee, **could** you mail this for me? *(more polite)*

USAGE NOTE You can also use ***please*** to make the request even more polite. Notice the word order.

Would you **close** the door, ***please***?
or
Would you ***please*** **close** the door?

IN WRITING **Requests** are much more common in **conversation** than in writing, but you can use requests in **informal notes**, **emails**, and **text messages**.

Can you **get** two oranges? *(conversation)*
Laura, **could** you **pick up** some bread on the way home? *(text message)*

2 Answers

There are **several ways to respond** to requests.

In **affirmative answers** to requests, we usually use expressions such as ***sure***, ***of course***, ***certainly***, ***I'd be glad to***, and ***no problem***.	A: **Would** you **shut** the window, please? B: ***Sure.*** or ***Of course.*** or ***Certainly.***
USAGE NOTE *Certainly* and *I'd be glad to* are more formal than other answers. *No problem* is the least formal.	A: Dan, **could** you **help** me carry these books? B: ***I'd be glad to***, Professor Chin. *(more formal)* A: **Can** you **lend** me your pen? B: **No problem.** *(least formal)*
USAGE NOTE In **negative answers**, we usually **apologize** and give an **explanation**.	A: **Could** you **deliver** this to Ron, please? B: ***I'm sorry***, ***but*** I **can't.** I'm expecting a client.
BE CAREFUL! Do not use *would* or *could* in response to polite requests.	NOT Sure I ~~would~~. NOT I'm sorry, but I ~~couldn't~~.

3 *Would you mind*

We also use the expression ***would you mind*** to make **polite requests**.

Use a **gerund** (verb + *-ing*) after ***would you mind***.	**Would you mind *making*** a copy of the report?
Would you mind is even more polite than *could* or *would*.	A: **Would you mind waiting**? Mr. Caras is in a meeting.
BE CAREFUL! When we answer this type of request with ***Not at all*** or ***Of course not***, it means that we will do what the person requests.	B: ***Not at all.*** or ***Of course not.*** *(OK. I'll do it.)*
USAGE NOTE In **negative answers**, we usually **apologize** and give an **explanation**.	C: ***I'm sorry***, I **can't.** I have another appointment in a half an hour.

PRONUNCIATION NOTE

15|02 **Pronunciation of *Could you, Would you, Will you, Can you***

In **informal conversation**, we often pronounce ***could you***, ***would you***, ***will you***, and ***can you*** as "couldja," "wouldja," "willya," and "canya."	A: **Could you** mail this for me? *(couldja)* B: Sure. **Would you** remind me later? *(wouldja)* A: **Will you** type this for me? *(willya)* B: No problem. **Can you** leave it on my desk? *(canya)*

REFERENCE NOTES

For general information on **modals**, see Unit 13, Grammar Notes 1–2, on page 177.
For *can* and *could* for **ability and possibility**, see Unit 13 on page 176; for **permission**, see Unit 14 on page 191.
For *can't* and *could* for **present conclusions**, see Unit 32 on page 440.
For *could* for **future possibility**, see Unit 31 on page 429.
For *will* for the **future**, see Unit 6 on page 76 and Unit 7 on page 93.
For a list of **modals and their functions**, see Appendix 19 on page 460.

STEP 3 FOCUSED PRACTICE

EXERCISE 1 DISCOVER THE GRAMMAR

GRAMMAR NOTES 1–3 **Raul's roommate, Emil, is having problems today. Underline Emil's requests. Then choose the appropriate response to each request.**

1. Raul, would you please drive me to Cal's Computer Shop? I have to bring my computer in.
  a. Yes, I would. (**b.**) I'd be glad to.

2. Would you mind lending me five dollars? I'm getting paid tomorrow.
  a. Not at all. **b.** Yes.

3. Raul, can you lend me your laptop for a minute? I have to email my teacher.
  a. Sorry, but I can't. **b.** No, I can't.

4. Will you pick up some milk on the way home this afternoon?
  a. No, I won't. **b.** I'm sorry, I can't. I'll be at work until 8:00.

5. Would you explain this text message from Kora? She uses weird abbreviations.
  a. I'd be glad to. **b.** No, I wouldn't.

6. Could you text me Jana's address? I lost it.
  a. No, I couldn't. **b.** Sorry, but I don't have it.

7. I'm in a real hurry. Will you help me do the dishes?
  a. Certainly. **b.** Of course not.

8. Could you lock the door on your way out? My hands are full.
  a. Yes, I could. **b.** Sure.

9. Kora, can you tell Ethan to come to the phone? It's important.
  a. No problem. **b.** Not at all.

EXERCISE 2 REQUESTS

A GRAMMAR NOTES 1, 3 Look at the pictures. What is each person thinking? Write the letter of the correct thought from the box.

a. Repair the copier.	~~d. File these reports.~~	g. Buy some cereal.
b. Call back later.	e. Shut the door.	h. Wait for a few minutes.
c. Get that book.	f. Close the window.	i. Wash your cups and dishes.

1. _d_

2. ____

3. ____

4. ____

5. ____

6. ____

7. ____

8. ____

9. ____

B What are the people in the pictures in A going to say? Complete their requests. Use the words in parentheses and the information from the pictures.

1. ___Could you file these reports, please?___ I've finished reading them.
(could)
2. ______________________ I can't think with all that noise in the hall.
(would)
3. ______________________ on the way home? We don't have any left.
(will)
4. ______________________ It's freezing in here.
(can)
5. ______________________ Mr. Rivera is still in a meeting.
(would you mind)
6. ______________________ It's getting messy in here.
(would you mind)
7. ______________________ I have to leave for a meeting now.
(could)
8. ______________________ I can't reach it.
(can)
9. ______________________ I need to make copies right away.
(could)

EXERCISE 3 REQUESTS AND ANSWERS

GRAMMAR NOTES 1–3 **Write polite requests. Use *can*, *could*, *will*, *would*, or *would you mind* and the correct form of the words in parentheses. Write appropriate answers. There can be more than one correct answer.**

1. MAN: ___Would you mind lending me your phone___? The battery in mine is dead.
a. (lend me your phone)

WOMAN: ___No problem___. But I'm in a hurry.
b.

______________________?
c. (please / keep your conversation short)

MAN: ______________________. I just need to text my friend.
d.

2. STUDENT: Excuse me, Professor Ruiz. ______________________?
a. (explain reflexive pronouns)

I don't understand them.

PROFESSOR: ______________________ right now. I'm expecting a call.
b.

______________________?
c. (come back in 20 minutes)

3. WOMAN: ______________________? It's blocking my driveway.
a. (move your car)

MAN: ______________________. I'll do it right away. I'm really
b.

sorry. I didn't notice.

4. MANAGER: ______________________? Our sales people need it for their
a. (please / distribute this report)

meeting this afternoon.

ASSISTANT: ______________________. I can't leave my desk right now.
b.

But I can ask Tania to do it.

EXERCISE 4 *COULD YOU, WOULD YOU (MIND), WILL YOU, CAN YOU*

15|03 PRONUNCIATION NOTE Listen to the short informal conversations. What do you hear? Complete the requests with *could you*, *would you (mind)*, *will you*, and *can you*.

1. ____Could you____ lend me some money?
2. ________________ call me when you get home?
3. ________________ turning the TV down?
4. ________________ explain the meaning of this word to me?
5. ________________ give me a ride home?
6. ________________ help me carry these books?

EXERCISE 5 EDITING

GRAMMAR NOTES 1–3 Read Marta's response to an email from her boss. (Her answers are in red.) There are eight mistakes in making and responding to requests. The first mistake is already corrected. Find and correct seven more.

Date: 04-11-16 12:14:39 EST
From: MartaCampos@dataline.com
To: JohnSanchez@dataline.com
CC: AnnChen@dataline.com
Subject: sales meeting—Reply

>>><JohnSanchez@dataline.com> 04/11/16 10:37 am>>>

The meetings are going well, but they are going to go on an extra day. Could you ~~call please~~ *please call* Doug Rogers to try to reschedule our sales meeting?

Not at all. I'll do it right away.

We'll need three extra copies of the monthly sales report. Would you ask Ann to take care of that?

Yes, I would. (Ann—could you do this?)

I won't have time to return Emma Lopes's call this week. Would you mind to call her and telling her I'll call her back next week?

No problem. Could you email me her phone number?

I hate to ask, but will you mind working on Saturday? We'll need the extra time to go over the new information I've gotten.

Sorry, but I couldn't. My in-laws are coming for a visit. But Rob Lin says he can come into the office to help out.

One last thing. I was going to pick up those new business cards, but I won't be back in time. Would you mind asking the printer to deliver them to the office? I'd really appreciate that.

Yes, I would. I'll call and ask him to do it right away.

And this will cheer you up—it looks like our office will receive the award for Communication Excellence this year.

Great! Can I told everyone, or is it a secret?

STEP 4 COMMUNICATION PRACTICE

EXERCISE 6 LISTENING

15|04 **A** Marta Campos has planned a busy weekend. Read the list. Then listen to the conversations. Listen again and check (✓) the things that belong on her schedule.

- ☐ **1.** drive Kevin to the library Saturday morning
- ☑ **2.** take Diana to the dentist
- ☐ **3.** take the kids to the library in the afternoon
- ☐ **4.** babysit for Amanda's daughter
- ☐ **5.** go to Amanda's party
- ☐ **6.** go to the movies
- ☐ **7.** walk Mom's dog
- ☐ **8.** pick up the car at the garage
- ☐ **9.** go to the gym with John

15|04 **B** Work with a partner. Listen again to the conversations. Discuss your answers in A. Why did or why didn't you check each item?

EXAMPLE: A: I didn't check item 1.
B: Right. Kevin asked his mother to drive him, but she answered, "Sorry, I can't."
A: She's taking Diana to the dentist.

EXERCISE 7 WHAT ABOUT YOU?

A CONVERSATION **Before you talk about your plans for the weekend, fill out your schedule.**

B **Work in a group. Talk about your weekend plans. Ask group members to help you with some of the things on your schedule.**

EXAMPLE: A: Ali, what are you doing Saturday afternoon?
B: I want to go to the mall, but my car broke down. Could you give me a ride?
C: Sure, I'd be glad to . . .

EXERCISE 8 COULD YOU . . . ?

ROLE PLAY **Work with a partner. Look at the pictures in Exercise 2. Role-play each situation. Take turns making and responding to requests. Use your imagination.**

EXAMPLE: A: Could you please file these reports for me?
B: Sure. I'll be glad to in just a minute. I need to file this one first before I lose it.
A: OK. Thanks.

FROM GRAMMAR TO WRITING

A BEFORE YOU WRITE **Read the three situations below. Work with a partner. Brainstorm several requests for each situation.**

1. Your roommate is going away for the weekend. Your sister from out of town will be visiting you. What can you ask your roommate?
2. You work at a restaurant on Mondays, Wednesdays, and Fridays. You have to go to the dentist, but the dentist can only see you on Wednesday. What can you ask a coworker?
3. You're in school. You have to leave class early in order to help your parents. What can you ask a classmate?

B WRITE **For each situation, write a text or email message making one or more requests. Use ideas from your brainstorming sessions. Then exchange messages with a partner. Write responses to your partner's requests. Try to avoid the common mistakes in the chart.**

EXAMPLE:

Hi Viktor. My sister is visiting tomorrow. Could you please lend her your bike for a ride in the park? Thanks. —Kunio	Hi Kunio. I'm really sorry, but I can't. My bike broke down this week. You can rent a bike in the park, though. —Viktor

Common Mistakes Using *Can*, *Could*, *Will*, *Would*, and *Would you mind* for Requests

Use the **base form** of the verb after ***can***, ***could***, ***will***, or ***would***. Do not use the gerund.	**Will** you **make** copies for me? NOT Will you ~~making~~ copies for me?
Put ***please*** **before the base form** of the verb or at the **end of the sentence**. Do not put *please* after the base form.	Could you ***please*** **send** me an email? Could you **send** me an email ***please***? NOT Could you ~~send please~~ me an email?
Use the **gerund** (verb + *-ing*) after ***would you mind***. Do not use the base form of the verb.	Would you mind **texting** me? NOT Would you mind ~~text~~ me?

C CHECK YOUR WORK **Read your six messages. Underline all the modals and expressions for requests. Circle *please*. Use the Editing Checklist to check your work.**

Editing Checklist

Did you use . . . ?

- ☐ the base form of the verb after *can, could, will,* or *would*
- ☐ the gerund after *would you mind . . .*
- ☐ *please* correctly
- ☐ an apology and explanation in a negative answer to a request

D REVISE YOUR WORK **Read your messages again. Can you improve your writing? Make changes if necessary.**

UNIT 15 **REVIEW**

Test yourself on the grammar of the unit.

A Circle the correct words to complete the conversations.

1. A: Would you mind to turn / turning off the TV? I'm trying to read.
   a.
   B: Yes, I would. / I'm sorry, I can't. I need to watch the news for a homework assignment.
   b.
2. A: Will you please text / text please me when you get home?
   a.
   B: Not at all. / No problem. I'll probably be home by nine.
   b.
3. A: Could you picked / pick up some dessert on the way home?
   a.
   B: I'd be glad to. / Yes, I could. How about ice cream?
   b.

B Read the statements in parentheses. Then complete the questions to make requests.

1. Would you mind ______________________________?
   (Please lend me five dollars.)
2. Could ______________________________?
   (I'd like you to drive me to school.)
3. Will ______________________________?
   (Please explain this sentence to me.)
4. Can ______________________________?
   (I'd like you to carry this suitcase for me.)
5. Would ______________________________?
   (Please distribute the report.)
6. Would you mind ______________________________?
   (I'd like you to walk the dog tonight.)

C Find and correct eight mistakes.

1. JASON: Hi, Tessa. It's Jason. Could you taking some photos of the game today?

   TESSA: Sorry, Jason, but I couldn't. My camera is broken. Maybe Jeri can help.

2. JASON: Hi, Jeri. Would you came to the game today? I need someone to take photos.

   JERI: Jason, can you mind calling me back in a few minutes? I'm busy right now.

   JASON: Sorry, Jeri, I can't, but I'll email you. Would you give me please your email address?

   JERI: Not at all. It's Rainbows@local.net.

3. JERI: Hi, Jason, it's Jeri. I'm sending you those photos. You could call me when you get them?

   JASON: Thanks, Jeri. The photos are great. Now, will teach me how to put them on Facebook?

Now check your answers on page 478.

UNIT 16

Advice: *Should, Ought to, Had better*

INTERNET RULES

OUTCOMES
- Give and ask for advice
- Identify main points in a short text about rules and advice
- Recognize statements of advice in a radio show
- Discuss possible solutions to everyday situations, giving reasons and explanations
- Write an email or letter of complaint, giving advice on making improvements

STEP 1 GRAMMAR IN CONTEXT

BEFORE YOU READ

How do you communicate with people on the Internet? Discuss the questions.

1. Is it important to be polite on the Internet? Why or why not?
2. Do you behave differently online than face-to-face with people?
3. What are some rules you follow?

READ

16|01 **Read this article about being polite on the Internet. If you don't understand a cyber[1] word, look up its meaning on the next page.**

Netiquette 101

Email, bulletin boards, and chat rooms open up a new world of communication—and sometimes misunderstanding. To avoid problems, you should know these simple rules of netiquette:

- When should you post to a bulletin board or chat room? Newbies shouldn't jump in right away—they really ought to lurk a little first. Look through old messages for answers to common questions. Many websites also have FAQs for basic information. After that, post when you have something new to say. You should keep your post short and simple.
- Should you use capital letters to make a strong statement? NO! A MESSAGE ALL IN CAPITAL LETTERS SEEMS LIKE SHOUTING. You should follow the normal rules for capital (big) and lowercase (small) letters.

- Did someone make you angry? Wait a minute! You'd better not reply right away. Count to 10 first. Don't flame another board or chat room member. You should never forget that people on the Internet are real people with real feelings.
- Emoticons can help avoid misunderstandings. You should learn how to use them to show your feelings.
- Internet safety is part of netiquette. When you post to a bulletin board or a chat room, you should always protect your identity by using a screen name. Never give your real name or other personal information.

Practice these five rules of netiquette, and most of your emoticons will be smileys! ☺

1 *cyber:* about computers or the Internet

Cyber Words

bulletin board an Internet site where members can post ideas about a special interest

chat room a site for online conversations in "real" time

emoticon a picture of a feeling, for example: 

FAQs Frequently Asked Questions

flame to send insulting messages to someone

lurk to read messages on a bulletin board but not post any messages

netiquette Internet etiquette (rules for polite behavior)

newbie (or newb) someone new to an Internet site

post to send messages to a bulletin board or chat room

AFTER YOU READ

A VOCABULARY **Complete the sentences with the words from the box.**

avoid	behavior	communication	identity	normal	protect

1. Never give your real ________________ in a chat room. Always use a screen name.
2. It's ________________ for newbies to lurk on a site before they post. Many people do that.
3. ________________ websites where members flame other members.
4. Emoticons improve your online ________________. They show your feelings.
5. People's ________________ in chat rooms is often different from how they act in real life.
6. ________________ yourself on the Internet. Never tell anyone your passwords.

B COMPREHENSION **Read the statements. Check (✓) *OK* or *Not OK*.**

	OK	Not OK
1. Read some messages before you post.	☐	☐
2. Reply immediately when you're angry.	☐	☐
3. Use all capital letters in your posts.	☐	☐
4. Use emoticons to show feelings.	☐	☐
5. Use your real name in chat rooms.	☐	☐
6. Write long, complicated messages.	☐	☐
7. Think about people's feelings when you post a message.	☐	☐

C DISCUSSION **Work with a partner. Compare your answers in B. Why did you check *OK* or *Not OK*?**

STEP 2 GRAMMAR PRESENTATION

ADVICE: *SHOULD, OUGHT TO, HAD BETTER*

Statements

Subject	*Should / Ought to / Had better**	Base Form of Verb
I You He She We You They	**should (not)** **ought to** **had better (not)**	**reply**.

* *Should* and *ought to* are modals. *Had better* is similar to a modal.
These forms do not have *-s* in the third-person singular.

Contractions

should not	=	**shouldn't**
had better	=	**'d better**

***Yes / No* Questions**

Should	Subject	Base Form of Verb
Should	I he she we they	**reply**?

Short Answers

Affirmative			Negative		
Yes,	you he she you they	**should**.	**No**,	you he she you they	**shouldn't**.

***Wh-* Questions**

Wh- Word	*Should*	Subject	Base Form of Verb	
How When Where	**should**	I he she we they	**send**	it?

GRAMMAR NOTES

1 *Should* and *Ought to*

Use the modals ***should*** and ***ought to*** to say that something is **advisable** (a good idea).

• ***should*** • ***ought to***	Derek **should answer** that email. You **ought to send** Mia a copy, too.
USAGE NOTE ***Should*** is much more **common** than *ought to* in conversation.	You **should check out** this website!
IN WRITING ***Should*** is common in both informal and formal writing.	You **should post** some of your vacation photos. *(email)* Internet users **should be** aware of proper Internet etiquette. *(newspaper)*
USAGE NOTE We often soften advice with ***maybe***, ***perhaps***, or ***I think***.	Ryan, ***maybe*** you **should spend** less time on the Internet.

2 *Had better*

Use the expression ***had better*** for **strong advice**—when you believe that something bad will happen if the person does not follow the advice.

• ***had better***	Kids, you**'d better get** offline now or you won't have time for your homework.
USAGE NOTE We mostly use the expression ***had better*** in **conversation**, and we usually use the contraction ***'d better***. The full form *had better* is very formal.	You**'d better** choose a screen name. *(common)* You **had better** choose a screen name. *(rare)*
Had better always refers to the **present** or the **future**. It never refers to the past (even though it uses the word *had*).	You**'d better call** them ***now***. They're waiting. You**'d better post** that ***tomorrow*** or it'll be late.

3 Negative Statements

Use ***should not*** and ***had better not*** in negative statements.

The negative of ***should*** is ***should not*** or ***shouldn't***.	You **shouldn't post** right away.
The negative of ***had better*** is ***had better not*** or ***'d better not***. Notice the word order.	You**'d better not use** your real name. NOT You~~'d not better~~ use your real name.
USAGE NOTE We do not usually use the negative of ***ought to*** in American English. We use ***shouldn't*** instead.	We **shouldn't** post long messages. We **ought not to** post long messages. *(rare)*

4 Questions and Short Answers

Use ***should*** for questions. We do not usually use *ought to* or *had better* for questions.	
• ***should***	When **should** I **sign on**?
Use ***should*** to ask for advice.	A: **Should** I **join** this chat room?
USAGE NOTE You can use ***should*** in **short answers**, but we often use other **expressions**.	B: Yes, you **should**. It's fun. C: ***Sure. Why not?*** D: ***Not really.*** It's a waste of time.

PRONUNCIATION NOTE

16|02 **Pronunciation of *Ought to* and *Had better***

In **informal conversation**, we often pronounce ***ought to*** "oughta." Notice that the "t" in "oughta" sounds like a quick "d."	A: I **ought to get** a new computer. *(I oughta get)*
For ***had better***, we usually pronounce ***had*** as the contraction ***'d***, and sometimes we leave out ***had*** and just say "better."	B: You **had better get** a flash drive, too. *(You'd better get* or *You better get)*

REFERENCE NOTES

For general information on **modals**, see Unit 13, Grammar Notes 1–2, on page 177.
For a list of **modals and their functions**, see Appendix 19 on page 460.

STEP 3 FOCUSED PRACTICE

EXERCISE 1 DISCOVER THE GRAMMAR

A GRAMMAR NOTES 1–4 **Read these posts to an online bulletin board for high school students. Underline the words that give or ask for advice.**

Subject: HELP!

From: Hothead

MY BRAIN IS EXPLODING!!! SAVE ME!! What should I do? I'm taking all honors courses this year, and I'm on the debate team, in the school congress, and on the soccer team. OH! And, I'd better not forget piano lessons! I'm so busy I shouldn't even be online now.

From: Tweety

First of all, you should stop shouting. You'll feel better. Then you really ought to ask yourself, "Why am I doing all this?" Is it for you, or are you trying to please somebody else?

From: Loki

Tweety's right, Hothead. Do you really want to do all that stuff? No? You'd better not do it then. You'll burn out before you graduate.

From: gud4me

You're such a loser. You should get a life. I mean a NORMAL life. Do you have any friends? Do you ever just sit around and do nothing?

From: Tweety

Hey, gud4me, no flaming allowed! That's bad cyber behavior. We really shouldn't fight—it never helps communication.

B **Check all the advice from the posts in A.**

- ☐ **1.** Take all honors courses.
- ☑ **2.** Stop shouting.
- ☐ **3.** Feel better.
- ☐ **4.** Don't do things you don't want to do.
- ☐ **5.** Get a life.
- ☐ **6.** Don't fight.

EXERCISE 2 STATEMENTS WITH *SHOULD*, *OUGHT TO*, AND *HAD BETTER*

GRAMMAR NOTES 1–3 **Read these posts to a chat room about learning English. Complete the posts. Use the correct form (affirmative or negative) of the words in parentheses. Use contractions when possible.**

CURLY: I think I ___should watch___ more movies to improve my English. Any ideas?
1. (should / watch)

USEDIT: I loved *The Uninvited*. But you ___had better not rent___ it if you don't like scary films.
2. (had better / rent)

AGURL: That's right. And you ___had better keep___ the remote in your hand. That way you can fast-forward through the scary parts.
3. (had better / keep)

592XY: I think you ___ought to see___ *Groundhog Day*. The same thing happens again and again. It's an old movie, but it's great listening practice—and it's funny!
4. (ought to / see)

PATI: You ___should turn on___ the English subtitles. They really help.
5. (should / turn on)

USEDIT: But you ___shouldn't use___ the subtitles right away. At first, you really
6. (should / use)

___should listen___ a few times. That's what rewind buttons are for!
7. (should / listen)

592XY: Good advice. And you really ___ought to read___ a plot summary before you watch. You can find one online. It's so much easier when you know the story.
8. (ought to / read)

AGURL: Curly, you're a math major, right? Then you really ___ought to watch___ my favorite movie, *The Da Vinci Code*. It's about solving a mystery with math clues.
9. (ought to / watch)

CURLY: Thanks, guys. Those are great ideas. But you ___had better not give___ me any more advice, or I'll never work on my other courses!
10. (had better / give)

EXERCISE 3 STATEMENTS WITH *SHOULD*, *OUGHT TO*, AND *HAD BETTER*

GRAMMAR NOTES 1–3 **Rewrite the Internet safety tips in parentheses. Use *should*, *ought to*, or *had better*. Choose between affirmative and negative.**

The Internet is a wonderful place to visit and hang out. Here are some tips to make your trip there a safe one!

1. I often use my real name online. Is that a problem?

Yes! ___You should always use a screen name.___
(Always use a screen name.)

Protect your identity!

2. Someone in my chat group just asked for my address.

___You had better not give out any personal information___
(Don't give out any personal information.)

People can use it to steal your identity and your money.

3. **My brother wants my password to check out a group before joining.**

You shouldn't give it to anyone
(Don't give it to anyone.)

Not even your brother! He might share it, and then people can steal your information.

4. **I sent a file to someone, and she told me it had a virus.**

You had better not get virus protection and use it
(Get virus protection and use it.)

A virus can hurt your computer and destroy important files (and other people's too).

5. **I update my virus protection every month. Is that really necessary?**

Yes! You ought to always keep your protection up-to-date
(Always keep your virus protection up-to-date.)

Program it to update automatically. Remember: *Old* virus protection is *no* virus protection!

6. **I got an email about a home-based business. I could make $15,000 a month.**

You had better not believe any "get rich quick" offers
(Don't believe any "get rich quick" offers.)

They sound good, but people almost always lose money.

7. **I got an interesting email. I don't know who sent it, but it's got a file attached.**

You shouldn't open any email from strangers
(Don't open any email attachments from strangers.)

They could contain dangerous viruses.

8. **The Internet sounds too dangerous for me!**

Not really. You ought to be careful ,
(Be careful!)

but enjoy yourself—it's an exciting world out there!

EXERCISE 4 QUESTIONS AND SHORT ANSWERS WITH *SHOULD*

GRAMMAR NOTE 4 **Complete these posts to an online bulletin board. Use the words from the box to complete the questions. Give short answers.**

buy one online	forward the email	~~try to repair it~~
check the spelling	say to make them stop	use emoticons
flame him	start posting	use my birthday

1. **Q:** My computer is seven years old and has problems. Should I try to repair it ?

   A: No, you shouldn't . That's very old for a computer! Buy a new one!

2. **Q:** I just joined an online discussion group. When ______________________? Right away?

   A: You should really just read for a while. It's always a good idea to "lurk" before you post.

3. **Q:** I just received a warning about a computer virus. The email says to tell everyone I know about it. ______________________?

   A: ______________________. These warnings are almost always false.

4. **Q:** I hate to go shopping, but I really need a jacket. ______________________?

   A: ______________________. It's safe. Just buy from a company you know.

5. Q: I type fast and make spelling mistakes. Is that bad? ______________________?

A: ______________________. Use a spell checker! Mistakes are bad netiquette!

6. Q: My friends email me a lot of jokes. I don't want to hurt their feelings, but I *really* don't want to keep getting these jokes. What ______________________?

A: You should be honest and say you are too busy to read them. These jokes can waste an awful lot of time!

7. Q: I always forget my password. ______________________ so I don't forget?

A: ______________________. It's too easy to guess. Protect your identity.

8. Q: A newb on our board is asking dumb questions. ______________________?

A: ______________________! Your behavior should be as polite online as offline.

9. Q: ______________________ in emails? Those smileys are awfully cute.

A: Sure, go ahead. They're fun. But don't use them in business emails.

EXERCISE 5 *OUGHT TO* OR *OUGHTA*; *HAD BETTER* OR *BETTER*

16|03 PRONUNCIATION NOTE Listen to the sentences. Check (✓) *More Formal* if you hear *ought to* or *had better*. Check (✓) *Less Formal* if you hear "oughta" or "better."

	More Formal	Less Formal
1. Do you think I ought to buy a new computer?	☐	☑
2. I think you had better get good virus protection.	☐	☐
3. Maybe you ought to get a tablet.	☐	☐
4. You had better read some reviews.	☐	☐
5. Do you think I ought to wait until next month?	☐	☐
6. I really think you had better get one now.	☐	☐

EXERCISE 6 EDITING

GRAMMAR NOTES 1–4 **Read these posts to a bulletin board for international students in the United States. There are twelve mistakes in the use of *should*, *ought to*, and *had better*. The first mistake is already corrected. Find and correct eleven more.**

Comments

Justme | My friend asked me to dinner, and she told me I should ~~to bring~~ bring some food! What kind of an invitation is that? What I should bring to this strange dinner party?

Sasha | LOL![1] The invitation is totally normal. Your friend is having a potluck—a dinner party where everybody brings something. It's really a lot of fun. You know, you really ought bring a dish from your country. People will enjoy that.

Toby | HELP! My first day of class, and I lost my wallet! What ought I do first? My student ID, credit card, and cash are all gone.

R2D2 | First of all, you'd not better panic because you need to be calm so you can speak clearly. You should to call your credit card company right away. Did you lose your wallet at school? Then you ought to going to the Lost and Found Department at your school.

Smiley | What should an international student does to make friends? At my college, people always smile and say, "Hi, how are you?" but they don't wait for an answer!

4gud | New students should joining some clubs and international student organizations. They also ought to find a student in each class to study with and ask about homework assignments.

Newguy | Hi. I'm new to this board. I'm from Vietnam, and I'm going to school in Canada next year. How should I will get ready?

Smiley | Welcome Newguy! I'm at school in Montreal, and you won't believe how cold it gets here. You're better bring a lot of warm clothes!

Sasha | You ought check the school's website. They might have a Vietnam Students Association. If they do, you should email the association with your questions. Good luck!

1 *LOL:* abbreviation for *Laughing out Loud*

STEP 4 COMMUNICATION PRACTICE

EXERCISE 7 LISTENING

16|04 **A** A radio show host, Tim Tommando, is giving advice to callers about buying a new computer. Listen to the show. Then read the advice in the list. Listen again and check (✓) the statements that agree with the host's advice.

- ☐ **1.** Repair a seven-year-old computer.
- ☑ **2.** Read online computer reviews.
- ☐ **3.** Throw away your old computer.
- ☐ **4.** Always buy the cheapest computer.
- ☐ **5.** Order a computer from a big online company.
- ☐ **6.** Shop at a local computer store.
- ☐ **7.** Consider a service contract.
- ☐ **8.** Get the most memory you can afford.

16|04 **B** Listen to the show again. Work with a partner. First, compare your answers in A. Then, discuss Tim's advice. Do you agree with the advice?

EXAMPLE: A: Tim says you shouldn't repair a seven-year-old computer.
B: I agree. You shouldn't repair an old computer. You should buy a new one even if your old one is still working. You should always have the newest technology.
A: I don't agree. I think you should keep using your computer as long as it lasts.

EXERCISE 8 WHAT SHOULD I DO?

PROBLEM SOLVING **Work in a group. Each group member chooses a problem to ask the group about. Group members discuss the problem and give advice.**

1. I was studying for exams, and I forgot my girlfriend's birthday. She's really angry at me. What should I do?

EXAMPLE: A: You'd better send flowers and take her to a nice restaurant.
B: I think you should apologize and tell her you were really busy.
C: Yes, but you'd better not just send her an email or text. Call her!
D: And in the future, you really should use one of those online apps that remind you about important events. You'll never forget again.

2. My boss emails me jokes that aren't really funny. Should I email back and say they're funny?

3. I sent an email to a friend. I thought it was a private communication between him and me, but he forwarded it to other people. I was really embarrassed. Was he wrong in forwarding it without asking me? Should I say something to him?

4. I have some friends that constantly send me "instant messages" when I'm online. I know they are just being friendly, but these interruptions annoy me when I'm working at my computer. What should I do? I don't want to hurt their feelings.

5. I work during the day and go to school at night. I don't have much time to go out. How do I make new friends? Should I join online interest groups?

EXERCISE 9 THEY REALLY OUGHT TO DO SOMETHING!

PICTURE DISCUSSION **Work with a partner. Look at a classroom at the EFL Computer Training Institute. Give advice for ways to improve the institute. Then compare your ideas with the ideas of another pair.**

EXAMPLE: A: They should empty the trash.
B: Yes, and they really ought to . . .

FROM GRAMMAR TO WRITING

A BEFORE YOU WRITE **Look again at the picture in Exercise 9. Make a list of four problems.**

1. ______________________________
2. ______________________________
3. ______________________________
4. ______________________________

B WRITE **Use your list to write an email to Mr. Thompson, the owner of the school. Give him advice on improvements the institute should make. Use *First*, *Second*, *In addition*, and *Finally*, to introduce each improvement. Try to avoid the common mistakes in the chart.**

EXAMPLE: Dear Mr. Thompson:

I am a student at the EFL Computer Training Institute. My classes are very good, but the Institute really should make some improvements. First, I really think someone should repair the copier. It's been broken for weeks. Second, . . . In addition, . . . Finally, . . .

Common Mistakes in Using *Should*, *Ought to*, and *Had better* for Advice

Use the **base form** of the verb after ***should***, ***ought to***, or ***had better***. Do not add *-s* to the base form after *he*, *she*, or *it*.	Someone **should repair** the copier. NOT Someone should ~~repairs~~ the copier.
Use ***ought to*** and ***had better*** in **formal writing**. Do not use *oughta* and *better*.	You **ought to** make these repairs right away. NOT You ~~oughta~~ make these repairs right away. You**'d better** do this before someone gets hurt. NOT You ~~better~~ do this before someone gets hurt.
Use ***should*** with ***maybe***, ***perhaps***, or ***I think*** to be more polite.	I ***think*** someone **should make** these repairs immediately. *(more polite)*

C CHECK YOUR WORK **Read your email. Underline all the words and expressions that give advice. Circle words or expressions that make the advice more polite. Use the Editing Checklist to check your work.**

Editing Checklist

Did you use . . . ?

- ☐ the base form of the verb after *should, ought to,* or *had better*
- ☐ the correct written forms of *ought to* and *had better*
- ☐ *maybe, perhaps,* or *I think* with *should* to soften the advice if you want to be more polite

D REVISE YOUR WORK **Read your email again. Can you improve your writing? Make changes if necessary.**

UNIT 16 **REVIEW**

Test yourself on the grammar of the unit.

A Choose the correct answer to complete each sentence.

1. Doug should _____ that Internet group. I think he'd like it.
   a. join **b.** joins **c.** to join
2. He ought _____ some postings before he posts his own.
   a. read **b.** reads **c.** to read
3. He should _____ a long message.
   a. n't post **b.** no post **c.** post no
4. He'd _____ give too much personal information. It could be dangerous.
   a. better **b.** better not **c.** not better
5. He'd better _____ careful.
   a. be **b.** not be **c.** not being

B Complete the conversations with the words in parentheses and with short answers.

1. A: ___should___ I ___call___ Suzanne tomorrow?
   a. (should / call)
   B: You ___had better do___ it tonight. She's been expecting to hear from you.
   b. (had better / do)
2. A: How ___should___ I ___contact___ Professor Lions? Email?
   a. (should / contact)
   B: No. You ___ought to call___ her. She prefers the phone.
   b. (ought to / call)
3. A: ___Should___ I ___ask___ her for help?
   a. (should / ask)
   B: ___Yes___, you ___should___. That's part of her job.
   b.
4. A: ___Should___ I ___do___ it right now?
   a. (should / do)
   B: ___No___, you ___shouldn't___. It's much too late.
   b.
   A: You're right. I ___had better wait___ until tomorrow morning.
   c. (had better / wait)

C Find and correct six mistakes.

1. Vanessa should gets a new computer. She ~~should no~~ *shouldn't* keep her old one.
2. She'd better not ~~buying~~ *buy* the first one she sees.
3. She ~~ought~~ *ought to* read reviews before she decides on one.
4. ~~Ought~~ *Should* she get one online or should she ~~goes~~ *go* to a store?

Now check your answers on page 479.

[illegible] Review

Test yourself on the grammar of the unit.

A Choose the correct answer to complete each sentence.

[illegible]

B Complete the conversations with the words in parentheses [illegible]

[illegible]

C [illegible]

[illegible]

Now check your answers on page [illegible].

Appendices

1 Irregular Verbs

When two forms are listed, the more common form is listed first.

BASE FORM	SIMPLE PAST	PAST PARTICIPLE
arise	arose	arisen
awake	awoke	awoken
be	was or were	been
beat	beat	beaten/beat
become	became	become
begin	began	begun
bend	bent	bent
bet	bet	bet
bite	bit	bitten
bleed	bled	bled
blow	blew	blown
break	broke	broken
bring	brought	brought
build	built	built
burn	burned/burnt	burnt/burned
burst	burst	burst
buy	bought	bought
catch	caught	caught
choose	chose	chosen
cling	clung	clung
come	came	come
cost	cost	cost
creep	crept	crept
cut	cut	cut
deal	dealt	dealt
dig	dug	dug
dive	dove/dived	dived
do	did	done
draw	drew	drawn
dream	dreamed/dreamt	dreamed/dreamt
drink	drank	drunk
drive	drove	driven
eat	ate	eaten
fall	fell	fallen
feed	fed	fed
feel	felt	felt
fight	fought	fought
find	found	found
fit	fit/fitted	fit
flee	fled	fled
fling	flung	flung
fly	flew	flown
forbid	forbid/forbade	forbidden
forget	forgot	forgotten
forgive	forgave	forgiven
freeze	froze	frozen
get	got	gotten/got
give	gave	given
go	went	gone
grind	ground	ground
grow	grew	grown

BASE FORM	SIMPLE PAST	PAST PARTICIPLE
hang	hung	hung
have	had	had
hear	heard	heard
hide	hid	hidden
hit	hit	hit
hold	held	held
hurt	hurt	hurt
keep	kept	kept
kneel	knelt/kneeled	knelt/kneeled
knit	knit/knitted	knit/knitted
know	knew	known
lay	laid	laid
lead	led	led
leap	leaped/leapt	leaped/leapt
leave	left	left
lend	lent	lent
let	let	let
lie *(lie down)*	lay	lain
light	lit/lighted	lit/lighted
lose	lost	lost
make	made	made
mean	meant	meant
meet	met	met
pay	paid	paid
prove	proved	proven/proved
put	put	put
quit	quit	quit
read /rid/	read /rɛd/	read /rɛd/
ride	rode	ridden
ring	rang	rung
rise	rose	risen
run	ran	run
say	said	said
see	saw	seen
seek	sought	sought
sell	sold	sold
send	sent	sent
set	set	set
sew	sewed	sewn/sewed
shake	shook	shaken
shave	shaved	shaved/shaven
shine *(intransitive)*	shone/shined	shone/shined
shoot	shot	shot
show	showed	shown
shrink	shrank/shrunk	shrunk/shrunken
shut	shut	shut
sing	sang	sung
sink	sank/sunk	sunk
sit	sat	sat
sleep	slept	slept
slide	slid	slid

BASE FORM	SIMPLE PAST	PAST PARTICIPLE	BASE FORM	SIMPLE PAST	PAST PARTICIPLE
speak	spoke	spoken	swing	swung	swung
speed	sped/speeded	sped/speeded	take	took	taken
spend	spent	spent	teach	taught	taught
spill	spilled/spilt	spilled/spilt	tear	tore	torn
spin	spun	spun	tell	told	told
spit	spit/spat	spat	think	thought	thought
split	split	split	throw	threw	thrown
spread	spread	spread	understand	understood	understood
spring	sprang	sprung	upset	upset	upset
stand	stood	stood	wake	woke	woken
steal	stole	stolen	wear	wore	worn
stick	stuck	stuck	weave	wove/weaved	woven/weaved
sting	stung	stung	weep	wept	wept
stink	stank/stunk	stunk	win	won	won
strike	struck	struck/stricken	wind	wound	wound
swear	swore	sworn	withdraw	withdrew	withdrawn
sweep	swept	swept	wring	wrung	wrung
swim	swam	swum	write	wrote	written

2 Non-Action Verbs

APPEARANCE
appear
be
look *(seem)*
represent
resemble
seem
signify

VALUE
cost
equal
weigh

EMOTIONS
admire
adore
appreciate
care
detest
dislike
doubt
envy
fear
forgive
hate
like
love
miss
regret
respect
trust

MENTAL STATES
agree
assume
believe
consider
disagree
disbelieve
estimate
expect
feel *(believe)*
find *(believe)*
forget
guess
hesitate
hope
imagine
know
mean
mind
presume
realize
recognize
remember
see *(understand)*
suppose
suspect
think *(believe)*
understand
wonder

POSSESSION AND RELATIONSHIP
belong
come from *(origin)*
contain
have
own
possess

SENSES AND PERCEPTIONS
feel
hear
hurt
notice
observe
perceive
recognize
see
seem
smell
sound
taste

WANTS AND PREFERENCES
desire
hope
need
prefer
want
wish

3 Verbs and Expressions Used Reflexively

allow yourself
amuse yourself
ask yourself
avail yourself of
be hard on yourself
be pleased with yourself
be proud of yourself
be yourself
behave yourself
believe in yourself
blame yourself
buy yourself
cut yourself
deprive yourself of
dry yourself
enjoy yourself
feel proud of yourself
feel sorry for yourself
forgive yourself
help yourself
hurt yourself
imagine yourself
introduce yourself
keep yourself (busy)
kill yourself
look after yourself
look at yourself
prepare yourself
pride yourself on
push yourself
remind yourself
see yourself
take care of yourself
talk to yourself
teach yourself
tell yourself
treat yourself
wash yourself

4 Transitive Phrasal Verbs

(s.o. = someone   s.t. = something)

PHRASAL VERB	MEANING
ask s.o. **over**	*invite to one's home*
blow s.t. **out**	*stop burning by blowing air on it*
blow s.t. **up**	*make explode*
bring s.o. or s.t. **back**	*return*
bring s.o. **up**	*raise (a child)*
bring s.t. **up**	*bring attention to*
burn s.t. **down**	*burn completely*
call s.o. **back**	*return a phone call*
call s.t. **off**	*cancel*
call s.o. **up**	*contact by phone*
calm s.o. **down**	*make less excited*
carry s.t. **out**	*complete (a plan)*
clean s.o. or s.t. **up**	*clean completely*
clear s.t. **up**	*explain*
close s.t. **down**	*close by force*
count on s.t. or s.o.	*depend on*
cover s.o. or s.t. **up**	*cover completely*
cross s.t. **out**	*draw a line through*
do s.t. **over**	*do again*
drink s.t. **up**	*drink completely*
drop s.o. or s.t. **off**	*take someplace in a car and leave there*
empty s.t. **out**	*empty completely*
end up doing s.t.	*do something you didn't plan to do*
figure s.o. **out**	*understand (the behavior)*
figure s.t. **out**	*solve, understand after thinking about it*
fill s.t. **in**	*complete with information*
fill s.t. **out**	*complete (a form)*
find s.t. **out**	*learn information*
get off s.t.	*leave (a bus, a couch)*
get over s.t.	*recover from*
give s.t. **back**	*return*
give s.t. **up**	*quit, abandon*
give up doing s.t.	*quit, stop*
go on doing s.t.	*continue*
hand s.t. **in**	*give work (to a boss/teacher), submit*
hand s.t. **out**	*distribute*
hand s.t. **over**	*give*
help s.o. **out**	*assist*
keep s.o. or s.t. **away**	*cause to stay at a distance*
keep s.t. **on**	*not remove (a piece of clothing/ jewelry)*
keep on doing s.t.	*continue*
keep s.o. or s.t. **out**	*not allow to enter*
lay s.o. **off**	*end employment*
leave s.t. **on**	1. *not turn off (a light/radio)* 2. *not remove (a piece of clothing/ jewelry)*
leave s.t. **out**	*not include, omit*
let s.o. **down**	*disappoint*
let s.o. or s.t. **in**	*allow to enter*
let s.o. **off**	*allow to leave (from a bus/car)*
light s.t. **up**	*illuminate*
look for s.o. or s.t.	*try to find*
look s.o. or s.t. **over**	*examine*
look s.t. **up**	*try to find (in a book/on the Internet)*
make s.t. **up**	*create*
pass s.t. **on**	*give to others*
pass s.t. **out**	*distribute*
pass s.o. or s.t. **over**	*decide not to use*
pass s.o. or s.t. **up**	*decide not to use, reject*
pay s.o. or s.t. **back**	*repay*
pick s.o. or s.t. **out**	*choose*
pick s.o. or s.t. **up**	1. *lift* 2. *go get someone or something*
pick s.t. **up**	1. *get (an idea/a new book)* 2. *answer the phone*
point s.o. or s.t. **out**	*indicate*
put s.t. **away**	*put in an appropriate place*
put s.t. **back**	*return to its original place*
put s.o. or s.t. **down**	*stop holding*
put s.t. **off**	*delay*
put off doing s.t.	*delay*
put s.t. **on**	*cover the body (with clothes/lotion)*
put s.t. **together**	*assemble*
put s.t. **up**	*erect*
set s.t. **up**	1. *prepare for use* 2. *establish (a business)*
shut s.t. **off**	*stop (a machine/light)*
straighten s.o. **out**	*change bad behavior*
straighten s.t. **up**	*make neat*
switch s.t. **on**	*start (a machine/light)*
take s.o. or s.t. **back**	*return*
take s.t. **off/out**	*remove*
take over s.t.	*get control of*
talk s.o. **into**	*persuade*
talk s.t. **over**	*discuss*
tear s.t. **down**	*destroy*
tear s.t. **off**	*remove by tearing*
tear s.t. **up**	*tear into small pieces*
think about doing s.t.	*consider*
think s.t. **over**	*consider*
think s.t. **up**	*invent*
throw s.t. **away/out**	*put in the trash, discard*
try s.t. **on**	*put clothing on to see if it fits*
try s.t. **out**	*use to see if it works*
turn s.t. **around**	*make it work well*
turn s.o. or s.t. **down**	*reject*
turn s.t. **down**	*lower the volume (a TV/radio)*
turn s.t. **in**	*give work (to a boss/teacher), submit*
turn s.o. or s.t. **into**	*change from one form to another*
turn s.o. **off**	[slang] *destroy interest in*
turn s.t. **off**	*stop (a machine/light), extinguish*
turn s.t. **on**	*start (a machine/light)*
turn s.t. **up**	*make louder (a TV/radio)*
use s.t. **up**	*use completely, consume*
wake s.o. **up**	*awaken*
work s.t. **out**	*solve, find a solution to a problem*
write s.t. **down**	*write on a piece of paper*
write s.t. **up**	*write in a finished form*

5 Intransitive Phrasal Verbs

PHRASAL VERB	MEANING
blow up	*explode*
break down	*stop working (a machine)*
burn down	*burn completely*
call back	*return a phone call*
calm down	*become less excited*
catch on	1. *begin to understand* 2. *become popular*
clear up	*become clear*
close down	*stop operating*
come about	*happen*
come along	*come with, accompany*
come by	*visit*
come back	*return*
come in	*enter*
come off	*become unattached*
come on	1. *do as I say* 2. *let's go*
come out	*appear*
come up	*arise*
dress up	*wear special clothes*
drop in	*visit by surprise*
drop out	*quit*
eat out	*eat in a restaurant*
empty out	*empty completely*
find out	*learn information*
fit in	*be accepted in a group*
follow through	*complete*
fool around	*act playful*
get ahead	*make progress, succeed*
get along	*have a good relationship*
get away	*go on vacation*
get back	*return*
get by	*survive*
get through	*finish*
get together	*meet*
get up	1. *get out of bed* 2. *stand*
give up	*quit*
go ahead	*begin or continue to do something*
go away	*leave*
go on	*continue*
grow up	*become an adult*
hang up	*end a phone call*
help out	*assist*
keep away	*stay at a distance*
keep on	*continue*
keep out	*not enter*
keep up	*go as fast*
lie down	*recline*
light up	*illuminate*
look out	*be careful*
make up	*end a disagreement, reconcile*
pass away	*die*
play around	*have fun*
run out	*not have enough*
set out	*begin an activity or a project*
show up	*appear*
sign up	*register*
sit down	*take a seat*
slip up	*make a mistake*
stand up	*rise*
start over	*start again*
stay up	*remain awake*
straighten up	*make neat*
take off	*depart (a plane)*
tune in	1. *watch or listen to (a show)* 2. *pay attention*
turn up	*appear*
wake up	*stop sleeping*
watch out	*be careful*
work out	1. *be resolved* 2. *exercise*

6 Irregular Plural Nouns

SINGULAR	PLURAL
analysis	analyses
basis	bases
crisis	crises
hypothesis	hypotheses
half	halves
knife	knives
leaf	leaves
life	lives
loaf	loaves
shelf	shelves
wife	wives
man	men
woman	women
child	children
foot	feet
tooth	teeth
goose	geese
mouse	mice
person	people
deer	deer
fish	fish
sheep	sheep

7 Non-Count Nouns

Non-count nouns are singular.

ACTIVITIES	COURSES OF STUDY	FOOD		IDEAS AND FEELINGS	LIQUIDS AND GASES	MATERIALS	VERY SMALL THINGS	WEATHER
baseball	archeology	bread	fruit	anger	air	ash	dust	fog
biking	art	broccoli	ice cream	beauty	blood	clay	pepper	ice
exploring	economics	butter	lettuce	fear	gasoline	cotton	rice	rain
farming	English	cake	meat	freedom	ink	glass	salt	snow
football	geography	cheese	pasta	friendship	milk	gold	sand	wind
golf	history	chicken	pizza	happiness	oil	leather	sugar	
hiking	mathematics	chocolate	salad	hate	oxygen	paper		
running	music	coffee	soup	hope	paint	silk		
sailing	photography	corn	spaghetti	loneliness	smoke	silver		
soccer	psychology	fat	spinach	love	soda	stone		
swimming	science	fish	tea	truth	water	wood		
tennis		flour	yogurt			wool		

NAMES OF CATEGORIES

clothing	(BUT: coats, hats, shoes ...)
equipment	(BUT: computers, phones, TVs ...)
food	(BUT: bananas, eggs, vegetables ...)
furniture	(BUT: beds, chairs, lamps, tables ...)
homework	(BUT: assignments, pages, problems ...)
jewelry	(BUT: bracelets, earrings, necklaces ...)
mail	(BUT: letters, packages, postcards ...)
money	(BUT: dinars, dollars, euros, pounds ...)
time	(BUT: minutes, months, years ...)
work	(BUT: jobs, projects, tasks ...)

OTHER

Some non-count nouns don't fit into any list.
You must memorize these non-count nouns.

advice
garbage/trash
help
information
luggage
news
traffic

8 Proper Nouns

Write proper nouns with a capital letter. Notice that some proper nouns use the definite article *the*.

PEOPLE

• first names	Anne, Eduardo, Mehmet, Olga, Shao-fen
• family names	Chen, García, Haddad, Smith
• family groups	the Chens, the Garcias, the Haddads, the Smiths
• titles	Doctor, Grandma, President, Professor
• title + names	Mr. García, Professor Smith, Uncle Steve

PLACES

• continents	Africa, Asia, Australia, Europe, South America
• countries	Argentina, China, France, Nigeria, Turkey, the United States
• provinces/states	Brittany, Ontario, Szechwan, Texas
• cities	Beijing, Istanbul, Rio de Janeiro, Toronto
• streets	the Champs-Elysées, Fifth Avenue
• structures	Harrods, the Louvre, the Petronas Towers
• schools	Midwood High School, Oxford University
• parks	Central Park, the Tivoli Gardens
• mountains	the Andes, the Himalayas, the Pyrenees
• oceans	the Atlantic, the Indian Ocean, the Pacific
• rivers	the Amazon, the Ganges, the Seine
• lakes	Baikal, Erie, Tanganyika, Titicaca
• canals	the Suez Canal, the Panama Canal
• deserts	the Gobi, the Kalahari, the Sahara

DOCUMENTS

the Bible, the Koran, the Constitution

LANGUAGES

Arabic, Chinese, Portuguese, Russian, Spanish

NATIONALITIES

Brazilian, Japanese, Mexican, Saudi, Turkish

RELIGIONS

Buddhism, Christianity, Hinduism, Islam, Judaism

COURSES

Introduction to Computer Sciences, Math 201

PRODUCT BRANDS

Adidas, Dell, Kleenex, Mercedes, Samsung

TIME

• months	January, March, December
• days	Monday, Wednesday, Saturday
• holidays	Bastille Day, Buddha Day, Christmas, Hanukah, New Year's Day, Ramadan

9 Adjectives That Form the Comparative and Superlative in Two Ways

The more common form of the comparative and the superlative is listed first.

ADJECTIVE	COMPARATIVE	SUPERLATIVE
cruel	crueler/more cruel	cruelest/most cruel
deadly	deadlier/more deadly	deadliest/most deadly
friendly	more friendly/friendlier	most friendly/friendliest
handsome	more handsome/handsomer	most handsome/handsomest
happy	happier/more happy	happiest/most happy
lively	livelier/more lively	liveliest/most lively
lonely	lonelier/more lonely	loneliest/most lonely
lovely	lovelier/more lovely	loveliest/most lovely
narrow	narrower/more narrow	narrowest/most narrow
pleasant	more pleasant/pleasanter	most pleasant/pleasantest
polite	more polite/politer	most polite/politest
quiet	quieter/more quiet	quietest/most quiet
shallow	shallower/more shallow	shallowest/most shallow
sincere	more sincere/sincerer	most sincere/sincerest
stupid	stupider/more stupid	stupidest/most stupid
true	truer/more true	truest/most true

10 Irregular Comparisons of Adjectives, Adverbs, and Quantifiers

ADJECTIVE	ADVERB	COMPARATIVE	SUPERLATIVE
bad	badly	worse	the worst
far	far	farther/further	the farthest/furthest
good	well	better	the best
little	little	less	the least
many/a lot of	—	more	the most
much*/a lot of	much*/a lot	more	the most

* *Much* is usually only used in questions and negative statements.

11 Participial Adjectives

-ED	-ING	-ED	-ING	-ED	-ING
alarmed	alarming	disturbed	disturbing	moved	moving
amazed	amazing	embarrassed	embarrassing	paralyzed	paralyzing
amused	amusing	entertained	entertaining	pleased	pleasing
annoyed	annoying	excited	exciting	relaxed	relaxing
astonished	astonishing	exhausted	exhausting	satisfied	satisfying
bored	boring	fascinated	fascinating	shocked	shocking
confused	confusing	frightened	frightening	surprised	surprising
depressed	depressing	horrified	horrifying	terrified	terrifying
disappointed	disappointing	inspired	inspiring	tired	tiring
disgusted	disgusting	interested	interesting	touched	touching
distressed	distressing	irritated	irritating	troubled	troubling

12 Order of Adjectives Before a Noun

1 When **adjectives from different categories** are used before a noun, they usually go in the order as displayed in the chart below. Do not use a comma between these adjectives. Remember that we do not usually use more than three adjectives before a noun.

EXAMPLES: I bought an **antique Greek flower** vase. NOT a ~~Greek antique~~ flower vase
She took some **easy college** courses. NOT some ~~college easy~~ courses
We sat at an **enormous round wooden** table. NOT a ~~wooden enormous round~~ table

OPINION	SIZE*	AGE	SHAPE	COLOR	ORIGIN	MATERIAL	NOUNS USED AS ADJECTIVES	
beautiful	enormous	antique	flat	blue	Asian	cotton	college	
comfortable	huge	modern	oval	gray	European	gold	flower	
cozy	little	new	rectangular	green	Greek	plastic	kitchen	**+ NOUN**
easy	tall	old	round	purple	Pacific	stone	mountain	
expensive	tiny	young	square	red	Southern	wooden	vacation	

* **EXCEPTION:** *Big* and *small* usually go first in a series of adjectives: *a small comfortable apartment.*

2 When **adjectives from the same category** are used before a noun, they do not follow a specific order. Use a comma between these adjectives.

EXAMPLES: We rented a **beautiful, comfortable, cozy** apartment. or
We rented a **cozy, comfortable, beautiful** apartment. or
We rented a **comfortable, cozy, beautiful** apartment.

13 Verbs Followed by Gerunds (Base Form of Verb + *-ing*)

acknowledge
admit
advise
allow
appreciate
avoid
ban
can't help
celebrate
consider
delay
deny
detest
discontinue
discuss
dislike
end up*
endure
enjoy
escape
excuse
explain
feel like
finish
forgive
give up*
go
go on*
imagine
justify
keep *(continue)*
keep on*
limit
mention
mind *(object to)*
miss
permit
postpone
practice
prevent
prohibit
put off*
quit
recall
recommend
report
resent
resist
risk
suggest
support
think about*
tolerate
understand

*A few phrasal verbs like these are followed by a gerund.

14 Verbs Followed by Infinitives (*To* + Base Form of Verb)

agree
aim
appear
arrange
ask
attempt
can('t) afford
can't wait
claim
choose
consent
decide
deserve
expect
fail
help*
hesitate
hope
hurry
intend
learn
manage
mean *(intend)*
need
neglect
offer
pay
plan
prepare
pretend
promise
refuse
request
rush
seem
struggle
threaten
volunteer
wait
want
wish
would like

* *Help* is often followed by the base form of the verb (example: *I helped paint the kitchen*).

15 Verbs Followed by Gerunds or Infinitives

begin
can't stand
continue
forget*
hate
like
love
prefer
remember*
regret*
start
stop*
try

*These verbs can be followed by either a gerund or an infinitive, but there is a big difference in meaning *(see Unit 26)*.

16 Verbs Followed by Object + Infinitive

advise
allow
ask*
beg*
cause
challenge
choose*
convince
encourage
expect*
forbid
force
get
help**
hire
instruct
invite
need*
order
pay*
permit
persuade
prefer*
promise*
remind
request
require
teach
tell
urge
want*
warn
would like*

*These verbs can also be followed by an infinitive without an object (example: *ask to leave* or *ask someone to leave*).
** *Help* is often followed by the base form of the verb, with or without an object (example: *I helped (her) paint the kitchen*).

17 Adjective + Preposition Combinations

accustomed to
afraid of
amazed at/by
angry at
ashamed of
aware of
awful at
bad at
bored with/by
capable of
careful of
certain about
concerned about
content with
curious about
different from
disappointed with
excited about
famous for
fond of
glad about
good at
happy about
interested in
nervous about
opposed to
pleased about
ready for
responsible for
sad about
safe from
satisfied with
shocked at/by
sick of
slow at/in
sorry for/about
surprised at/about/by
terrible at
tired of
used to
worried about

18 Verb + Preposition Combinations

admit to	believe in	dream about/of	pay for	succeed in	think about
advise against	choose between	feel about	plan on	talk about	wonder about
apologize for	complain about	insist on	rely on	thank someone for	worry about
approve of	decide on	object to	resort to		

19 Modals and Their Functions

FUNCTION	MODAL OR EXPRESSION	TIME	EXAMPLES
Ability	**can** **can't**	Present	Sam **can swim**. He **can't skate**.
	could **couldn't**	Past	We **could swim** last year. We **couldn't skate**.
	be able to* **not be able to***	All verb forms	Lea **is able to run** fast. She **wasn't able to run** fast last year.
Permission	**can** **can't** **could** **may** **may not**	Present or future	**Can** I **sit** here? **Can** I **call** tomorrow? Yes, you **can**. No, you **can't**. Sorry. **Could** he **leave** now? **May** I **borrow** your pen? Yes, you **may**. No, you **may not**. Sorry.
Requests	**can** **can't** **could** **will** **would**	Present or future	**Can** you **close** the door, please? Sure, I **can**. Sorry, I **can't**. **Could** you please **answer** the phone? **Will** you **wash** the dishes, please? **Would** you please **mail** this letter?
Advice	**should** **shouldn't** **ought to** **had better**** **had better not****	Present or future	You **should study** more. You **shouldn't miss** class. We **ought to leave**. We**'d better go**. We**'d better not stay**.
Necessity	**have to*** **not have to***	All verb forms	He **has to go** now. I **had to go** yesterday. I **will have to go** soon. He **doesn't have to go** yet.
	have got to* **must**	Present or future	He**'s got to leave**! You **must use** a pen for the test.
Prohibition	**must not** **can't**	Present or future	You **must not drive** without a license. You **can't drive** without a license.

*The meaning of this expression is similar to the meaning of a modal. Unlike a modal, the verb changes for present tense third-person singular.

**The meaning of this expression is similar to the meaning of a modal. Like a modal, it has no *-s* for third-person singular.

FUNCTION	MODAL OR EXPRESSION	TIME	EXAMPLES
Possibility	**must** **must not** **have to***	Present	This **must be** her house. Her name is on the door. She **must not be** home. I don't see her car. She **had to know** him. They went to school together.
	have got to* **may** **may not** **might** **might not** **could**	Present or future	He**'s got to be** guilty. We saw him do it. She **may be** home now. It **may not rain** tomorrow. Lee **might be sick** today. He **might not come** to class. They **could be** at the library. It **could rain** tomorrow.
Impossibility	**can't**	Present or future	That **can't be** Ana. She left for France yesterday. It **can't snow** tomorrow. It's going to be too warm.
	couldn't	Present	He **couldn't be** guilty. He was away . . .

*The meaning of this expression is similar to the meaning of a modal. Unlike a modal, the verb changes for present tense third-person singular.

20 Spelling Rules for the Simple Present: Third-Person Singular (*He*, *She*, *It*)

1 Add ***-s*** for most verbs.

work works
buy buys
ride rides
return returns

2 Add ***-es*** for verbs that end in ***-ch***, ***-s***, ***-sh***, ***-x***, or ***-z***.

watch watch**es**
pass pass**es**
rush rush**es**
relax relax**es**
buzz buzz**es**

3 Change the ***y*** to ***i*** and add ***-es*** when the base form ends in **consonant + *y***.

study stud**ies**
hurry hurr**ies**
dry dr**ies**

4 Do not change the ***y*** when the base form ends in **vowel + *y***. Add ***-s***.

play play**s**
enjoy enjoy**s**

5 A few verbs have **irregular forms**.

be **is**
do **does**
go **goes**
have **has**

21 Spelling Rules for Base Form of Verb + *-ing* (Progressive and Gerund)

1 Add ***-ing*** to the base form of the verb.

read	read**ing**
stand	stand**ing**

2 If the verb ends in a **silent *-e***, drop the final ***-e*** and add ***-ing***.

leave	leav**ing**
take	tak**ing**

3 In **one-syllable** verbs, if the last three letters are a consonant-vowel-consonant combination (CVC), double the last consonant and add ***-ing***.

C V C
↓ ↓ ↓
s i t — sit**ting**

C V C
↓ ↓ ↓
p l a n — plan**ning**

EXCEPTION: Do not double the last consonant in verbs that end in ***-w***, ***-x***, or ***-y***.

sew	sew**ing**
fix	fix**ing**
play	play**ing**

4 In verbs of **two or more syllables** that end in a consonant-vowel-consonant combination, double the last consonant only if the last syllable is stressed.

admi´t	admit**ting**	*(The last syllable is stressed, so double the* **-t**.*)*
whi´sper	whisper**ing**	*(The last syllable is not stressed, so don't double the* **-r**.*)*

5 If the verb ends in ***-ie***, change the ***ie*** to ***y*** before adding ***-ing***.

die	**dying**
lie	**lying**

Stress

´ shows main stress.

22 Spelling Rules for Base Form of Verb + *-ed* (Simple Past and Past Participle of Regular Verbs)

1 If the verb ends in a **consonant**, add ***-ed***.

return	return**ed**
help	help**ed**

2 If the verb ends in ***-e***, add ***-d***.

live	live**d**
create	create**d**
die	die**d**

3 In **one-syllable** verbs, if the last three letters are a consonant-vowel-consonant combination (CVC), double the last consonant and add ***-ed***.

C V C
↓ ↓ ↓
h o p — hop**ped**

C V C
↓ ↓ ↓
g r a b — grab**bed**

EXCEPTION: Do not double the last consonant in **one-syllable** verbs that end in ***-w***, ***-x***, or ***-y***.

bow	bow**ed**
mix	mix**ed**
play	play**ed**

4 In verbs of **two or more syllables** that end in a consonant-vowel-consonant combination, double the last consonant only if the last syllable is stressed.

prefe´r	prefer**red**	*(The last syllable is stressed, so double the* **-r**.*)*
vi´sit	visit**ed**	*(The last syllable is not stressed, so don't double the* **-t**.*)*

5 If the verb ends in **consonant + *y***, change the ***y*** to ***i*** and add ***-ed***.

worry	worr**ied**
carry	carr**ied**

6 If the verb ends in **vowel + *y***, add ***-ed***. (Do not change the ***y*** to ***i***.)

play	play**ed**
annoy	annoy**ed**

EXCEPTIONS:

lay	la**id**
pay	pa**id**
say	sa**id**

23 Spelling Rules for the Comparative (*-er*) and Superlative (*-est*) of Adjectives

1 With **one-syllable** adjectives, add ***-er*** to form the comparative. Add ***-est*** to form the superlative.

cheap	cheap**er**	cheap**est**
bright	bright**er**	bright**est**

2 If the adjective ends in ***-e***, add ***-r*** or ***-st***.

nice	nice**r**	nice**st**

3 If the adjective ends in **consonant + *y***, change ***y*** to ***i*** before you add ***-er*** or ***-est***.

pretty	prett**ier**	prett**iest**

EXCEPTION:

shy	shy**er**	shy**est**

4 In **one-syllable** adjectives, if the last three letters are a consonant-vowel-consonant combination (CVC), double the last consonant before adding ***-er*** or ***-est***.

C V C
↓ ↓ ↓

b i g	big**ger**	big**gest**

EXCEPTION: Do not double the last consonant in adjectives that end in ***-w*** or ***-y***.

slow	slow**er**	slow**est**
gray	gray**er**	gray**est**

24 Spelling Rules for Adverbs Ending in *-ly*

1 Add ***-ly*** to the corresponding adjective.

nice	nice**ly**
quiet	quiet**ly**
beautiful	beautiful**ly**

EXCEPTION:

true	tru**ly**

2 If the adjective ends in **consonant + *y***, change the ***y*** to ***i*** before adding ***-ly***.

easy	eas**ily**

3 If the adjective ends in ***-le***, drop the ***e*** and add ***-y***.

possible	possibl**y**

4 If the adjective ends in ***-ic***, add ***-ally***.

basic	basic**ally**
fantastic	fantastic**ally**

25 Spelling Rules for Regular Plural Nouns

1 Add ***-s*** to most nouns.

book	book**s**
table	table**s**
cup	cup**s**

2 Add ***-es*** to nouns that end in ***-ch***, ***-s***, ***-sh***, or ***-x***.

watch	watch**es**
bus	bus**es**
dish	dish**es**
box	box**es**

3 Add ***-s*** to nouns that end in **vowel + *y***.

day	day**s**
key	key**s**

4 Change the ***y*** to ***i*** and add ***-es*** to nouns that end in **consonant + *y***.

baby	bab**ies**
city	cit**ies**
strawberry	strawberr**ies**

5 Add ***-s*** to nouns that end in **vowel + *o***.

radio	radio**s**
video	video**s**
zoo	zoo**s**

6 Add ***-es*** to nouns that end in **consonant + *o***.

potato	potato**es**
tomato	tomato**es**

EXCEPTIONS:

kilo	kilo**s**
photo	photo**s**
piano	piano**s**

26 Contractions with Verb Forms

1 SIMPLE PRESENT, PRESENT PROGRESSIVE, AND IMPERATIVE

Contractions with *Be*

I am	=	I**'m**
you are	=	you**'re**
he is	=	he**'s**
she is	=	she**'s**
it is	=	it**'s**
we are	=	we**'re**
you are	=	you**'re**
they are	=	they**'re**

Simple Present	Present Progressive
I**'m** a student.	I**'m studying** here.
He**'s** my teacher.	He**'s teaching** verbs.
We**'re** from Canada.	We**'re living** here.

I am not	=	I**'m not**		
you are not	=	you**'re not**	or	you **aren't**
he is not	=	he**'s not**	or	he **isn't**
she is not	=	she**'s not**	or	she **isn't**
it is not	=	it**'s not**	or	it **isn't**
we are not	=	we**'re not**	or	we **aren't**
you are not	=	you**'re not**	or	you **aren't**
they are not	=	they**'re not**	or	they **aren't**

Simple Present	Present Progressive
She**'s not** sick.	She**'s not reading**.
He **isn't** late.	He **isn't coming**.
We **aren't** twins.	We **aren't leaving**.
They**'re not** here.	They**'re not playing**.

Contractions with *Do*

do not	=	**don't**
does not	=	**doesn't**

Simple Present	Imperative
They **don't live** here.	**Don't run!**
It **doesn't snow** much.	

2 SIMPLE PAST AND PAST PROGRESSIVE

Contractions with *Be*

was not	=	**wasn't**
were not	=	**weren't**

Contractions with *Do*

did not	=	**didn't**

Simple Past	Past Progressive
He **wasn't** a poet.	He **wasn't singing**.
They **weren't** twins.	They **weren't sleeping**.
We **didn't see** her.	

3 FUTURE

Contractions with *Will*

I will	=	I**'ll**
you will	=	you**'ll**
he will	=	he**'ll**
she will	=	she**'ll**
it will	=	it**'ll**
we will	=	we**'ll**
you will	=	you**'ll**
they will	=	they**'ll**
will not	=	**won't**

Future with *Will*

I**'ll take** the train.
It**'ll be** faster that way.
We**'ll go** together.
He **won't come** with us.
They **won't miss** the train.

Contractions with *Be going to*

I am going to	=	I**'m** going to
you are going to	=	you**'re** going to
he is going to	=	he**'s** going to
she is going to	=	she**'s** going to
it is going to	=	it**'s** going to
we are going to	=	we**'re** going to
you are going to	=	you**'re** going to
they are going to	=	they**'re** going to

Future with *Be going to*

I**'m going to buy** tickets tomorrow.
She**'s going to call** you.
It**'s going to rain** soon.
We**'re going to drive** to Boston.
They**'re going to crash!**

4 PRESENT PERFECT AND PRESENT PERFECT PROGRESSIVE

Contractions with *Have*

I have	=	I**'ve**
you have	=	you**'ve**
he has	=	he**'s**
she has	=	she**'s**
it has	=	it**'s**
we have	=	we**'ve**
you have	=	you**'ve**
they have	=	they**'ve**
have not	=	**haven't**
has not	=	**hasn't**

You**'ve** already **read** that page.
We**'ve been writing** for an hour.
She**'s been** to Africa three times.
It**'s been raining** since yesterday.
We **haven't seen** any elephants yet.
They **haven't been living** here long.

5 MODALS AND SIMILAR EXPRESSIONS

cannot or can not	=	**can't**
could not	=	**couldn't**
should not	=	**shouldn't**
had better	=	**'d better**
would prefer	=	**'d prefer**
would rather	=	**'d rather**

She **can't dance**.
We **shouldn't go**.
They**'d better decide**.
I**'d prefer** coffee.
I**'d rather take** the bus.

27 Capitalization and Punctuation Rules

	USE FOR . . .	EXAMPLES
capital letter	• the first-person pronoun *I*	Tomorrow **I** will be here at 2:00.
	• proper nouns	His name is **Karl**. He lives in **Germany**.
	• the first word of a sentence	**When** does the train leave? **At** 2:00.
apostrophe (')	• possessive nouns	Is that **Marta's** coat?
	• contractions	**That's** not hers. **It's** mine.
comma (,)	• after items in a list	He bought **apples, pears, oranges,** and **bananas**.
	• before sentence connectors *and*, *but*, *or*, and *so*	They watched TV**, and** she played video games. She's tired**, so** she's going to bed now.
	• after the first part of a sentence that begins with *because*	***Because* it's raining,** we're not walking to the office.
	• after the first part of a sentence that begins with a preposition	***Across from* the post office,** there's a good restaurant.
	• after the first part of a sentence that begins with a time clause or an *if*-clause	***After* he arrived,** we ate dinner. ***If* it rains,** we won't go.
exclamation point (!)	• at the end of a sentence to show surprise or a strong feeling	You're here**!** That's great**!** Stop**!** A car is coming**!**
period (.)	• at the end of a statement	Today is Wednesday**.**
question mark (?)	• at the end of a question	What day is today**?**

28 Pronunciation Table

A|01 These are the pronunciation symbols used in this text. Listen to the pronunciation of the key words.

VOWELS

SYMBOL	KEY WORD	SYMBOL	KEY WORD
i	beat, feed	ə	banana, among
ɪ	bit, did	ɚ	shirt, murder
eɪ	date, paid	aɪ	bite, cry, buy, eye
ɛ	bet, bed	aʊ	about, how
æ	bat, bad	ɔɪ	voice, boy
ɑ	box, odd, father	ɪr	beer
ɔ	bought, dog	ɛr	bare
oʊ	boat, road	ɑr	bar
ʊ	book, good	ɔr	door
u	boot, food, student	ʊr	tour
ʌ	but, mud, mother		

CONSONANTS

SYMBOL	KEY WORD	SYMBOL	KEY WORD
p	pack, happy	z	zip, please, goes
b	back, rubber	ʃ	ship, machine, station,
t	tie		special, discussion
d	die	ʒ	measure, vision
k	came, key, quick	h	hot, who
g	game, guest	m	men
tʃ	church, nature, watch	n	sun, know, pneumonia
dʒ	judge, general, major	ŋ	sung, ringing
f	fan, photograph	w	wet, white
v	van	l	light, long
θ	thing, breath	r	right, wrong
ð	then, breathe	y	yes, use, music
s	sip, city, psychology	t̬	butter, bottle

29 Pronunciation Rules for the Simple Present: Third-Person Singular (*He*, *She*, *It*)

1 The third-person singular in the simple present always ends in the letter ***-s***. There are, however, three different pronunciations for the final sound of the third-person singular.

/s/	/z/	/ɪz/
talks	loves	dances

2 The final sound is pronounced **/s/** after the voiceless sounds **/p/**, **/t/**, **/k/**, and **/f/**.

top	to**ps**
get	ge**ts**
take	ta**kes**
laugh	lau**ghs**

3 The final sound is pronounced **/z/** after the voiced sounds **/b/**, **/d/**, **/g/**, **/v/**, **/m/**, **/n/**, **/ŋ/**, **/l/**, **/r/**, and **/ð/**.

describe	descri**bes**
spend	spen**ds**
hug	hu**gs**
live	li**ves**
seem	see**ms**
remain	remai**ns**
sing	si**ngs**
tell	te**lls**
lower	low**ers**
bathe	ba**thes**

4 The final sound is pronounced **/z/** after all **vowel sounds**.

agree	agr**ees**
try	tr**ies**
stay	sta**ys**
know	kn**ows**

5 The final sound is pronounced **/ɪz/** after the sounds **/s/**, **/z/**, **/ʃ/**, **/ʒ/**, **/tʃ/**, and **/dʒ/**. **/ɪz/** adds a syllable to the verb.

miss	mi**sses**
freeze	free**zes**
rush	ru**shes**
massage	massa**ges**
watch	wa**tches**
judge	ju**dges**

6 ***Do*** and ***say*** have a change in vowel sound.

do **/du/**	does **/dʌz/**
say **/seɪ/**	says **/sɛz/**

30 Pronunciation Rules for the Simple Past and Past Participle of Regular Verbs

1 The regular simple past and past participle always end in the letter ***-d***. There are three different pronunciations for the final sound of the regular simple past and past participle.

/t/	/d/	/ɪd/
race**d**	live**d**	attend**ed**

2 The final sound is pronounced /t/ after the voiceless sounds /p/, /k/, /f/, /s/, /ʃ/, and /ʧ/.

hop	ho**pped**
work	wor**ked**
laugh	lau**ghed**
address	addre**ssed**
publish	publi**shed**
watch	wa**tched**

3 The final sound is pronounced /d/ after the voiced sounds /b/, /g/, /v/, /z/, /ʒ/, /dʒ/, /m/, /n/, /ŋ/, /l/, /r/, and /ð/.

rub	ru**bbed**
hug	hu**gged**
live	li**ved**
surprise	surpri**sed**
massage	massa**ged**
change	chan**ged**
rhyme	rhy**med**
return	retur**ned**
bang	ban**ged**
enroll	enro**lled**
appear	appea**red**
bathe	ba**thed**

4 The final sound is pronounced /d/ after all **vowel sounds**.

agree	agr**eed**
die	di**ed**
play	pl**ayed**
enjoy	enj**oyed**
snow	sn**owed**

5 The final sound is pronounced /ɪd/ after /t/ and /d/. /ɪd/ adds a syllable to the verb.

start	star**ted**
decide	deci**ded**

Glossary of Grammar Terms

action verb A verb that describes an action.

Alicia **ran** home.

adjective A word that describes a noun or pronoun.

That's a **great** idea.
It's **wonderful**.

adverb A word that describes a verb, an adjective, or another adverb.

She drives **carefully**.
She's a **very** good driver.
She drives **really** well.

adverb of frequency An adverb that describes how often something happens.

We **always** watch that program.

adverb of manner An adverb that describes how someone does something or how something happens. It usually ends in *-ly*.

He sings **beautifully**.

adverb of time An adverb that describes when something happens.

We'll see you **soon**.

affirmative A statement without a negative, or an answer meaning *Yes*.

He **works**. *(affirmative statement)*
Yes, he **does**. *(affirmative short answer)*

article A word that goes before a noun.

The indefinite articles are *a* and *an*.

I ate **a** sandwich and **an** apple.

The definite article is *the*.

I didn't like **the** sandwich. **The** apple was good.

auxiliary verb (also called **helping verb**) A verb used with a main verb. *Be*, *do*, and *have* are often auxiliary verbs. Modals (*can*, *should*, *may*...) are also auxiliary verbs.

I **am** exercising right now.
Does he exercise every day?
She **should** exercise every day.
They**'ve** learned how to swim.
They **can** swim very well.
We **may** go to the pool tomorrow.

base form The simple form of a verb without any endings (*-s*, *-ed*, *-ing*) or other changes.

be, have, go, drive

capital letter The large form of a letter. The capital letters are: *A*, *B*, *C*, *D*, . . .

Alicia lives in the **U**nited **S**tates.

clause A group of words that has a subject and a verb. A sentence can have one or more clauses.

We are leaving now. *(one clause)*
When he calls, we'll leave. *(two clauses)*

common noun A word for a person, place, or thing (but not the name of the person, place, or thing).

Teresa lives in a **house** near the **beach**.

comparative The form of an adjective or adverb that shows the difference between two people, places, or things.

Alain is **shorter** than Brendan. *(adjective)*
Brendan runs **faster** than Alain. *(adverb)*

comparison A statement that shows the difference between two people, places, or things. A comparison can use comparative adjectives and comparative adverbs. It can also use *as . . . as*.

Alain is **shorter than** Brendan.
Alain isn't **as tall as** Brendan.
He runs **faster than** Brendan.

consonant A letter of the alphabet. The consonants are:

b, c, d, f, g, h, j, k, l, m, n, p, q, r, s, t, v, w, x, y, z

continuous See **progressive**.

contraction A short form of a word or words. An apostrophe (') replaces the missing letter or letters.

she's = she is
hasn't = has not
can't = cannot
won't = will not

count noun A noun that you can count. It has a singular and a plural form.

one **book**, two **books**

definite article ***the***

This article goes before a noun that refers to a specific person, place, or thing.

Please bring me **the book** on the table. I'm almost finished reading it.

dependent clause (also called **subordinate clause**) A clause that needs a main clause for its meaning.

When I get home, I'll call you.

direct object A noun or pronoun that receives the action of a verb.

Marta kicked **the ball**. I saw **her**.

formal Language used in business situations or with adults you do not know.

Good afternoon, Mr. Rivera. Please have a seat.

gerund A noun formed with verb + *-ing*. It can be the subject or object of a sentence.

Swimming is great exercise.
I enjoy **swimming**.

helping verb See **auxiliary verb**.

imperative A sentence that gives a command or instructions.

Hurry!
Don't touch that!

indefinite article ***a*** or ***an***

These articles go before a noun that does not refer to a specific person, place, or thing.

Can you bring me **a book**? I'm looking for something to read.

indefinite past Past time, but not a specific time. It is often used with the present perfect.

I've already **seen** that movie.

indefinite pronoun A pronoun such as *someone, something, anyone, anything, anywhere, no one, nothing, nowhere, everyone,* and *everything*. An indefinite pronoun does not refer to a specific person, place, or thing.

Someone called you last night.
Did **anything** happen?

indirect object A noun or pronoun (often a person) that receives something as the result of the action of the verb.

I told **John** the story.
He gave **me** some good advice.

infinitive *to* + base form of the verb

I want **to leave** now.

infinitive of purpose *(in order) to* + base form

This form gives the reason for an action.

I go to school **(in order) to learn** English.

informal Language used with family, friends, and children.

Hi, Pete. Sit down.

information question See ***wh-*** **question**.

inseparable phrasal verb A phrasal verb whose parts must stay together.

We **ran into** Tomás at the supermarket.

intransitive verb A verb that does not have an object.

We **fell**.

irregular A word that does not change its form in the usual way.

good → **well**
bad → **worse**

irregular verb A verb that does not form its past with *-ed*.

leave → **left**

main clause A clause that can stand alone as a sentence.

When I get home, **I'll call you**.

main verb A verb that describes an action or state. It is often used with an auxiliary verb.

She **calls** every day.
Jared is **calling**.
He'll **call** again later.
Does he **call** every day?

modal A type of auxiliary verb. It goes before a main verb or stands alone as a short answer. It expresses ideas such as ability, advice, obligation, permission, and possibility. *Can, could, will, would, may, might, should, ought to,* and *must* are modals.

Can you swim?
Yes, I **can**.
You really **should** learn to swim.

negative A statement or answer meaning *No*.

He **doesn't** work. *(negative statement)*
No, he **doesn't**. *(negative short answer)*

non-action verb (also called **stative verb**) A verb that does not describe an action. It describes such things as thoughts, feelings, and senses.

I **remember** that word.
Chris **loves** ice cream.
It **tastes** great.

non-count noun A noun that you usually do not count (*air, water, rice, love, . . .*). It has only a singular form.

The **rice** is delicious.

noun A word for a person, place, or thing.

My **sister**, **Anne**, works in an **office**.
She uses a **computer**.

object A noun or pronoun that receives the action of a verb. Sometimes a verb has two objects.

She wrote **a letter to Tom**.
She wrote **him a letter**.

object pronoun A pronoun (*me, you, him, her, it, us, them*) that receives the action of a verb.

I gave **her** a book.
I gave **it** to **her**.

paragraph A group of sentences, usually about one topic.

participial adjective An adjective that ends in *-ing* or *-ed*. It comes from a verb.

That's an **interesting** book.
She's **interested** in the book.

particle A word that looks like a preposition and combines with a main verb to form a phrasal verb. It often changes the meaning of the main verb.

He looked the word **up**.
(He looked for the meaning in the dictionary.)
I ran **into** my teacher.
(I met my teacher accidentally.)

past participle A verb form (verb + *-ed*). It can also be irregular. It is used to form the present perfect. It can also be an adjective.

We've **lived** here since April.
She's **interested** in math.

phrasal verb (also called **two-word verb**) A verb that has two parts (verb + particle). The meaning is often different from the meaning of its separate parts.

He **grew up** in Texas. *(became an adult)*
His parents **brought** him **up** to be honest. *(raised)*

phrase A group of words that forms a unit but does not have a main verb. Many phrases give information about time or place.

Last year, we were living **in Canada**.

plural A form that means two or more.

There **are** three **people** in the restaurant.
They are eating dinner.
We saw **them**.

possessive Nouns, pronouns, or adjectives that show a relationship or show that someone owns something.

Zach is **Megan's** brother. *(possessive noun)*
Is that car **his**? *(possessive pronoun)*
That's **his** car. *(possessive adjective)*

predicate The part of a sentence that has the main verb. It tells what the subject is doing or describes the subject.

My sister **works for a travel agency**.

preposition A word that goes before a noun or a pronoun to show time, place, or direction.

I went **to** the bank **on** Monday. It's **next to** my office.
I told him **about** it.

Prepositions also go before nouns, pronouns, and gerunds in expressions with verbs and adjectives.

We rely **on** him.
She's accustomed **to** getting up early.

progressive (also called **continuous**) The verb form *be* + verb + *-ing*. It focuses on the continuation (not the completion) of an action.

She**'s reading** the paper.

We **were watching** TV when you called.

pronoun A word used in place of a noun.

That's my brother. You met **him** at my party.

proper noun A noun that is the name of a person, place, or thing. It begins with a capital letter.

Maria goes to **Central High School.**

It's on **High Street.**

punctuation Marks used in writing (period, comma, . . .). They make the meaning clear. For example, a period (**.**) shows the end of a sentence. It also shows that the sentence is a statement, not a question.

"Come in**,"** she said**.**

quantifier A word or phrase that shows an amount (but not an exact amount). It often comes before a noun.

Josh bought **a lot of** books last year, but he only read **a few.**

He doesn't have **much** time.

question See ***yes/no* question** and ***wh-* question**.

question word See ***wh-* word**.

reciprocal pronoun A pronoun (*each other* or *one another*) that shows that the subject and object of a sentence refer to the same people and that these people have a two-way relationship.

Megan and Jason have known **each other** since high school.

All the students worked with **one another** on the project.

reflexive pronoun A pronoun (*myself, yourself, himself, herself, itself, ourselves, yourselves, themselves*) that shows that the subject and the object of the sentence refer to the same people or things.

He looked at **himself** in the mirror.

They enjoyed **themselves** at the party.

regular A word that changes its form in the usual way.

play → play**ed**
fast → fast**er**
quick → quick**ly**

sentence A group of words that has a subject and a main verb. It begins with a capital letter and ends with a period (**.**), question mark (**?**), or exclamation point (**!**).

Computers are very useful.

EXCEPTION: In imperative sentences, the subject is *you*. We do not usually say or write the subject in imperative sentences.

Call her now!

separable phrasal verb A phrasal verb whose parts can separate.

Tom **looked** the word **up** in a dictionary.

He **looked** it **up.**

short answer An answer to a *yes/no* question.

A: Did you call me last night?

B: **No, I didn't.** or **No.**

singular one

They have **a sister.**

She works in **a hospital.**

statement A sentence that gives information. In writing, it ends in a period.

Today is Monday**.**

stative verb See **non-action verb**.

subject The person, place, or thing that the sentence is about.

Ms. Chen teaches English.

Her class is interesting.

subject pronoun A pronoun that shows the person or thing (*I, you, he, she, it, we, they*) that the sentence is about.

I read a lot.

She reads a lot too.

subordinate clause See **dependent clause**.

superlative The form of an adjective or adverb that is used to compare a person, place, or thing to a group of people, places, or things.

Cindi is **the best** dancer in the group. *(adjective)*
She dances **the most gracefully**. *(adverb)*

tense The form of a verb that shows the time of the action.

simple present: Fabio **talks** to his friend every day.

simple past: Fabio **talked** to his teacher yesterday.

third-person singular The pronouns *he*, *she*, and *it* or a singular noun. In the simple present, the third-person-singular verb ends in *-s*.

Tomás works in an office. *(Tomás = he)*

time clause A clause that begins with a time word such as *when*, *before*, *after*, *while*, or *as soon as*.

I'll call you **when I get home**.

time expression A phrase that describes when something happened or will happen.

We saw Tomás **last week**.
He'll graduate **next year**.

transitive verb A verb that has an object.

She **paints** beautiful pictures.

two-word verb See **phrasal verb**.

verb A word that describes what the subject of the sentence does, thinks, feels, senses, or owns.

They **run** two miles every day.
I **agree** with you.
She **loved** that movie.
We **smell** smoke.
He **has** a new camera.

vowel A letter of the alphabet. The vowels are:

a, **e**, **i**, **o**, **u**

***wh-* question** (also called **information question**) A question that begins with a *wh-* word. You answer a *wh-* question with information.

A: **Where** are you going?
B: To the store.

***wh-* word** (also called **question word**) A word such as *who*, *what*, *when*, *where*, *which*, *why*, *how*, and *how much*. It often begins a *wh-* question.

Who is that?
What did you see?
When does the movie usually start?
How long is it?

***yes/no* question** A question that begins with a form of *be* or an auxiliary verb. You can answer a *yes/no* question with *yes* or *no*.

A: **Are** you a student?
B: **Yes**, I am. or **No**, I'm not.

A: **Do** you come here often?
B: **Yes**, I do. or **No**, I don't.

Unit Review Answer Key

Note: In this answer key, where a short or contracted form is given, the full or long form is also correct (unless the purpose of the exercise is to practice the short or contracted forms).

UNIT 1

A
1. are you taking
2. I don't
3. often speak
4. He's talking
5. Do

B
1. are…doing
2. 'm…playing
3. Do…want
4. don't eat
5. 'm feeling **or** feel
6. looks
7. doesn't taste
8. are…shouting
9. Are
10. talk

C I live in Qatar, but right now I ~~stay~~ *'m staying* in Wisconsin. I'm studying English here. I ~~have~~ *'m having* a good time this summer, but in some ways it's a pretty strange experience. Summer in Wisconsin ~~feel~~ *feels* like winter in Qatar! Every weekend, I go to the beach with some classmates, but I ~~go never~~ *never go* into the water—it's too cold! I'm ~~enjoy~~ *enjoying* my time here though, and my culture shock is going away fast.

UNIT 2

A
1. b
2. c
3. a
4. c
5. a
6. c

B
1. called
2. didn't answer
3. Did…go
4. Yes…did
5. went
6. did…see
7. saw
8. didn't like

C The poet Elizabeth Alexander was born in New York City, but she didn't ~~grew~~ *grow* up there. Her father ~~taked~~ *took* a job with the government, and her family moved to Washington, D.C. As a child, she ~~have~~ *had* a loving family. Her parents were active in the civil rights movement, and Alexander ~~gots~~ *got* interested in African-American history. In her first book, she wrote about important African leaders. She met Barack Obama at the University of Chicago. They both ~~teached~~ *taught* there in the 1990s. On January 20, 2009, she ~~reads~~ *read* a poem at President Obama's inauguration.

UNIT 3

A
1. Did…hear
2. saw
3. turned
4. Were…driving **or** Did…drive
5. was working
6. was raining
7. was finishing
8. was leaving **or** left
9. stopped
10. looked

B
1. …Danielle was watching TV, I was studying
2. I closed my book…the show *Dr. Davis* came on
3. Dr. Davis was talking to his patient…the electricity went off
4. …the electricity went off, we lit some candles
5. We were talking (**or** We talked) about a lot of things…we were waiting for the lights to come on

C When I turned on the TV for the first episode of *Dr. Davis*, I ~~unpacked~~ *was unpacking* boxes in my freshman dorm room. I stopped and watched for an hour. After that, I ~~wasn't missing~~ *didn't miss* a single show while I was attending school. While I was solving math problems, Dr. Davis was solving medical mysteries. And *just* ~~while~~ *when* my dumb boyfriend broke up with me, the beautiful Dr. Grace left Davis for the third time. I even watched the show from the hospital when I ~~was breaking~~ *broke* my leg. The show just ended. I was sad when I ~~see~~ *saw* the last episode, but I think it's time for some real life!

UNIT 4

A
1. did
2. used to
3. Did
4. play
5. used to
6. used to

B
1. a. used to look
   b. used to have
   c. used to wear
   d. wouldn't get
2. a. used to play
   b. would practice
   c. Did…use(d) to go
   d. used to love

C
1. As a little girl, Yi Ling ~~would~~ *used to* live in Singapore.
2. In 1998, her family ~~used to move~~ *moved* to England.
3. Singapore used to ~~being~~ *be* a part of Malaysia. Today, it is a separate country.

4. The Singapore River used to ~~had~~ have hundreds of small boats on it.
5. The water ~~would~~ used to be very dirty.
6. In the past, flights from England to Singapore would ~~took~~ take several days. Planes used to make many stops to refuel.

UNIT 5

A
1. h
2. d
3. f
4. a
5. g
6. e
7. c
8. b

B
1. work
2. did she
3. told
4. did she leave
5. start
6. is her boss
7. does

C
A: What did you ~~did~~ do with my law book? I can't find it.
B: Nothing. Where ~~you saw~~ did you see it last?
A: In the living room. I was watching *Judge Judy* on TV. ~~What~~ What's Zack's phone number?
B: I'm not sure. ~~Why you~~ Why do you want to know?
A: He took the class last year. I'll call him. Maybe he still has his book.
B: Good idea. What time does he ~~gets~~ get out of work?

UNIT 6

A
1. We're going
2. I'll meet
3. It's going to rain
4. is giving
5. is going to fall

B
1. does…leave **or** will…leave **or** is…leaving **or** is…going to leave
2. 're going to feel **or** you'll feel
3. is going to land **or** will land **or** lands
4. is going to get
5. 'll pay **or** I'm paying **or** I'm going to pay
6. 's going to rain
7. does…start **or** will…start **or** is…starting **or** is…going to start
8. Is…going to call **or** Will…call **or** Is…calling
9. won't forget **or** isn't going to forget
10. 'll speak

C
1. When will Dr. Starr ~~gets~~ get home tomorrow?
2. His lecture starts at 7:00, so I think I ~~go~~ 'll go **or** 'm going to go.
3. Do you want to go with me, or are you ~~study~~ studying **or** going to study tonight?

4. What ~~you are~~ are you going to do next weekend?
5. I'm ~~going~~ going to be home all day.

UNIT 7

A
1. graduate
2. finish
3. When
4. Will
5. learning
6. until
7. Are you

B
1. works **or** 's working
2. won't register **or** isn't going to register
3. 'll spend **or** 's going to spend
4. studies **or** is studying
5. won't look **or** isn't going to look
6. graduates
7. 'll take **or** 's going to take

C
A: Are you going to call Phil when ~~we'll finish~~ we finish dinner?
B: No, I'm too tired. I'm just going to watch TV ~~after~~ before I go to sleep.
A: Before I wash the dishes, I'm ~~going~~ going to answer some emails.
B: I'll help you~~,~~ as soon as ~~I'll drink~~ I drink my coffee.
A: No rush. I have a lot of emails. I won't be ready to clean up until ~~you'll finish~~ you finish.

UNIT 8

A
1. for
2. since
3. for
4. for
5. Since
6. For
7. Since

B
1. 've been
2. haven't had
3. has loved
4. 've competed
5. 's won
6. haven't seen

C
1. Marta and Tomás ~~lived~~ have lived here since they got married in 2013.
2. Tomás has been a professional tennis player since he ~~has come~~ came to this country.
3. He has won several competitions ~~for~~ since then.
4. Since I have known Tomás, he ~~had~~ has had three different coaches.
5. I haven't ~~see~~ seen Marta for several weeks.
6. She ~~have~~ has been in Brazil since April 1.
7. I've wanted to visit Brazil ~~since~~ for years, but I haven't had any vacation time since I got this new job.

UNIT 9

A 1. already
2. still
3. yet
4. Has
5. told
6. yet

B 1. a. has already graduated **or** has graduated already
b. still haven't had
2. a. Have…delivered…yet
b. still hasn't set
c. 's already started **or** 's started already
3. a. still haven't arrived
b. has arrived yet
c. have…met…yet

C A: I can't believe it's the 10th already. And we still ~~didn't~~ *haven't* finished planning.

B: We haven't checked the guest list for a while. Who hasn't ~~replies~~ *replied* yet?

A: Sally hasn't called about the invitation ~~already~~ *yet*. I wonder if she's coming.

B: Maybe she just forgot. Have you called ~~yet her~~ *her yet*?

A: I've already ~~call~~ *called* her a couple of times. She hasn't called back ~~still~~ *yet*. **or** She *still* hasn't called back ~~still~~.

UNIT 10

A 1. ever
2. just
3. been
4. Has
5. lately
6. has

B 1. Have…seen
2. 've…been
3. has…read
4. 's given
5. 've…wanted
6. has taken
7. 's…shown

C 1. I've ~~lately~~ traveled a lot *lately*.
2. We've ~~returned just~~ *just returned* from an African safari.
3. I've never ~~have~~ *had* so much fun before.
4. Have you ~~been ever~~ *ever been* on a safari?
5. No, but I've recently ~~went~~ *gone* **or** *been* hot-air ballooning.
6. My wife and I ~~has~~ *have* decided to go next summer.
7. I've ~~saw~~ *seen* a lot of great photos on a hot-air ballooning website.

UNIT 11

A 1. When did you move to Vancouver?
2. How long have you been an engineer?
3. Did you work in Vancouver for a long time?
4. When did you get married?
5. How many years have you lived in Singapore?
6. Has your wife lived in Singapore long?

B 1. 've been
2. saw
3. 've crossed
4. haven't seen
5. took
6. was
7. has learned
8. ordered
9. didn't learn

C Tina and Ken lived apart for a while, but then Tina found a job in Singapore. She ~~has moved~~ *moved* there last month. Here are some of their thoughts:

KEN: I'm so glad Tina is finally here. Last year ~~has been~~ *was* the hardest time of my life.

TINA: Before I got here, I didn't ~~understood~~ *understand* Ken's experiences. But ~~I was~~ *I've been* in culture shock since I ~~arrive~~ *arrived*. Now I know what a difficult time Ken had at first. But he never gave up.

UNIT 12

A 1. has written
2. has been writing
3. I've been reading
4. has read
5. I've had
6. I've been taking

B 1. a. have…lived (**or** been living)
b. 've been
c. 've been enjoying
2. a. Have…read
b. has…written
3. a. 've been trying
b. 've been studying
4. a. has…been
b. Has…chosen

C 1. Janet hasn't ~~been writing~~ *written* a word since she sat down at her computer.
2. Since I've known Dan, he's ~~been having~~ *had* five different jobs.
3. I've ~~drunk~~ *been drinking* coffee all morning. I think I've ~~been having~~ *had* at least 10 cups!
4. We've ~~been lived~~ *been living* **or** *lived* here for several years, but we're moving next month.

UNIT 13

A 1. speak
2. was able to
3. will be able to
4. can't
5. couldn't

B 1. could speak **or** was able to speak
2. was able to win
3. can speak **or** is able to speak
4. can't write **or** isn't able to write
5. 'll be able to improve **or** can improve
6. can travel **or** will be able to travel
7. can't afford **or** isn't able to afford
8. will be able to make **or** can make
9. could communicate **or** was able to communicate
10. can visit **or** will be able to visit

C A: I can't ~~to see~~ *see* the board. The guy in front of me is very tall.

B: Let's change seats. ~~You be~~ *You'll be* able to see from this seat.

A: Thanks. I don't want to miss anything. I ~~no can~~ *can't* believe what a great teacher Ms. Acosta is.

B: I know. My sister had her last semester. She ~~could~~ *was able to* get an A on her final exam!

A: ~~Were~~ *Was* your sister able to speak any Spanish before taking that class?

B: No. She couldn't speak a word!

A: That's amazing!

UNIT 14

A 1. come
2. Do
3. borrow
4. if
5. please shut

B 1. I borrow a pen
2. my sister leave
3. I open a window
4. my friend and I (**or** we) come early
5. I ask a question

C 1. A: Do you mind if I ~~changed~~ *change* the date of our next meeting?

B: ~~Yes, I do.~~ *Not at all.* **or** *No, I don't.* **or** *No problem.* When would you like to meet?

2. A: Could I ~~calling~~ *call* you tonight?

B: Sorry, but you ~~couldn't~~ *can't*. I won't be home.

3. A: Mom, ~~I may~~ *may I* have some more ice cream?

B: No, you ~~mayn't~~ *may not*. You've already had a lot. You'll get sick.

4. A: Do you mind if my son ~~turn~~ *turns* on the TV?

B: ~~Not at all.~~ *Sorry, (but)* I can't study with the TV on.

5. A: Can my sister ~~borrows~~ *borrow* your bike?

B: Could I ~~letting~~ *let* you know tomorrow?

A: Sure. No problem.

UNIT 15

A 1. a. turning
b. I'm sorry, I can't.
2. a. please text
b. No problem.
3. a. pick
b. I'd be glad to.

B 1. lending me five dollars
2. you drive me to school
3. you (please) explain this sentence to me (please)
4. you carry this suitcase for me
5. you (please) distribute the report (please)
6. walking the dog tonight

C 1. JASON: Hi, Tessa. It's Jason. Could you ~~taking~~ *take* some photos of the game today?

TESSA: Sorry, Jason, but I ~~couldn't~~ *can't*. My camera is broken. Maybe Jeri can help.

2. JASON: Hi, Jeri. Would you ~~came~~ *come* to the game today? I need someone to take photos.

JERI: Jason, ~~can~~ *would* you mind calling me back in a few minutes? I'm busy right now.

JASON: Sorry, Jeri, I can't, but I'll email you. Would you ~~give me please~~ *please give me* your email address?

JERI: ~~Not at all.~~ *Sure.* **or** *No problem.* **or** *Of course.* **or** *Certainly.* It's Rainbows@local.net.

3. JERI: Hi, Jason, it's Jeri. I'm sending you those photos. ~~You could~~ *Could you* call me when you get them?

JASON: Thanks, Jeri. The photos are great. Now, ~~will teach~~ *will you teach* me how to put them on Facebook?

UNIT 16

A 1. a 2. c 3. a 4. b 5. a

B 1. a. Should…call
b. 'd better do
2. a. should…contact
b. ought to call
3. a. Should…ask
b. Yes…should
4. a. Should…do
b. No…shouldn't
c. 'd better wait

C 1. Vanessa should ~~gets~~ get a new computer. She ~~should no~~ shouldn't keep her old one.
2. She'd better not ~~buying~~ buy the first one she sees.
3. She ~~ought~~ ought to read reviews before she decides on one.
4. ~~Ought~~ Should she get one online or should she ~~goes~~ go to a store?

UNIT 17

A 1. a 2. b 3. c 4. c 5. a

B 1. Music is
2. photos show
3. Money makes
4. Clothing shows
5. Food goes

C One night in ~~june~~ June, 1,400 ~~Years~~ years ago, a volcano erupted in today's El Salvador and buried a village of the great Mayan civilization. Archaeologists have already found many large ~~building~~ buildings from this time, but only a ~~little~~ few homes of farmers and workers. The village of El Ceren contains perfect examples of ~~a great deal of~~ many **or** a lot of **or** a great many everyday objects. The archaeologists have found some knives (with ~~foods~~ food still on them), ~~much~~ many **or** a lot of pots, ~~a lot~~ a lot of garden tools, some fabrics, and a book. On the wall of one room, they found a few ~~word~~ words in an unknown language. There is still a lot to learn from this time capsule, called "the ~~pompeii~~ Pompeii of Latin America."

UNIT 18

A 1. a 2. a 3. Ø 4. an 5. Some 6. Ø 7. the 8. the

B 1. a. the
b. the
2. a. a
b. a
c. an

C Yesterday, I downloaded two movies. One was ^a comedy, the other was ~~a~~ an Argentinian thriller. We watched ~~a~~ the comedy first. It was really funny. ~~A~~ The thriller wasn't that good. There wasn't enough action in it. Tonight, I think I'd rather read ~~the~~ a book than watch a movie. I recently bought ~~the~~ a book of fables and a mystery. I think I'll read ~~a~~ the mystery before I go to sleep.

UNIT 19

A 1. annoying
2. late
3. perfect
4. hard
5. surprisingly

B 1. interesting old house
2. big cheerful yellow kitchen **or** cheerful big yellow kitchen
3. peaceful residential street
4. nice young international students
5. didn't seem friendly at all (**or** at all friendly)
6. charming little Greek restaurant
7. really beautiful garden
8. wonderful old round wooden table
9. decide pretty quickly
10. rent awfully fast

C The conditions in Parker Dorm are pretty ~~shocked~~ shocking. The rooms are ~~terrible~~ terribly small, and the furniture is incredibly ugly. The locks on the doors don't work ~~good~~ well, so your stuff is never ~~safely~~ safe. The dorm counselors are great—they're all really nice, friendly people—but they can't make up for the ~~badly~~ bad conditions.

UNIT 20

A 1. as
2. better
3. more
4. less
5. longer
6. the more impatient

B 1. more expensive than
2. bigger
3. larger than
4. more convenient
5. farther

C Last night, I had dinner at the new Pasta Place on the corner of Main Street and Grove. This new Pasta Place is just as good ~~than~~ as the others, and it has just as many sauces to choose from. No one makes a

~~more good~~ better traditional tomato sauce ^than them. But there are much ~~interestinger~~ more interesting choices. Their mushroom cream sauce, for example, is as ~~better~~ good as I've ever had. Try the mushroom and tomato sauce for a healthier ~~than~~ meal. It's just as delicious. The new branch is already popular. The later it is, ~~longer~~ the longer the lines. My recommendation: Go early for a ~~more short~~ shorter wait. And go soon. This place will only get ~~more popular~~ more and more popular!

UNIT 21

A
1. the coldest
2. the highest
3. the driest
4. the rainiest
5. the most expensive
6. the cheapest

B
1. the worst
2. the most fantastic
3. the most popular
4. the most crowded
5. the most difficult
6. the best
7. the funniest

C Small towns aren't ~~most~~ the most dynamic places to visit, and that's just why we love to vacation on Tangier Island. This tiny island is probably ~~the less~~ the least popular vacation spot in the United States. Almost no one comes here. But it's also one of ~~the most safest~~ the safest places to visit. And you'll find some of ~~the goodest~~ the best seafood and ~~the beautiful~~ the most beautiful beaches here. It's one of ~~the easy~~ the easiest places to get around (there are no cars on the island). If you get bored, just hop on the ferry. You're only a few hours from Washington, D.C., and a few more hours from New York and ~~the excitingest~~ the most exciting nightlife ever.

UNIT 22

A
1. well
2. doesn't run
3. more accurately
4. of
5. as well
6. the more tired he gets
7. harder
8. better

B
1. well
2. faster
3. the most accurately
4. the hardest
5. the worst

C Last night's game was a very exciting one. The Globes played the best they've played all season. But they still didn't play as ~~good~~ well as the Stars. The Stars hit the ball more ~~frequent~~ frequently and ran ~~more fast~~ faster than the Globes, and their pitcher, Kevin Rodriguez, threw the ball more accurately. Their catcher, Scott Harris, handled ~~better the ball~~ the ball better than the Globes' catcher. The Globes are good, but they are ~~less good than~~ not as good as the Stars. All in all, the Stars just keep playing ~~good~~ better and better. And the better they play, the ~~hardest~~ harder it is for their fans to get tickets! These games sell out quicker than hotcakes, so go early if you want to get a chance to see the Stars.

UNIT 23

A
1. not liking
2. smoking
3. feeling
4. joining
5. swimming
6. not eating
7. improving

B
1. Laughing is
2. suggests **or** suggested watching
3. Telling…helps **or** will help
4. advises **or** advised against drinking
5. enjoy taking
6. think about smoking

C
1. You look great. Buying these bikes ~~were~~ was a good idea.
2. I know. I'm happy about ~~lose~~ losing weight, too. ~~Didn't~~ Not exercising was a bad idea.
3. It always is. Hey, I'm thinking of ~~rent~~ renting a movie. What do you suggest ~~to see~~ seeing?
4. I've been looking forward to ~~see~~ seeing *Grown Ups*. Have you seen it yet?
5. Not yet. Do you recommend it? You're so good at ~~choose~~ choosing movies.

UNIT 24

A
1. to read
2. to meet
3. to finish
4. to go
5. to play
6. to call

B 1. invited Mary to visit us
2. agreed to come
3. wants to make new friends
4. told her to come early
5. decided not to invite Tom
6. needs to finish his project

C 1. A: I want ~~invite~~ *to invite* you to my party.
B: Thanks. I'd love ~~coming~~ *to come*.
2. A: I plan ~~to not~~ *not to* get there before 8:00.
B: Remember ~~getting~~ *to get* the soda. Don't forget!
3. A: Sara asked ~~I~~ *me* to help her.
B: I agreed ~~helping~~ *to help* her, too.
4. A: I promised ~~pick up~~ *to pick up* some ice cream.
B: OK. But let's do it early. I prefer ~~don't~~ *not to* arrive late.

UNIT 25

A 1. get
2. in order not
3. to use
4. too
5. clearly enough

B 1. easy enough to program
2. too hard for me to use
3. too fast for me to understand
4. too far for us to walk
5. to get there by 6:30
6. early enough for us to walk
7. too heavy for us to cross
8. my phone to get directions
9. clearly enough for it to work
10. a taxi to save time

C Is sixteen too young ~~for~~ *to* drive? It's really hard to ~~saying~~ *say*. Some kids are mature enough to drive at sixteen, but some aren't. I think most sixteen-year-olds are still too immature ~~drive~~ *to drive* with friends in the car, though. It's ~~for them easy~~ *easy for them* to forget to pay attention with a lot of kids in the car. In order ~~preventing~~ *to prevent* accidents, some families have a "no friends" rule for the first year. I think that's a reasonable idea. And I think there should be a "no cell phone" rule, too—for talking or texting.

UNIT 26

A 1. starting
2. to finish
3. trying
4. to join
5. seeing
6. to call
7. Studying

B 1. doing
2. to take
3. working **or** to work
4. sitting
5. taking
6. to get
7. studying **or** to study

C I hate clutter. But before now, I wasn't able to prevent it from ~~to happen~~ *happening*. I even put off going home because seeing the mess made me feel bad. Then I remembered recently ~~to read~~ *reading* an interesting magazine article about clutter. I decided ~~trying~~ *to try* one of the recommended tactics. I learned that I need ~~cleaning~~ *to clean* up every night before I go to bed. Just ten minutes can make a big difference. I've stopped ~~to avoid~~ *avoiding* going home now, and I enjoy being in my nice, neat apartment. ~~To clean~~ *Cleaning* up every night isn't always easy, but it's really worth it!

UNIT 27

A 1. me
2. myself
3. each other
4. herself
5. yourselves
6. itself
7. one another
8. myself

B 1. talk to each other
2. greet each other
3. help yourself
4. enjoying themselves
5. drove herself

C When I first met Nicole, I told myself, "I'm not going to like working with ~~herself~~ *her*." Negative self-talk! I was really wrong. Nicole has helped ~~myself~~ *me* out with so many things. When she ~~oneself~~ *herself* didn't know something, she always found out for me. That way, both of ~~ourselves~~ *us* learned something. After I learned the job better, we helped ~~each other's~~ *each other* **or** *one another* out. The job ~~themselves~~ *itself* isn't that challenging, but I'm really enjoying myself. All of us in the office have become good friends. We all like ~~each another~~ *each other* **or** *one another*. That makes it a great place to work. I feel lucky to be here.

UNIT 28

A
1. out
2. up
3. on
4. out
5. up
6. over

B
1. Joe gets up early.
2. He turns on the TV. **or** He turns the TV on.
3. He sits down with Ana.
4. They get along well.
5. They look over his schedule. **or** They look his schedule over.
6. They talk it over.
7. They put it away.
8. They put on their coats. **or** They put their coats on.

C As soon as Ina ~~wakes out~~ wakes up, she quickly gets dressed, ~~puts off~~ puts on her mosquito repellent, and goes out with her classmates into the rain forest. They ~~keep up~~ keep on walking until they find what they are looking for—chimpanzees. They've been studying the chimps for weeks. The chimps are really intelligent. They know which plants have medicinal qualities, and which plants don't. Somehow these amazing animals have ~~figured out it~~ figured it out!

At the end of each day, Ina and her classmates go back to their camp. It's late, and they're tired. But, before they ~~turn on~~ turn off the lights to go to bed, they ~~talk up~~ talk over their plans for the next day. Everyone is tired but excited to be doing such interesting work.

UNIT 29

A
1. don't have to
2. Does
3. can't
4. 've got to
5. had
6. have

B
1. don't have to do
2. have to pick up **or** 'll have to pick up **or** 're going to have to pick up
3. 've…had to stand
4. don't have to wait **or** won't have to wait **or** aren't going to have to wait
5. can't smoke
6. has to move **or** will have to move **or** is going to have to move
7. can't sit
8. have to have **or** 'll have to have
9. had to eat

C
1. He can't ~~boards~~ board the plane yet.
2. Passengers ~~must not~~ don't have to stay in their seats when the seat belt light is off.
3. Passengers: Please note that you ~~gotta~~ have to **or** must pay extra for luggage over 50 pounds (23 kg).
4. You don't ~~have got to~~ have to show your passport right now, but please have it ready.
5. Paul ~~will has~~ will have **or** has to unpack some of his stuff. His suitcase is much too heavy.

UNIT 30

A
1. a
2. b
3. c
4. a
5. c

B
1. a. 're supposed to be
   b. isn't supposed to start
2. a. are…supposed to sit
   b. 're supposed to go
3. a. Was (**or** Am)…supposed to wear
   b. 're (**or** were) supposed to wear
4. a. isn't (**or** wasn't) supposed to rain
   b. was (**or** is) supposed to be

C
1. Dahlia was ~~suppose~~ supposed to drive. She was ~~supposed not~~ not supposed to fly.
2. She ~~is~~ was supposed to wear her blue dress, but she changed her mind.
3. What are we supposed to ~~doing~~ do after the ceremony?
4. My parents ~~will~~ were supposed to fly home tomorrow, but they're staying another day.
5. It was ~~no~~ not supposed to be this cold, and it ~~didn't suppose~~ wasn't supposed to rain.

UNIT 31

A
1. Will
2. might
3. going to
4. may
5. get
6. could
7. Maybe

B
1. a. Are…going to go
   b. may **or** might **or** could
2. a. Is…going to be
   b. may not (be) **or** might not (be)

3. a. are…going to work
   b. may stay **or** might stay **or** could stay
4. a. may not open **or** might not open
   b. may open **or** might open **or** could open

C Suddenly, weather forecasts all over the world are predicting terrible storms. Climatologist Jack Hall understands weather trends, and he thinks that a new ice age could ~~to begin~~ *begin* very quickly. His son Sam is in New York with his high school class. One student is sick and ~~mayn't~~ *may not* live without medicine. ~~May those kids~~ *Will those kids* **or** *Are those kids going to* survive by themselves? They ~~maybe~~ *may* **or** *might* not. Jack bundles up and starts walking to New York to save them. There ~~might could~~ *may* **or** *might* **or** *could* be a happy ending. Or the world could end. You'll have to watch to find out!

UNIT 32

A
1. must
2. has got to
3. could
4. can't
5. Could
6. could

B
1. a. couldn't be
   b. could be
2. a. could…want
   b. Could…be
   c. can't be
3. a. Could…lead
   b. might know

C
1. Jason has been coughing all morning. He might ~~having~~ *have* a cold.
2. Diana must not ~~likes~~ *like* fish. She left most of it on her plate.
3. ~~May~~ *Could* **or** *Can* the package be from your parents?
4. That's impossible! It ~~might not~~ *couldn't* **or** *can't* be true.
5. Is the bank still open? That's a good question. I don't know. It ~~might~~ *might be*.
6. She ~~could~~ *couldn't* **or** *can't* be a thief! I trust her completely!
7. ~~It's got~~ *It's got to* be a joke. I don't believe it's serious.

Information Gaps, Student B

UNIT 2

EXERCISE 12 CELEBRITY PROFILE

A INFORMATION GAP Work with a partner. Student B will follow the instructions below. Student A will follow the instructions on page 30.

STUDENT B

- Read the profile of an actor who is also a poet, painter, and musician. Ask your partner questions to complete the missing information.

  EXAMPLE: B: Where was Viggo born?
  A: He was born in New York.

- Answer your partner's questions.

  EXAMPLE: A: When was Viggo born?
  B: He was born on October 20, 1958.

- If you don't know how to spell something, ask your partner.

  EXAMPLE: B: How do you spell New York?
  A: Capital *N*, *e*, *w*, space, capital *Y*, *o*, *r*, *k*.

SCREEN-TIME PROFILE

Viggo Mortensen
actor, poet, painter, musician

Date of Birth: October 20, 1958

Place of Birth: *New York* ________

Mini Bio:

- lived in Argentina, Venezuela, and Denmark as a child
- attended school in ________
- learned to speak Spanish
- returned to the United States in 1969
- became a movie actor in 19____
- first movie was ________
- played the part of Aragorn in *Lord of the Rings* (This movie made him famous.)
- finished his first book of poems in 1993 (The title was *Ten Last Night*.)
- created ________ for the movie *A Perfect Murder* (He played the part of the artist.)
- wrote ________ for *Lord of the Rings*

B When you are finished, compare the profiles. Are they the same?

EXERCISE 7 PARTY CHORES

A INFORMATION GAP Work with a partner. Student B will follow the instructions below. Student A will follow the instructions on page 126.

STUDENT B

- Look at Gisela's "To Do" list. Ask your partner questions to find out which chores Gisela has already done. Check (✓) those chores.

  EXAMPLE: B: Has Gisela vacuumed the carpet yet?
  A: No, she hasn't. *or* No, not yet.

- Look at the picture of the Stangers' kitchen and at Karl's "To Do" list. Check (✓) the chores that Karl has already done. Then answer your partner's questions about Karl's chores.

  EXAMPLE: A: Has Karl bought a memory card yet?
  B: Yes, he has. *or* Yes, he's already gotten one.

To Do: Karl

- ☑ buy memory card for camera
- ☐ bake the cake
- ☐ put the turkey in the oven
- ☐ mop the floor
- ☐ wash the dishes
- ☐ cut up the vegetables

To Do: Gisela

- ☐ vacuum the carpet
- ☑ buy flowers
- ☐ wash the windows
- ☐ set the table
- ☐ hang the balloons
- ☐ wrap the gift

B Now compare lists with your partner. Are they the same?

UNIT 18

EXERCISE 10 STORY TIME

A INFORMATION GAP Work with a partner. Student B will follow the instructions below. Student A will follow the instructions on page 255.

STUDENT B

- Look at the picture. Answer your partner's questions.

  EXAMPLE: A: Who's the man in the black cape?
  B: He's the magician.

- Ask your partner for the information you need to finish labeling the picture.

  EXAMPLE: B: What's the magician holding?
  A: A magic wand.

- If you don't know how to spell something, ask your partner.

  EXAMPLE: B: How do you spell "wand"?
  A: *w, a, n, d*

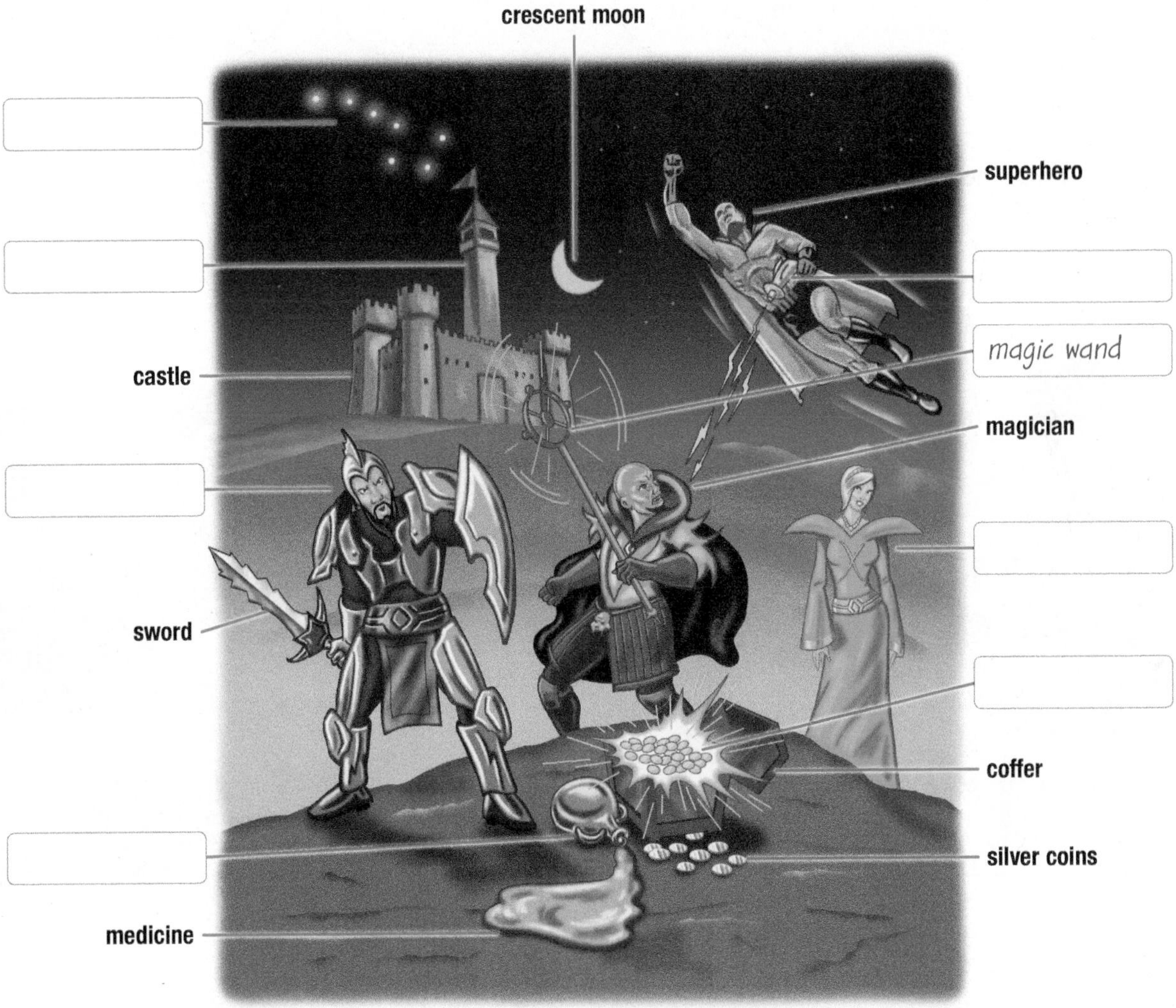

B When you are finished, compare pictures. Are the labels the same?

EXERCISE 12 AT THE SUPPORT GROUP

A INFORMATION GAP Work with a partner. Student B will follow the instructions below. Student A will follow the instructions on page 365.

STUDENT B

- Look at the picture. Answer your partner's questions.

EXAMPLE: A: What does Eva remember doing?
B: She remembers meeting Todd.

- Ask your partner questions to complete what people said at the support group meeting.

EXAMPLE: B: What does Todd hope to do?
A: He hopes to see Eva again.

B Now compare pictures with your partner. Are they the same?

Index

This index is for the full and split editions. All entries are in the full book. Entries for Volume A of the split edition are in black. Entries for Volume B are in blue.